Advance Praise for *The Cool Factor*

"Del Breckenfeld's, *The Cool Factor* gets the inside story on the music business partnering with major corporations fueling their brands."
—Billy F Gibbons, guitarist, singer, and songwriter with the multiplatinum ZZ Top and all around "Sharp Dressed Man."

"*The Cool Factor* presents a compelling picture on the power of music as a motivator—not just for marketing purposes, but more importantly, for understanding how music making at all ages enriches our everyday lives."
—Joe Lamond, President & CEO, NAMM

"In the *Cool Factor*, Del Breckenfeld shows us first hand how to get celebrities to partner with corporations for the purpose of positive outreach. Del and Fender have personally shared their expertise with us throughout the course of many years, specifically helping us raise significant funds for families devastated by Hurricane Katrina. We salute Del and strongly urge readers to pick up this book. It will help you discover how a brand can effectively be catapulted to new heights through partnership marketing with 'cool' products, musicians, and events."
—Don Felder, former lead guitarist and songwriter of The Eagles, best-selling author of *Heaven and Hell: My Life in the Eagles (1974–2001)*

"Del Breckenfeld knows cool. Fender, the brand he oversees, has such a high cool factor that even millions of non-musicians aspire to use its products. I love *The Cool Factor*—both the book and the idea. It's what most boring and predictable marketing is lacking today. Read it to find out how cool is your most effective secret weapon and learn how to add it to your marketing arsenal."
—David Meerman Scott, author of *The New Rules of Marketing and PR* and *World Wide Rave*

"Del has no equal when it comes to turning what's hip into a hit. He's that rare breed who's mastered the art of combining the very best of music and film, and creating ripples of contagious enthusiasm wherever he goes. It's time corporate America understood they can create and not just duplicate. *The Cool Factor* is the best big-picture primer I know for anyone looking to 'widespread' a little magic."

> —Dave Philips, CEO, Corner of The Sky Entertainment, and Executive Producer, *Evan Almighty* and *Where Music Meets Film*, live from the Sundance film festival

"A truly cool book that is so hot it can help turn any business into one people are talking about and sending money to. Read this one!"

> —Joe Vitale, author of *The Attractor Factor* and *The Key*

The
Cool Factor

The
Cool Factor

BUILDING YOUR BRAND'S IMAGE
——— THROUGH ———
PARTNERSHIP MARKETING

Del Breckenfeld

WILEY

John Wiley & Sons, Inc.

Library of Congress Cataloging-in-Publication Data:

Breckenfeld, Del, 1949–
   The cool factor : building your brand's image through partnership marketing / Del Breckenfeld.
       p. cm.
   Includes bibliographical references and index.
   ISBN 978-0-470-37196-1 (cloth)
1. Branding (Marketing) 2. Brand name products. 3. Imagery (Psychology)   I. Title.
   HF5415.1255.B74 2009
   978-0-470-37196-1   2008020133

Printed in the United States of America.

10 9 8 7 6 5 4 3 2 1

Dedicated to my parents, Ed and Anne, who gave my brothers
and I the dream, then the gift, of music

CONTENTS

ACKNOWLEDGMENTS

Before writing this, my first book, I had no idea how many people would be instrumental in bringing it to reality through their dedicated efforts and support—and now I do. Thanks to Bill Mendello, Rich Kerley, Bill Cummiskey, Jason Padgitt, Richard McDonald, Andy Rossi, and my boss, Mark VanVleet, from Fender Musical Instruments Corporation, who, at one time or another, had enough trust to allow me to expand the boundaries of what a musical instrument manufacturer could do. Also from FMIC, my hard-working and loyal assistant, Dave Collins, who jumped head first into this extremely challenging (but he will admit rewarding) department, entertainment marketing, and never ceases to amaze me with his seemingly endless drive and positive energy. And thanks to Paul Jernigan, Alex Perez, Rich Siegle, Tony Franklin, Justin Norvell, Keith Davis, Chris Suffolk, Lee Holtry, Gayle Castro, Rose Bishop, Kristy Swanson, Ryan Davidson, Larry, Hector, Carlos, Luis, and all my other friends at Fender who work so hard to keep our brand at the top. Thanks, too, to former Fender family members: Bob Heinrich, John Page, Jack Shelton, Al Guzman, Dan Smith, Keith Brawley, Rick Anderson, Bruce Bolen Sr., Chuck Hemich, and Joe Baffa, all of whom placed their trust in me as well. Special thanks to my ex-boss Ritchie Fliegler (who I'm sure at this moment is cruisin' with the top down somewhere in the Arizona desert in his 1964 Rangoon Red Ford Thunderbird), who shared the vision that the Fender brand should have the same power outside our industry that we have within, and had the bravado to prove it. And to the late Bill Shultz, who I am convinced that, without him, Fender would have never found the light following the dark days under CBS.

I am grateful for the many wonderful friends and associates I have worked with over the years in our industry—Elliot Kendall at Ume, Scotty Finck at Hollywood Records, Jeff Yapp and Carrie Bantin at MTV Networks, Jody Glisman-Best, formerly of Capitol EMI, Liz Erman at Warner's, the Jetsyn twins and their gang at Pier 3 Entertainment, Spencer Proffer and Steve Plunkett at Meteor 17, Joe Lamond, Dominique Agnew, Morgan Ringwald, and Jeff "Jelly" Livingston at NAMM; Warren Weideman, Mimi Clarke, and Gary Arnold at Best Buy; Dave Philips at Edmonds Entertainment, and all the record labels, managers, and incredible artists I have had the pleasure to know. Kudos to the Tobacco Rouges, Buster, Gambler, the Quarrymen, and the Glimmer Twins as well. I also want to thank my music teacher, Ms. Barnett, who helped bring out a talent in me I would never have realized I had.

Very special thanks to Greg Reitman of Blue Water Entertainment (Greg, "I got my book!") and his dad, Bert Davis, who, without them, this book certainly would have never happened; John Wiley & Sons Publishers, in particular, my Executive Editor (now Publisher), Matt Holt, who took a chance on a novice writer, and Jessica Campilango, Christine Moore, and Kate Lindsay for all their guidance; Debbie Shuck from the Fender Center for diligently translating and transcribing my ramblings; and finally, to my family: my mom for her loving support; my brothers Bruce and Ed, whose devotion to music still inspires me today; my sister-in law Sunniva Sorby, a true explorer of life; my stepson Kjell, who taught me how to kill at *Rock Band*; my two lovely daughters, Shanna for the endless hours of research, and Holly for putting it plain and simple: "Dad, don't worry about the book. Just write like you talk and you'll be fine"; and most of all to my beautiful and beloved wife Bettina, who, day after day, gives me the love and encouragement to actually make me believe I can do the things I didn't think I could do.

ABOUT THE AUTHOR

In one form or another, Del Breckenfeld has been in entertainment marketing all of his life. Even without a formal degree in marketing (he graduated from Northeastern Illinois University in Chicago with a major in music on a full-talent scholarship in his final years), he did, however, learn street marketing from the bottom up; starting with marketing and promoting his local high school band, and working his way through college playing music; finally signing a major record deal with EMI America Records (a subsidiary of Capitol Records in the United States); then touring with the major bands of the day, and ultimately ending up broke, like so many other musicians in similar circumstances. He then decided he needed to pursue another career in music that would at least give him a regular paycheck to support a growing family, and was fortunate to work for one of the innovative guitar companies of the 1980s, Dean Guitars. It was there that the owner, Dean Zelinsky, and Del developed a groundbreaking promotional program for Anheuser-Busch, where they got to work with some of the most astute marketers in the world. From there, he was able to climb the ladder to reach the pinnacle of the guitar industry—Fender Musical Instruments Corporation, where he was encouraged to expand the boundaries of traditional entertainment marketing. As he states, "When you are the industry leader, you want to always look ahead, not behind, to see who's gaining on you," (paraphrased from the great Satchel Paige).

Throughout his career, he has worked closely with some of the biggest names in music, movies, and TV, and has been involved in promotional campaigns with some of the world's most successful and well-known brands—all along learning the ins and outs of partnership marketing, and developing his own unique approach to brand building.

INTRODUCTION

If you ask someone, "What is *cool?*" he would probably reply that he can't tell you in exact words, but knows it when he sees it. So a better question might be, "Can we give examples of what we deem is cool?" To do that, we might have to make it relative—all the way back to the 1930s when the expression *cool* began to catch on in English slang. In the 1950s, it certainly would have been Marlon Brando in *The Wild One*, James Dean in *Rebel Without a Cause*, the Beat poets, Miles Davis's jazz (that is, the landmark recording "The Birth of the Cool"); or maybe the early rockers like Elvis, Gene Vincent, and Little Richard. In the 1960s, it may have been Steve McQueen's character in *The Great Escape*, Bob Dylan, the British Invasion led by the Beatles and the Rolling Stones, or the Who, with their Mod image and Carnaby Street fashion.

Each generation can be defined by its coolest actors, musicians, fashions, and trends. *Cool* was determined by the innovators that were most often the rebels of society, who in some way threatened the Establishment and were able to deliver this message through their music, acting, and, perhaps most important, their image. Back then, this message was delivered by relatively narrow choices in media—TV, movies, print, and radio. When I was a youngster, there were only three commercial TV networks, all of which broadcast to a huge audience and wide demographic. That's how Elvis was able to reach a massive audience with his first appearances and why the Beatles were able to reach an astounding seventy-three million viewers on their premier performance on the Ed Sullivan Show in 1964. For me, that latter performance was the Big Bang that still resonates today, as that was the moment I decided I would make the entertainment industry my lifelong ambition. The next day, after the Beatles sang "She Loves You," I, along with millions of other Baby Boomer boys, tried our best to force our shorn locks down onto our foreheads in a desperate attempt to imitate the Beatle bangs of our newfound heroes. I wanted to look like them, talk like them, dress like them, and most important, play guitar with my mates in a band like theirs (Paul McCartney once remarked that he would rather be in a band than drive a Rolls Royce). And the more I succeeded in my makeover, the more the girls took notice—the same ones who used to ignore my very existence just a few months before. And, of course, the girls wanted to be the "birds" who flocked around the Beatles, or in our case, the local musicians, who were the next best thing. Looking back, I realize that that was lifestyle marketing at its most effective and dynamic.

In 1964, in addition to the Beatles, you heard the Rolling Stones, the Beach Boys, Dean Martin, and Johnny Cash on one massive format—Top 40 radio. Movies were premiered in single-screen movie theaters, and James Bond was the coolest of the cool (once again, orbited by a bevy of beautiful and sometimes dangerous "Bond Girls"). Most magazines were aimed at targeted audiences, but still covered a wide range of related interests in one issue, and newspapers gave us the breaking news, sometimes two or three editions in a single *"Extra! Extra! Read All About It!"* day. If any performer, or product, for that matter, appeared in one or two of those outlets, chances are they would have reached just about every person in the United States.

That all gradually changed, however, with the introduction of cable and satellite TV, formatted radio, multiplex cinemas, specialty magazines, and the Biggest Daddy of them all—the World Wide Web. People today expect everything on demand, and we have created a system to facilitate that, not just in the United States, but globally. Even though it can be delivered on demand, the more the delivery system is subdivided and formatted to individual tastes, the harder it is to reach the widest possible audience with a single broadcast event. Case in point: over 65,000 CDs were released in 2006 (wait a minute, there's only 8,760 hours in a year, so even if the most dedicated music aficionado listened 24/7 he could only listen to . . . well, you get the point). Plus, according to the February 2008 issue of *Marketing, Inc.*, there are over 100 million blogs worldwide. That's why I believe that, small or large, individual, independent, or part of a large conglomerate, having a recognizable brand name has never been more essential to rising above the din to achieve and sustain success.

But how does brand (or band, for that matter) get its message through such a chaotic delivery system? The good news is that somehow, the innovators can still determine what is cool, and when certain people in the delivery system catch on, it becomes hot. In the number one best-seller, *The Tipping Point: How Little Things Can Make a Big Difference*, author Malcolm Gladwell's premise is that a small group of influential people can create an "epidemic" that becomes a fad for the masses.

Before the success of his book, Gladwell had published a 1997 article in *The New Yorker* in which he popularized the term *cool hunters,* marketers who looked for and identified the next big trends. Today, cool hunters have been replaced by people like Jane Buckingham, who charges companies such as Fox, Sony, Lancome, and T-Mobile $35,000 per year to receive her Cassandra Report; which features comprehensive studies on Generations X and Y, the 112 million U.S. residents between the ages of 14 and 34. Buckingham told the *Los Angeles Times* in a recent article that this is the demographic that "dictates what's cool to both those older and younger than them [sic]."

On the Web, users of sites like Myspace and YouTube can run the gamut from amateurs to professionals, and present everything in between through the same delivery system. A certain amount of reality is deemed cool, so even large corporations place content on those sites that are made to look amateurish even though they are produced by some of the slickest agencies in the world. Savvy marketers agree on one thing— if your brand is deemed cool—you rule!

I understand that if you are a marketer, you may be saying, "I have a much greater problem, which is that my brand is not cool. So even if I can reach a large audience, my brand may still not ignite enough interest for someone to purchase it." That is precisely my motivation for writing this book.

I never intended to write a how-to book on marketing, but rather to illustrate through examples—often backed up by my experiences—how a brand can be effectively driven to new heights by partnership marketing with cool products, celebrities, musicians, and events that have already established *The Cool Factor.* I will give firsthand insights on how the company I work for, Fender Musical Instruments Corporation, the best-selling and most recognizable brand name in electric guitars and amps, partners with many other larger corporations outside our industry that want to tap into Fender's cool factor. But this is not a book about the guitar industry or limited to the music industry; rather, it is a book that will demonstrate how the whole entertainment industry—and beyond—can offer countless opportunities for partnership marketing.

Fender® has three flagship models (and several other models and brands that dominate our industry) in its arsenal that are revered among musicians. So the primary question is what makes the Stratocaster®guitar, Telecaster®guitar, and P Bass® so cool in our world, even after more than 50 years? First of all, the founder, Leo Fender, created products that were uniquely different from other brands and then launched them through partnership marketing with the coolest artists of the day (a trend that Fender continues today).

When Leo Fender founded the company in 1946, he was the new kid on the block, as giants like Gibson and Martin were around for more than 50 and 100 years, respectively (and for the most part, looked it). Additionally, Leo himself was not a guitar player, so he relied on his artist partners to tell him how to improve his product and make it more appealing to musicians and ultimately, to the masses.

Leo did have an eye for design, so when the Stratocaster guitar was introduced in 1954 (using lots of chrome, and a few years later, custom colors from DuPont, just like the coolest cars of the era), there was nothing remotely comparable in the world of instruments (there we go again with being an innovator and a rebel!). Of course, the Stratocaster sounded and played great, and that's also why artists picked up on it. Without their influence, Fender would not have had the same powerful impact on the world.

The images of Buddy Holly playing his Strat on the Ed Sullivan Show and Jimi Hendrix playing (and burning) his Strat at the Monterey Pop Festival are timeless reflections in rock history. And although the look of the Stratocaster guitar and the other flagship models at Fender have not changed much over the years, they are still played by today's top artists. One reason is certainly the assumption that if one of the greatest and most influential guitarists of all time—Jimi Hendrix—and his legions of disciples deemed the Stratocaster guitar cool enough to play, then it's plenty cool enough for everyone else.

And that rule can apply to most brands—coolness by association. Al & Laura Ries state in their book, *The Origin of Brands*,

"What makes a brand fashionable (re: cool)? In a word, celebrities." (Al also co-wrote what I consider to be the bible of brand marketing, *Positioning: The Battle for Your Mind*.) Fenders were cool at their conception, but they were essentially launched with a stamp of approval from the coolest artists of the era who were searching for something new and different. And when they found it, they propelled it to perpetual stardom. As a result, many people who work with me tell me I must have "the coolest job in the world." That may be somewhat true, but quite a bit of that perception comes from the fact that if you are not in our industry, what we do day to day may seem mysterious. Ultimately, my purpose for this book is to give marketers in *any* field the magic key to unlock that mystery.

The premise of this book grew out of my experiences in the music and entertainment industry, in which I have been continuously working since the age of eleven—when my mom purchased a 1950s-era Kay acoustic arch top from one of her weekly "bridge girls," Marguerite Bugarewicz. Marguerite's son Ken had lost interest in the guitar purchased at Sears, so she wanted to give it—or throw it—away. My mom didn't feel right taking it for free, so she paid a whole five bucks for that guitar. Little did she know that that fin would open the door to a lifelong passion for music and respect for true artists, which also led to the only career I have ever known.

I didn't want to base the book, however, solely on my own instincts and experience, so I reached out to many old friends, including Warren Weideman, who created the first entertainment marketing company; and the Jetsyn twins, who were there with their company, Pier 3 Entertainment, at the dawn of the product placement boom, and are still going strong as other Johnny-come-latelies have folded. I also spoke to new friends like licensing guru Art Ford, with whom I worked at Sundance on the "Where Music Meets Film" events and who thinks this is the most exciting time to be an independent in our industry;

Tim Meyers, the talented young singer-songwriter who decided to go it alone without label support and is the first unsigned artist to be featured on a national ad campaign for retail giant Target; and the fascinating Karl T. Bruhn, whose lifelong dream is to introduce recreational music-making to the masses.

Along with these interviews, my research also introduced me to a new collection of wonderful books and authors I otherwise wouldn't have known. *This is Your Brain on Music, Unmarketable, Musicophilia*, and the hilarious *Rock On* are just some of the gems I have unearthed that have taught me that the adventure of discovery and learning never abates. For that, I will always be appreciative.

Note: The parent company of the Fender brand is the Fender Musical Instruments Corporation. For the purpose of simplification, I will refer to the company as *Fender*, and I will have a model name or the word *guitar* following Fender when referring to the instrument. I will also sometimes refer to marketing personnel as *marketeers* when I feel it is warranted to convey their expertise as opposed to just describing their occupation.

CHAPTER 1

The Birth of the Cool—A 101 Primer

For anything or anyone to be thought of as *cool*, they have to have two things going for them: first, they have to be imbued with the rebel spirit, and second, they have to be unique when compared with the norm of the day. They then, of course, must be exposed to the widest possible audience, who will publicly or secretly aspire to be like them, or who want to be associated with them. As Richard McDonald, FMIC's senior vice president of marketing, instills in us, everyone is an individual—so the first thing we do to express that individuality is to find others who share the same interests as us. A paradox? Not at all, because in that group will be the born leaders who will show us the way to individual expression. In other words, their guidance bestows upon us something to emulate or to associate with. People, places, and things can have a powerful influence on our lifestyles and buying habits, so brands associated with them can also be perceived as having the *Cool Factor*. Simply put, coolness by association.

According to the *American Heritage Dictionary of the English Language*,[1] we find the origin of the word from the Middle English *cole*, from the Old English *cöl*. It typically appears as an adjective: *What a cool ride*. But it can also be an adverb: *Play it cool*; a transitive verb: *Cool your jets*; an intransitive verb: *Take a break and cool off*; and a noun: *Keep your cool*.

Even though jazz music in the mid-1940s used the word to describe the notion that cool jazz was an emotional detachment (as opposed to the hot jazz of the preceding era), it probably first appeared as a title in Charlie Parker's *Cool Blues*,[2] released in 1947. I would like to mark the launch of the word in popular vernacular with the 1949–1950 recording of the landmark Miles Davis recording *Birth of the Cool*[3] (on which Charlie Parker appeared as well). That was Miles's statement on cementing a new direction in his music and it gives us—for the sake of argument—a perfect starting point. Even though it also appeared in Leonard Bernstein's musical *West Side Story*, its popularity as an often-used slang expression didn't come into its own until the 1960s.[4]

There were many other slang words that were just as popular in their respective eras: the 1940s gave us *crazy*; and, in addition to *cool*, the 1950s also gave us *neat*. The 1960s were well, *groovy*, and the 1970s were *rad*. In the 1980s, your street cred showed when you used *bad* to mean *good*, and in the 1990s everything cool was *def*. For better or worse, those decades also created *hot*, *fab*, *far out*, *snazzy*, *slick*, *totally tubular*, *tight*, *sweet*, *awesome*, *hip*, and *hep*. I have been trying to find a similar word to mark this decade but so far all I can come up with is *cool*. We have come full circle from The Bird and Miles when rapper Lupe Fiasco, known for his cutting-edge fashion to go along with his music, released his late 2007 CD, *The Cool*.[5] Use any of the other slang expressions and you would painfully date yourself. Think of the embarrassment that would ensue if your marketing director said at a top-level meeting, "Gee, your marketing campaign is *groovy!* Let's get the boys in the art department to come up with some *neat* graphics and we'll get ready for launch." Simply substitute the word *cool* for *groovy* and *neat* and your marketing director becomes suddenly, well, very cool. I have been at high-level entertainment meetings where the word *cool* is bandied back and forth as everyone nods assurances.

I am not a professor of linguistics, but even if I were, I don't think I could find a suitable explanation for why this word has remained in our everyday lingo for more than 50 years without anyone having tired of it. In fact, instead of dating us, using *cool* makes us appear extremely contemporary as we demonstrated in the preceding marketing director's language example. Even dating back to its usage in Black English, it has had a positive connotation. If I had to guess, I would say that it's a one-size-fits-all word that can be used anytime someone wants to convey positivity so that the person using it knows that the listener knows exactly what the speaker means.

Okay, better to use examples. On New Year's Day, the TV commentator on the Rose Bowl Parade telecast kept saying, "Now, here's a cool float." Later that day, the anchor on the evening news gave us "a cool new way to ring in the New Year," and after that segment, his co-anchor added, "Cool." The *Los Angeles Times* described the difference in Radiohead's "In Rainbows"[6] release on the Internet as a pay-what-you-want download, and the retail store release as having the bonus content, which consisted of little more than "some cool stickers."[7] You can do your own unscientific research like I did if you'd like, but I think you get the point.

So how about this concept? We need to rein in the usage of the word for the purpose of this book or we may get to the point of referring to everything as cool, which we know by definition cannot be so. If something or someone who we can all agree is cool, however, the main point is figuring out how that factor can be transferred to something or someone else. For example, most agree that Steve McQueen is the quintessential cool guy. In fact, his motorcycle-riding, Nazi-antagonizing character Captain Hilts in the movie, *The Great Escape*,[8] was nicknamed "The Cooler King"—pun definitely intended. From his first starring role in a TV series, *Wanted Dead or Alive*,[9] throughout the rest of his career, Steve continued to reestablish his credentials as one of the kings of cool through well-chosen roles like Bullitt[10] in the film of the same name, which featured one of the greatest car chases in film history with Steve barreling up and down the streets of San Francisco in a hot-rodded Mustang. McQueen still transfers that image today to products like the Swiss watchmaker Tag Hauer with its "Steve McQueen Monaco Edition"[11] even though he died almost 30 years ago. Even in rock music, Sheryl Crow wrote a tribute song to him titled, what else, "Steve McQueen."[12] The song's music video featured scenes from his best-known movies and went on to become a theme song for NASCAR.[13] So transferring the equity of a star like Steve McQueen to a product does work, but we can't just limit ourselves to rebel-type action stars.

What about the seemingly unhip occupation of politician? Today's politicos have no problem tapping the hottest celebrities and musicians to boost their campaigns. However, I personally don't think we have had a cool president since John F. Kennedy because today's candidates have to be careful not to stray outside the public's comfort zone. But for one night in June 1992, Bill Clinton was able to show some cool when he appeared on

Arsenio Hall's late-night talk show during his presidential bid, donning Blues Brothers'–style Ray-Ban shades and somewhat adequately blow sax on "Heartbreak Hotel" and "God Bless the Child." That appearance marked a major uptick in his image for younger voters and women in particular and also spiked Arsenio's ratings to 5.4 million viewers.[14] That worked so well because, relatively speaking, it was quite cutting edge for a presidential candidate at the time.

It may be wrong to think that image doesn't still resonate the same today, or maybe it's due to his reputation for philandering, but in a recent *Playboy* magazine poll, 58 percent of the respondents thought Bill Clinton was the sexiest president of the past 40 years (former actor and president Ronald Reagan was second with 22 percent). It looks like women will always dig entertainers. That did not carry over, unfortunately, to former Republican governor of Arkansas and 2008 presidential candidate Mike Huckabee, who had occasionally been seen strapping on an electric bass to perform at election primary rallies. One of the reasons is that unless you are a lead-singing bassist dripping with charisma like Paul McCartney or Sting, bass is just not as cool as a front man's instrument like the guitar or saxophone. Trust me, I know, because I was a professional bass player for many years and I chose the instrument because there was always someone better than me on guitar in the band.

Barack Obama was the first presidential candidate since JFK to have actually achieved the type of adulation usually reserved for rock stars. Besides possessing good looks and a great speaking voice, Obama was able to tap into an emotional and spiritual connection with his audience, not unlike so many great rock stars. The type of fervor his dramatic speeches garnered drew comparisons to the type of reactions elicited by gospel preachers. It's no surprise that many of our greatest soul singers—Sam Cooke, Aretha Franklin, Tina Turner, and Al Green, just to name a few—all got their start in church singing gospel praises of the Lord.

The association between rock music and cool goes back to the early pioneers in the Fifties. With their antiestablishment stances purveyed through their "jungle beats," coupled with rebellious ("Roll over Beethoven," "Jailhouse Rock"), sexual ("Tutti Frutti," "Rock Me All Night Long"), and downright peculiar ("Be-Bop-a-Lula," "You ain't nothing but a Hound Dog," "Don't you step on my Blue Suede Shoes") lyrics; and accentuated by sneers and outrageous clothes and hairstyles— you had the makings on one giant "up yours" to the placid Eisenhower postwar decade. No wonder teenagers embraced it, since we know that anything our parents warn us is dangerous is precisely what we want. David Letterman even created a catch-phrase for his late night show when he wants to proclaim his coolness—"I am rock 'n' roll."

Speaking of 1950s clothing, the black leather motorcycle jacket worn by Marlon Brando's character, Johnny Strabler, in *The Wild One*[15] and his badass motorcycle gang, the Black Rebels Motorcycle Club[16] symbolized the rebel coolness many of that era aspired to. From Gene Vincent and Elvis to the Hamburg-era Silver Beatles, donning a black leather biker jacket announced to the world that you were *bad*. When I was in school, we referred to our leather-clad schoolmates as *greasers* because of the massive amount of Brylcreem ("A Little Dab'll Do Ya") in their hair to get that pompadour just right. In the United Kingdom of the 1950s, they were known as Teds (short for *Teddy boys*) and in the 1960s as *rockers*. Even the parody that actor Henry Winkler created for his leather-jacketed character, Fonzie, in the retro-1950s TV sitcom "Happy Days," was, in a word, cool, as confirmed in this dialogue from *Pulp Fiction*[17] between Samuel L. Jackson's character Jules and Amanda Plummer's character Yolanda:

Jules: We're all going to be like three little Fonzies here. And what's Fonzie like? Come on, Yolanda, what's Fonzie like?

Yolanda: Cool?
Jules: What?
Yolanda: Cool.
Jules: Correctamundo!

Back to the prototype outlaw motorcycle rider epitomized by Brando. Harley-Davidson couldn't have flourished selling $25,000 motorcycles if the company sold only to the true vagabond biker. That's why the typical Harley rider today averages around 50 years old and could very well be a doctor, lawyer, or business professional. By trading their business uniform for an HD uniform (riders refer to the *HD* in Harley clothing as *hundred dollars* because that's what a typical article costs), the weekend rider can borrow a little of the rebel equity without having to actually terrorize a town as Brando's biker gang did in *The Wild One*. In fact, you don't even have to ride a bike; simply don a Harley black leather jacket with branded Harley T-shirt and the image is transferred to you. No wonder licensed apparel is reported to be up to 20 percent of Harley's gross profits.

In the same way, brands can greatly enhance their cool factor by associating with celebrities, musicians, events, and other brands that the majority of us deem to be cool.

CHAPTER 2

The Prime Marketing Motivators—Too Much of a Good or Bad Thing?

E ver since high school, I knew I wanted to be in the music business in one capacity or another. Those aspirations, however, took a slight rerouting when I took my first marketing class. From the first day, I thought to myself, "These marketing guys from Madison Ave. seem to be the rock stars of their own world." Not unlike the American Movie Channel TV series *Mad Men*, I pictured these marketeers as a new breed of cool, sophisticated executives that had the inside track on what the rest of us desired, and they knew exactly how to drive it home through their creative ad campaigns.

We all seemed to embrace their messages of living the American Dream through sharp cars, brand new housing developments, and efficient new products that made our lives easier

and therefore gave us more free time to enjoy our new acquisitions. They were able to make simple chores like doing the
laundry seem glamorous. Heck, they even made smoking look
cool. America didn't seem to mind them advertising products as
long as they also brought us great entertainment. Single-sponsor
TV series were some of the most popular of the 1950s—*The
Alcoa (Aluminum) Hour, The Philco Television Playhouse, The Dinah
Shore Show* ("See the USA in Your Chevrolet" sung by the host
during the show), *The Goodyear Theatre*, and the *Texaco Star
Theater*, starring none other than Mr. Television himself, Milton
Berle. I decided if my music career didn't pan out, I was certain
that marketing was my calling!

I put that idea on hold for over a decade, as my music career
did take an upward path; but when I was ready to return to a
real-world job, I revisited my dream of getting into marketing,
still with a foot in the music industry, working for Dean Guitars.
I began to reacquaint myself with the rules of traditional
marketing that still applied; but when I began to examine
the new techniques I was shocked and somewhat disappointed
to learn how much had changed. Marketing was intruding
more and more into people's lives, which made consumers
appear less involved in decision making. We had always had
subliminal messages in marketing, but the new techniques went
far beyond that. With buzz words like *network* and *viral marketing*, everyone was in danger of becoming a marketing statistic
that marketeers could manipulate into a buying frenzy. The
Internet, cable TV, cell phones, and even our own friends and
families became just another tool in the endless assault on our
defenseless senses.

Today, the cause and effect of the lead stories of local nightly
news—car chases, gang shootings, robberies, and so on—are
immediately followed by commercials that encourage us to feel
better about our life with the purchase of a new car, or some new
drug for a symptom we didn't know we had (that pesky little war

in Iraq usually doesn't make it in until after the first commercial break, at least in the Los Angeles newscasts). Furthermore, Neil Postman puts forth the following observation in his book, *Amusing Ourselves to Death: Public Discourse in the Age of Show Business*[1]: "The viewers also know that no matter how grave any fragment of the news may appear, it will shortly be followed by a series of commercials that will, in an instant, defuse the import of the news; in fact, render it banal." Douglas Rushkoff, in his book, *Coercion: Why We Listen to What "They" Say,*[2] talks about what he calls a simple marketing technique like inducing "regression and transference." "All this means is making a person feel small, like a child, and then stepping in as the person's new parent figure," states Rushkoff. Even if the news isn't scary enough, the following commercial may intimidate us even further "before introducing the nice gray-haired announcer"—the new parent figure.

Today's marketeers have devoted much energy to finding ways around how we are to pay for all of these nonessential items. We are no longer constrained by the amount of disposable income we have. No money for more stuff? No problem, we'll just extend your already overmaxed credit card. Can't afford or qualify for a larger home? Again, no problem, we'll just be more creative in our loan processing—can somebody say, "Subprime interest-only loans?" (I knew you could.) Can't afford a three-year loan on that SUV that marketeers convinced you that you've always wanted? We'll just make the loan five years, no money down, with a higher interest rate. (Of course, so the vehicle won't be worth as much as you owe on the loan when you try to sell it because you can no longer afford the cost of gas to fill it up.) And unless you can hire a lawyer to decipher the fine print for every transaction in which you are about to partake, there is little defense the typical consumer has to counteract this onslaught. We know, unfortunately, where these practices have landed the average person. All of a sudden, it didn't look so cool to be a marketing guru.

The more sophisticated the means become, the less sophisticated and creative the techniques become. You don't have to be a marketing wiz to know how powerful sex, greed, and fear are as motivators. Yet, even though we know this, we still find ourselves falling prey to their siren's song. And people in big business and politics know this; so when all else fails, they will always revert back to using these tactics. The obvious problem is that since we are not all on a level playing field when it comes to understanding this, it's too easy to rely on these devices to sell your product; whether it be going further into debt for a new car or adding to our enormous federal budget deficit for a new jet fighter. The other problem is that those who use such methods also find out that there's always someone willing to push the limits to be sexier or scarier. And once you reach the limits, you lose your impact.

As far as sex, I'm not talking about pornography here. A February 2008 story in the *Washington Post* reported that mainstream lingerie brand, Victoria's Secret saw sales decline 8 percent at their stores that had been open for at least one year, which is a key measure of a retailer's health. Their CEO, Sharen J. Turney, announced the brand had gotten too sexy, and was ready to set a new course.[3] No doubt this decision also had something to do with the steady decline in viewership from the 12 million who witnessed the first Victoria's Secret infomercial in 2001, to the 7.5 million who tuned in to the 2007 edition.[4]

When I worked for a new guitar company called Dean Guitars in the 1980s, the founder, Dean Zelinsky, was a brilliant young marketeer who also lived the rock and roll lifestyle, which of course, included being surrounded by beautiful young women (read: *groupies*). Dean knew that guitars were sexy in and of themselves, but he also knew that many young males played guitar to get lucky with the ladies, like the rock stars they emulated. Dean promoted this through ads that featured gorgeous and scantily clad women. Many of these women were aspiring Playboy Playmates, or had already achieved that notoriety.

While other companies had celebrity artists at their exhibits in our industry's biggest trade show, Dean and I had beautiful women in a fashion show in our booth. This was so outrageous for our industry that it turned guitar marketing upside down, and our sales exploded. It didn't hurt that ZZ Top used our famous spinning-fur guitars in their breakout video, *Legs*, which coincidentally featured Playboy Playmates. And even though we had many of the top bands of the day like Heart,[5] Kansas, and the Cars using our guitars, other companies cried foul and said we couldn't sell our guitars and that's why we had to revert to sexy models. Well pretty soon, music videos without beautiful sexy girls were rare and other guitar companies jumped on the bandwagon.

Not too long after, Dean sold his company and the others mostly fell by the wayside except for the ones like Fender, which refused to play that trendy game. That was 20 years ago, and even though this type of promoting has lost its novelty shock value, the new buyers' guide for *Guitar World* magazine no longer uses artists, but—you got it—scantily clad Playmates. And for the past few years, the Dean trade show booth once again features the sexy rocker girls. The more things change . . .

Whether we play an instrument or not, music is an integral part of our daily life that we can't escape—even when we want to. From the music in waiting rooms, elevators, and malls, to when we are on hold on a business call, to the commercials that assault us, we have little choice in the matter if we are to exist in the modern world. As the accompaniment to movies and TV, we understand that music is a key element of a dramatic or romantic scene. I have attended many rough cuts of movies before the music was added, and no matter how wonderful the actors played out their parts, the end result with the right soundtrack added is always many times more effective. Just picture the movie *Jaws*, without the ominous musical accompaniment alerting us that the threatening behemoth is lurking somewhere below, and the ocean shots would actually have a serene, calming effect. And somewhere in the United States, a teacher is demonstrating to a film class how one can dramatically alter the mood of the opening scene in *Forrest Gump* by simply replacing the lilting music under the gently drifting feather, with a more menacing soundtrack.

Music has the power to trigger certain emotions and feelings and prompt memories of past events that we thought we have long forgotten. Quentin Tarantino visualized the opening scene *Pulp Fiction* set to Dick Dale's surf classic "Misirlou."[6] He apparently didn't want the other songs on the soundtrack to be so recognizable that they would distract the audience from his scene, so music supervisor Karyn Rachtman looked for either lesser-known songs from major artists, or cover versions of famous songs. The strongest compliment to a filmmaker and composer is when a particular soundtrack song is forever linked with a movie or specific scene, whether that piece was licensed from an existing work, or written specifically for the production. That makes sense, but why do marketers determine that we need music all the time, most everywhere we go? Do they actually believe they can program the overworked, beaten-to-death cliché "The Soundtrack of Your Life"? Hardly. To examine that further, we first look at why music has such a hold on our psyche.

In author Daniel J. Levitin's fascinating book, *This is Your Brain on Music: The Science of a Human Obsession*,[7] he writes about the cerebellum—the evolutionarily oldest part of our brain—being involved in emotions and planning of movements. He goes on further to explain that the cerebellum is sometimes referred to as the reptilian brain and says, "Although it weighs only 10 percent as much as the rest of the brain, it contains 50 to 80 percent of the neurons. The function of this oldest part of the brain is something that is crucial to music: timing." It seems that music taps into primitive brain structures involved with motivation, reward, and emotion. What's even more intriguing is that Dr. Levitin presents research that shows children as young as one year recognize and prefer music they were exposed to in the womb. Pretty powerful stuff indeed!

When I was pre-kindergarten age and home each day, the radio was constantly on. I remember hearing my mother sing along with the hits of the day—"Que Sera Sera," "Secret Love," "Come on-a My House," and "How Much Is that Doggie in the Window?" (it was the 1950s, after all). As soon as my dad got home from work, he would spin Prez Prado and Henry Mancini on our top-of-the-line Grundig hi-fi.

It's no wonder that even at an early age, music was a key ingredient in my life. The soundtrack to my cowboy-and-Indian adventures with my friends was "The Ballad of Davy Crockett." And when I ran with the football, I now know that it was pretty embarrassing that I would sing the instrumental theme song from the TV series *Combat*. I don't think I realized at that time that I wanted to be a musician, but I do recall a deliveryman coming to our back door one time during a birthday party for one of the neighbors, and the girls started squealing that he looked like Elvis. I clearly recall that when my mom tipped him, he curled his lip in true king fashion and replied, "Ahh, thank you very much, ma'am," to which one of the girls practically fainted. Even then, I knew that there must be something to this musician thing.

As I grew older, and had a small amount of disposable income from my allowance, I began to seek out the type of music that spoke to me and my generation. As a teenager growing up in the

1960s, there was certainly no shortage of new music to embrace. Songs appeared to become more and more personal, as artists, led by Bob Dylan and the Beatles, wrote their own lyrics and music. No matter if the subject matter was love found or lost, or more political in nature, these artists appeared to be singing directly to me—and I couldn't get enough. In *This is Your Brain on Music*, Levitin sheds some light on this emotional connection: "We make ourselves vulnerable to our favorite artists because they make themselves vulnerable to us."

We all have our own version of my story, no matter when or in what part of the world you grew up in. And because music as an emotional connection is such a motivator, right up there with sex and fear in the minds of most marketers, it comes as no surprise that it can also push the abuse envelope. In Martin Howard's book, *We Know What You Want: How They Change Your Mind*,[8] the author exposes the tactics that influence us to "buy, think, and believe." Howard demonstrates music examples such as department store customers exposed to Muzak ("Our art is to capture the emotional power of music and put it to work for your business") shop 18 percent longer and make 17 percent more purchases. Grocery stores slow down the Muzak beats per minute to reap 38 percent more purchases. And the opposite is just as eye opening—quicker beats in fast food restaurants increase the rate at which patrons chew their food. In other words, the faster you can make them eat, the faster you can turn the table.

It appears that nothing is out of the reach of the enormous arms of corporations. In the 1970s, punk was a very powerful under-ground movement in attitude and music as a reaction to the corporatizing of the arts. So you might think that that would be the last bastion of works untouched by corporate hands. In Anne

Elizabeth Moore's book, *Unmarketable: Brandalism, Copyfighting, Mocketing, and the Erosion of Integrity,*[9] the author bemoans the hijacking of the punk culture by large corporations. The very nature of punk was so anticorporate that freedom of expression couldn't be compromised by financial influence. This was why so many indie bands and labels thought it would be the height of hypocrisy to protect their copyrights, and therefore became ripe for the picking by major corporations looking for that cutting-edge image. Moore writes about Nike's SB shoe division committing nothing short of plagiary by mixing Dischord Records and Minor Threat's "label and band's cachet" with the company's "Major Threat" campaign. After Nike sort of apologized for the cannibalization in a carefully well-worded lawyer-doctored statement, the label posted this on its web site: "It is disheartening to us to think that Nike may be successful in using this imagery to fool kids into thinking that the general ethos of the label, and Minor Threat in particular, can somehow be linked to Nike's mission." But the label determined that by not suing the $14 billion Nike, they would not compromise their antiestablishment ethos. The label went further in dismissing the experience as just "another familiar example of mainstream corporations attempting to assimilate underground culture to turn a buck."

Even when an artist is deceased and the control of his likeness has been transferred to the estate, that likeness can be just as valuable a commodity—whether or not the artist would have approved the usage. One ad that caused outrage in the music community was an ad campaign for Dr. Martens in Britain that featured retouched photos of Kurt Cobain, Joey Ramone, the Clash's Joe Strummer, and the Sex Pistols' bassist Sid Vicious—each wearing a white angel's toga and a pair of Docs.

An offshoot of the punk mantra is Do it Yourself, or DIY—music, art, and almost anything else to convey an individual's (your) freedom of expression. Graffiti became one of the most recognizable forms of DIY because it was so pervasive in major cities across the United States and was thereby being seen by millions of people every day. So it should come as no surprise that ad agencies would find a way to exploit it for a viral underground marketing campaign.

That's just what Critical Massive, an interactive marketing agency based in Calgary, Alberta, Canada, did for their clients like U.S. Cellular, White Castle, and M&Ms candy. Referred to as *Graffadi*, it has been utilized for marketing for Verizon, Nissan, *Time*, and yes, (no surprise here) Nike. As Moore so eloquently writes, "This . . . use of underpaid artists and urban neighborhoods for the purposes of expanding product awareness and, hopefully, profit, or, in other words, exploitation." But isn't Graffadi illegal? No worries, as one industry guide to Graffadi covers this inconvenience by suggesting that advertisers should stipulate that they will reimburse artists for fines and legal fees. An *Ad Age* columnist editorialized that "something like this is much cheaper than producing and running a national television commercial." In other words, a small price to pay for street cred.

In the 1990s, when punk became mainstream for the music biz after the tremendous success of Nirvana's anti–Madison Ave teen angst anthem, "Smells Like Teen Spirit,"[10] a troubled Kurt Cobain had to come to grips with his dilemma of achieving popularity by having to work with major corporations without compromising his integrity to his fans. It's no wonder that for Nirvana's first big cover story in *Rolling Stone* magazine in 1992, Kurt expressed his disdain by wearing the now-famous DIY T-shirt emblazoned with the inscription *Corporate Magazines Still Suck*. Score one for Punk ethics.

Although I may not agree with all the marketing tactics of using these powerful motivators to sell just about any product, I was still fascinated by marketing, and loved music more than ever. Maybe it was just simply that I felt the need to justify my career path in marketing, but I truly believed that I owed it to myself to explore all the ways I could harness my love of music to focus on the positive aspects of music marketing, and maybe even bring a little of this magic to others.

In his book, *Musicophilia: Tales of Music and the Brain,*[11] neurologist and author Oliver Sacks documented remarkable instances of the healing power of music. His interest in music neuroscience began when he first heard about the phenomenon from nurses at Beth Abraham Hospital in 1966, where he observed the patients he wrote about in his book *Awakenings.*[12] "On weekends there was singing in religious services—and these people who'd been frozen for many years seemed liberated by the music and could move, sing, and even dance." Sacks goes on to say, "Music voice and auditory stimuli are functionally more closely linked to memory and emotion than visual phenomena, therefore they hold an ability to transport one into realms of emotion and memory."[13] Listening to music has even been touted as a way to help stroke victims recover specific and cognitive functions. In Finland, in a six-month study of 60 recent victims of stroke ages 35 to 75, researchers found that exposure to music for at least one hour per day improved verbal memory by an astonishing 60 percent.[14]

One of the people I feel most fortunate to work with at Fender is Tony Franklin, who is on our artist relations team based on the West Coast. Not only is he a highly regarded artist at the top of his field as a musician who has played with some of the biggest names in our industry, but I have always felt that he brings a certain spiritualism to his day-to-day responsibilities with Fender. I asked him for an explanation of how he sees music's impact in our everyday lives. The following is what he told me.

"I believe that music is something far deeper, far more meaningful than we can simply comprehend with our ears. It touches us deeply on a soul level. It is a spiritual vibration, and truly 'inspired' music speaks to us on a level that is way beyond the five senses. I read a book called *Talks with Great Composers*, which explored the inspiration of the classic composers and how they went about their writing process. A large portion of the book was focused on Johannes Brahms, taken from an actual conversation that Brahms had with the author. The conversation took place in 1895, and Brahms agreed to do the interview on the condition that the book would not be published until at least fifty years after his passing; the reason being, in Brahms's opinion, that many of the great composers were not fully recognized until fifty years or more after they died. If we look at the lives of a number of great composers, this indeed is true. Brahms considered his inspiration (and that of other truly inspired writers) to be divine in nature.

"Brahms would enter an almost trance-like state when he wrote, as if he were simply a conduit for the musical message that was being given to him. Of course, he had to have the musical knowledge and skills to be able to 'translate' the gift that was coming his way, but the initial inspiration, the 'raw' data was coming from a place that he considered to be divine. He had no idea when the inspirations would come, but he came to recognize when the inspiration was being given to him, and would respond accordingly. With this kind of writing, these composers were not writing for themselves, or following a trend; they were simply honoring the moment, being true to the muse, with a sense of duty, capturing the message that was being delivered through them. For many of these composers, their works were ahead of their time, hence the reason they were not fully appreciated until many years after their passing.

"Apparently when Handel wrote the *Messiah*, he locked himself in his room for twenty-one days, requesting not to be disturbed. When he emerged, he simply said, 'I have been touched by God.'

"Music doesn't have to be a grand classical piece to be inspired. Any music that stands the test of time, and continues to touch us, or move, or inspire us, is part of the grand spiritual vibration of music. We've all turned on the radio or played a CD and heard a song that has changed our mood, changed our day, or changed our lives.

"The great artists of the past fifty years or more are those who honored the muse first, and took chances by creating music that had not been done before. Maybe there isn't so much room for innovation these days—Jimi Hendrix, the Beatles, Led Zeppelin, the Rolling Stones et cetera, left such big footprints, that there is little room to step, without stepping on them at least a little. But what all of these artists had was incredible heart and soul, a deep feeling and conviction for what they did. I don't see that in so much of today's music, though it is there.

"People often want to become 'famous', 'stars,' and 'wealthy' rather than a first-rate musician or a world-class vocalist. It is a well-worn cliché, 'Do what you love, the money will follow.' I believe this to be true, while also applying proper business etiquette, integrity, network-ing, and business principles.

"Music should not be a commodity. It is too personal and sacred. It is of the heart and soul. And yet, we need the business side of things to allow listeners to access and hear music. Reflecting back on those great composers, many of which [sic] died poor, misunderstood, and shunned—they were not afraid to give up everything to honor the muse, the spirit of music that shone through them. We need the business side of things, but the music is more important than the business. If every faculty of the entertainment business disappeared, music and entertainment would still continue. But if the music disappeared, then the music business would evaporate."

Wanting to bring all my research closer to home, I contacted a long-time friend and associate of mine with whom I had worked at Fender, Morgan Ringwald; who is now the director of market development at NAMM, The International Music Products Association, (formerly known as the National Association of Music Merchants). This 100-year-old nonprofit organization had several initiatives to promote and support music education; so when I met with Morgan to discuss this chapter, he immediately stopped me and said, "You need to talk with Karl T. Bruhn, who will tell you everything you need to know about 'Recreational Music Making and Wellness.'" I knew from my affiliation with NAMM that music making played a key role in building self-esteem in children and young adults, which often led to everything from improved social skills to better grades.

All I knew about RMM was that it was some type of marketing program that had to do with music making and wellness, and thanks to Morgan's recommendation, I quickly arranged a meeting with Mr. Bruhn. On a perfect, patented Southern California afternoon, Karl T. Bruhn and I sat down for lunch in a classic Mediterranean-inspired restaurant that would have not been out of place in the movie, *Casablanca*. I found out from the very distinguished-looking former senior vice president of the Yamaha Corporation that he was also the chairman of the Yamaha Music and Wellness Institute (YMWI, yamahainstitute.org).

He explained that the organization was established for two primary purposes: foremost is the performance of exemplary, cutting-edge scientific research documenting active music participation as an effective, integral healthy lifestyle strategy for people of all ages throughout the world. The second is a dedicated focus on providing engaging educational programs for the purpose of disseminating these original findings to professional and public audiences. Karl was quick to point out that "RMM is *not* the same old, same old," and that the benefits of RMM extend far beyond music. He stated that there are important differences between RMM and traditional music instruction that need to be understood.

First of all, unlike traditional education programs, RMM refers to any form of music-making that is not based on mastery of performance. I told Karl that when people found out I work for a guitar company, they would say time and time again, "I always wanted to play a musical instrument, but I know I could never become a rock star." (Note: in *This is Your Brain on Music*, author Daniel J. Levitin presents research of the "10,000-hour rule," which says that that is the time it takes to become proficient on an instrument). Karl smiled and told me, "RMM is not about inspiring extraordinary music-making; it's about inspiring extraordinary living. You see, the primary goal is wellness enhancement, enjoyment, communication, nurturing, support, creative self-expression, and a host of nonmusical outcomes."

I explained to Karl that I had done quite a bit of research on the power of music for this chapter and I that could also offer firsthand experience on how music had enhanced my life. Even now, the first thing I do when I get home from a tough day at work is to listen to some of my favorite music, or pick up my acoustic guitar and strum away.

Karl replied, "Listen, an article in *Newsweek* a few years ago stated that experts claim that sixty to ninety percent of doctor visits involve stress-related complaints. Furthermore, the *New York Times* reported that workplace stress costs the nation more than $300 billion each year. For the first time in the history of medicine, the successful reversal of key elements of the human stress response has been documented on the DNA level utilizing an RMM strategy." Karl's colleague, Dr. Barry Bittman, MD, of the Mind-Body Wellness Center in Meadville, Pennsylvania, was the study's principal investigator. Dr. Bittman is also president and CEO of the Yamaha Music and Wellness Institute.

Karl told me that the genome research that Dr. Bittman did ("Recreational Music-Making Modulates the Human Stress Response") is an unparalleled first for the music products industry, and perhaps the most significant strategic breakthrough in our understanding of the health benefits of music-making. "Even though computers and the Internet have brought us together," continued Karl, "they have also isolated us. RMM's format is based upon group activities and get-togethers for all ages, with the criteria being inclusive, regardless of talent."

I told Karl that although I have been in the music biz all my life, this was the first time I realized how important it is for our industry to promote the concept of recreational music making. From my conversations with him, I knew the benefits of promoting wellness through this program. I also recognized the opportunities to increase business, as we would be opening the doors to a completely new market segment of people who could be motivated to pick up an instrument, not necessarily to become a performer, but simply to enjoy music. (Note: According to the U.S. Gallop Poll in 2003, only 7.6 percent of U.S. adults over the age of 18 play a musical instrument, and only 6 percent of respondents learned to play after the age of 18.) There is clearly a vast underserved market out there that our industry has overlooked. That is one of reasons that Fender's late CEO, Bill Shultz (who was a close friend and associate of Karl's), supported the children's and young adults' music education programs offered by the nonprofit Fender Center in Corona, California.

Karl continued, "Our industry is making great progress with programs such as Lowery's Magic Organ course, [and] Remo's *Health*RHYTHMS programs (which incidentally has trained over 1,400 facilitators), Roland's Club Roland, and Yamaha's Clavinova Connection, but we still have a long way to go in promoting this to both the manufacturers and retailers in our industry and beyond."

He then explained to me that "market development is a process." He then proceeded to show me a model for our industry that I believe would work for any market development department, because it is based on market segments from innovators to laggards:

1. Have Capacity (time, money, interest, and so on)

- Currently shopping music stores for make, model, and price

2. Have Capacity (time, money, interest, and so on)

- Talking to friends and others whom they perceive to have knowledge of music products and music education and getting recommendations, ideas, and so forth concerning their interest in buying an instrument or taking music lessons—but have *not* yet visited a music store.

3. Have Capacity (time, money, interest, and so on)

- *Some* interest in learning to make their own music, or taking music lessons for themselves or their kids, but also interested in a big screen TV, trip to Europe, new car, and other sizable purchases.
- Again, this group may have *some* interest in music but it is *not* a big priority.
- Big discount ads usually get their attention only if they are already interested in buying a music instrument or having their children take music lessons (either privately or in public school).

4. Have Capacity (time, money, interest, and so on)

- This is the biggest group of all; however, as an industry, we generally don't seem to know how to reach them.

Typical ads about price and features don't get their attention.

5. Have No Capacity at this Time

- That is, a homeless person, out of work, and so on.

Karl further said, "Del, the number three and four groups are immense, and we, as an industry, are not reaching them with the same old, same old messages about discounts, and features et cetera. [They] are not working. The objective of our marketing efforts should be to move each of these groups up a notch. For example, number one, close the people who are currently shopping at a music store; then get the next group to move up and start shopping at a music store. Once again, market development is a process." I replied, "So you are saying that RMM has the capability to be the key ingredient in this process?"

"Precisely. Making your own music is not only fun but it can be good for your health. The benefits of RMM ultimately extend far beyond music—the public and members of our own industry need to know this." Then with a warm smile, he added, "During my lifetime RMM and wellness will be recorded as history—not news. And I'm seventy-eight years old."

Now I had the backup I was looking for—a statement from an industry expert that music is not only an extremely powerful motivator and marketing device, but when used in a positive manner, it has healing powers and affects our lives in the most profound biological, psychological, and sociological ways. I also realized I had to challenge myself to explore the ways these concepts and research data could be applied to all types of marketing.

CHAPTER 3

Expanding Your Brand's Identity— Partnership Marketing Outside Your Core Market

Even successful brands need help when going outside their comfort zone in marketing, and you should not be worried about diluting the brand when you do so as long as you set some parameters. When I was working with Dean Guitars in the mid–1980s, our sales manager approached me with an idea. "I just saw Van Halen last night and the bassist (Michael Anthony) was playing this bass that looked like a big bottle of Jack Daniels. It was so cool. We should do that with Budweiser." "Why Bud?" I asked. "Because I like Bud, and maybe we'll get some free cases of beer from them!" That was good enough for me to approach the owner with the idea of creating logoed guitars that could be used by Anheuser-Busch to tap into the world of rock.

Keep in mind that at this point, Bud was still using race cars with a fast jazz soundtrack in their commercials. Budweiser was one of the oldest and best-selling brands in U.S. history and they knew their market was "Joe Six-pack"—the blue-collar guy who downed a sixer each night after work, and much more on weekends. Joe was as loyal to his beer brand as he was to his brand of cars and trucks (U.S.-made, of course). Dean and I knew A-B had to be ripe for new ideas, so we worked together on a logoed guitar with a shape based on their famous "Bowtie" logo.

We approached licensing at their headquarters in St. Louis because we had a contact there, and besides, we knew we had to start somewhere. After about 10 minutes in licensing, we were whisked up to the top floor to meet the Vice President of Promotions, John Lodge, who asked us to open the guitar case so he could see firsthand "what was causing all the commotion downstairs." After glancing at the guitar and without batting an eye, he said, "I will need about a thousand of those right away." We tried not to show it, but we were floored—because that was about *quadruple* what we sold in a typical month.

But we didn't stop there. Once we had opened that huge gateway into the corporate world, we helped create a music sponsorship program that beer companies still use as a template today: sponsorships of bands on the highest touring levels, down to the local bands playing the clubs where beer is served. That was a simple plan, modeled after their sports marketing, which supported the major leagues, to the local tavern leagues, and everything in between. We created point-of-purchase displays, promotional lapel pins, and even placed guitars in their commercials. We had worked before with ZZ Top (see Chapter 2), who was now a huge commercial success, so it was only natural that we brought them to Bud for their next tour sponsorship. A-B then signed on to sponsor the Rolling Stones's *Steel Wheels* tour by paying an unprecedented $17 million. Most of that money went into TV ads, which debuted during the NBA playoffs, also unheard of for a rock 'n' roll band at that time. It seemed that Bud had built a brand new market through their music promotions and sponsorships overnight—without losing their core customer, Joe Six-pack; and Dean Guitars had a partner with enormous resources that allowed us to play with the big boys in our industry. Bud became a cool brand and A-B was approaching 50 percent of the beer market. (That was, of course, before the explosion of microbreweries.)

If you believe most marketing campaigns, bigger is definitely better. But that's not always the situation. Take the case (or should I say several cases) of microbreweries. At the time we were working with Bud, their marketing guys would always use *The Art of War*[1] analogies to describe their campaigns. "We'll find their window of vulnerability," and "This is how we can outflank our opponents," they would say in marketing meetings. But I have to admit that for such a large company, they could move fast if they needed to, and that's why we were able to make such an impact on their marketing.

For instance, I remember a time when they were discussing how Lone Star Beer was making inroads in the Texas market, because they had long-necked bottles that made the guys holding them look cooler than those who were holding the squat-necked bottles Bud had at the time. Whether these bottles were phallic symbols or not, Bud switched all of their bottles, not just in Texas, to the longnecks, which are still used today.[2]

Even though the marketers at Bud were able to move quickly against Lone Star, they focused most of their long-term marketing attention on the number two-ranking beer company, Miller Brewing. At the same time, craft beers and imports began to take a bigger chunk of the market. With names like Fat Tire, Gila Monster Amber Lager, Dogfish Head, and Ol' Bastard piquing their interest, consumers began to seek out those brands—first for the novelty, then the taste. Today, through aggressive marketing and acquisitions, Anheuser-Busch has held on to its

50.9 percent share of the shrinking beer market (Note: now owned by Belgium brewer InBev in a $52 billion merger), with numbers two and three, Miller and Molson Coors, now combining forces in an effort to attain a 30 percent market share. All others make up the remaining share but the telling point is that while domestic beers like Bud are down 1.7 percent since 2002, imported beers are up 24.4 percent and microbreweries are up 21.2 percent in the same period.[3] Keep in mind that the micros are accomplishing this with minuscule ad budgets compared to the big brands. I guess you can say being different and edgy does count, even in the beer market.

Remember this when you are ready to go outside your company's comfort zone: "Your brand can't be everything to everyone—focus on what you are trying to accomplish." Those are my words to live (and market) by. Before you can begin to build your brand's image, you must first decide the ideal new market you want to reach. Easy enough, right? Well, not as easy as you might think—because so many companies try to reach outside their target market and are thinking that's the surest way to increase sales. You can only do that when you have established your brand's recognition within your core market. During my years in the music business, I cannot tell you how many demos (an artist's sample of their music sent to record labels to garner their interest for a potential record deal) I received of an artist or band showcasing several different styles of music through five or six different songs. That approach never works—because it doesn't show an artist's sound or the unique style that makes them different from everyone else.

Remember the Coolness Law Number Two from Chapter 1? Your product has to be unique when compared with the norm of the day. So instead of a lottery approach whereby anyone can be your audience, you must commit to the market you want to reach. This, I believe, is the only credible way to build your brand. Once you have made that commitment, you can then seek out potential partners that are already established in that market that will help propel your brand to stratospheric heights.

As I demonstrated at the beginning of this chapter, Dean was a small but recognizable brand name established in the guitar industry. We were looking to promote our brand and sales outside our industry into what we considered the "real world," where Budweiser literally was king. At the same time, Anheuser-Busch was looking for a way to capture more market share by adding the next generation of drinkers. They determined that the younger demographic was less interested in racing and other traditional sports, and more passionate about rock music and live music events. Dean and I obviously came along at the perfect time, but both companies had already decided on the new market they were going to reach for. Otherwise, our respective partnerships probably wouldn't have come to be.

One of best examples of a major brand trying to be everything to everyone was Cadillac. By introducing the Cimarron model in 1981, the company tried to bridge the gap between the traditional Cadillac buyer—who was looking to the brand for luxury and prestige—and the more frugal buyer, who looks for savings through higher gas mileage. Because of the higher price tag that accompanies a Cadillac emblem, it did not register with the thrifty consumer—who was buying imports—that this would be any kind of bargain. By diluting the Cadillac brand with a smaller automobile, the vehicle did nothing to excite the status-seeking affluent consumer. When first introduced, the Cimarron sold about a third of what Cadillac had anticipated, and was put out of its misery after 1988. The damage had been done, however, to the Cadillac image. I use this example because it's a perfect segue into the story in Chapter 4 on how Cadillac was able to reposition itself and salvage the brand's image through a dynamic rock 'n' roll marketing campaign.

But even well-established artists in the music biz make the same mistakes. I have nothing against artists trying to expand their audiences by taking bold new directions, but sometimes they move a bit too far away from their established audience. Take Garth Brooks, for example. While riding high on record-breaking record and concert ticket sales, Brooks created an alter ego rock star, Chris Gaines. Originally intended to foreshadow a movie that never happened, the 1999 standalone CD never reached the sales expectations of a Brooks CD because it wasn't embraced by his loyal fans or the new audience he was trying to reach; and the next year Brooks announced a period of retirement from recording and touring.

Closer to home, I was ready to explore ways for Fender to promote the brand outside of traditional industry avenues. I knew that all our competitors shared the exact same outlets to promote our respective brands—we advertised in the same guitar magazines and other music industry publications that reached only the same audience month after month. By running product or artists ads, Fender and other brands were preaching to their respective choirs. The ads were necessary to reach that core market of two hundred thousand or so loyal readers. I also understood, however, the rest of the world out there included nonmusicians, or casual consumers, who may have not realized that they were potential customers for our brand. And that was whom we had to preach the gospel of Fender to.

I was intrigued by what Nike was able to accomplish when they faced the same marketing concerns in the mid-1980s. The company was looking to expand beyond just athletic shoes designed for a specific sport. When they asked Baby Boomers back then what sport they played, a good portion likely replied that they didn't play too many active sports like basketball, tennis, and so on anymore because of an injury or they were just getting too old. (I understand this, because I've been in the same boat: I severely tore my anterior cruciate ligament playing basketball with Janie Lane of Warrant in a pickup game. Even though I had surgery, my knee never fully recovered enough to allow me to play competitive sports again.) When asked what they did for exercise, the Boomers most likely replied that they walked their dog. "Okay, so you're a cross-trainer!" replied the Nike research team. The company's sales of cross-trainers totaled $92.5 million in 1987, and today, cross-training shoes generate $1.2 billion in sales, with Nike commanding 50 percent of the market.[4]

I was also fascinated by Nike's concept of image transfer, that is, cool ads, cool product. As Dan Wieden of the Weiden & Kennedy agency, which has handled all of Nike's advertising since 1985 puts it, "We don't set out to make ads. The ultimate goal is to make a connection." This seems to make sense, considering that both Wieden and Nike founder Phil Knight freely admit that they both "hate advertising."[5]

I had already experienced quite a bit of success working at Dean and at Washburn (my former companies) in creating promotions and campaigns by partnering with major corporations in the real world; so I had some guidelines that would help me explore new avenues at Fender. I also realized, though, that I couldn't explore these avenues as an extension of my responsibilities in artist relations, since I would have to have the resources to devote all of my energies to this new proposition.

I am a firm believer in dedicating face time whenever possible, as is most of the entertainment industry. E-mails and voicemail are good ways to communicate information, but nothing replaces in-person dialogue when developing long-term relationships and successful programs. It worked for me in artist relations, and I knew I would have to spend even more face time if I was to move into a new arena of marketing.

As I explain in more detail in Chapter 7, the success of the Fender Catalina Island Blues Festival made me realize the opportunity for creating the concept for a new division at Fender—a division that would promote the brand well beyond the typical musical instrument company markets. I used to complain to my girlfriend, Bettina (who later became my wife and was at the time on the team that created the festival), that Fender was missing all types of opportunities to promote the brand because we didn't have anyone to focus his efforts on these opportunities. At that time, I was the director of artist relations, so my primary responsibility was for the artist endorsement program. But I was empowered by the Catalina events and the fact that my department was seeing considerable growth in movie and TV placements. Bettina, in her wonderful, Norwegian, cut-to-the-basics way, said to me, "Stop complaining and create the job for yourself." It just so happened that I would be attending our annual marketing meetings at our corporate headquarters in Scottsdale, Arizona, and so I jumped at the chance to create the template for this new department.

I had some strong advice from a book I had just read, *The Innovator's Dilemma*.[6] Author Clayton M. Christensen uses a chapter to outline the need for a separate marketing division outside of a company's traditional marketing department that he describes as a *spin-out organization* to explore new markets. "How separate does the effort need to be?" writes Christensen. "The primary requirement is that the project cannot be forced to compete with projects in the mainstream organization for resources. Because values are the criteria by which prioritization decisions are made. Projects that are inconsistent with a company's mainstream values will naturally be accorded lowest priority." Christensen makes another key point in his demonstration as to why "outstanding companies that did everything right—were in tune with the competition, listened to customers, and invested aggressively in new technologies—still lost their market leadership when confronted with disruptive changes in technology and market structure."

A telling story on this front took place in the early 1950s when the chairman of Sony, Akio Morita, asked AT&T to grant him the license for their patented transistor technology, which AT&T had developed in 1947. He even went so far as to take up residence in an inexpensive New York City hotel to be able to constantly badger them, despite their resistance. After finally giving in, Sony asked what Morita planned to do with the technology, to which he replied, "We will build small radios." One of the executives at the document signing remarked, "Why would anyone care about smaller radios?" At that time, consumers were demanding better quality hi-fi radios. Sony introduced the *lo-fi* transistor radio for a new market for that was seeking a portable personal radio—beach-going teens, picnickers, fans at ballparks, and so on. It's not surprising that none of the leading manufacturers of table-top radios became an industry leader in personal radios, and that each and every one was eventually driven from the radio market.

Newly energized by Bettina's encouragement and my recent reading, I literally worked right up to my plane flight to create a template for a new department called Market Development. Thankfully, we had a young COO at the time named Bob Heinrich, who, once he finished reading my proposal, and with the blessing of our Chairman, Bill Shultz, gave me the job. The department was to be run by Vice President, Ritchie Fliegler, in Scottsdale, who had joined Fender at the same time as I, but had held different marketing positions at the company. Alex Perez, who had been my assistant in artist relations, took over my job to free me up for the position of Market Development Director–Promotions.

I was a little skeptical at first, because Ritchie and I had our differences of opinion on some of the things I was trying to accomplish. Bob commented that this might have been because Ritchie was an East Coast guy and I was "Hollywood." He suggested that Ritchie and I meet symbolically somewhere in the middle of the country, and when we did, we developed a close working relationship, and eventually a strong friendship. Ritchie and I were around the same age and had therefore shared similar experiences in music and lifestyle. Ritchie's fanaticism with classic cars helped open the door to many future partnerships for FMIC in the auto industry—including a partnership with Ford for the new Shelby Mustang that came with a matching co-branded Fender Stratocaster guitar.

Even though my job description remained the same, I thought a new title would be less restrictive than Market Development Director–promotions, so I suggested a different one: Director, Entertainment Marketing. I felt this was a moniker that covered a far wider range of responsibilities with great possibilities for future growth. Thankfully, Ritchie agreed. I presented my department's mission statement as follows:

"Entertainment Marketing is to become a fully integrated department to build and take advantage of relationships within the entertainment community to facilitate placements, promotional tie-ins, licensing, marketing support and charitable and educational programs."

At the time, I wasn't aware of any other music instrument company that had a similar department, although it was becoming more common in the corporate United States.

To acquire more information on the origins of entertainment marketing, I sat down with my good friend Warren Weideman, who was at the forefront of this concept at its inception. For our interview, we fittingly chose the historic Hollywood Roosevelt hotel, site of the first Academy Awards ceremony, located along the Hollywood Walk of Fame.

"I was actually interviewed by *Ad Age* back in the Eighties because I had worked at several movie studios, working on films targeted at young adults, marketing, and doing college promotions, and saw that there were a lot of movies that had great opportunities for product placement and I wondered, 'Who are these people putting product in the movies?' So I investigated four or five product placement companies and found that they all had product placement, but no one did promotions. And I thought there's a need for that in the marketplace. So, myself and a gentleman from the Miller Brewing Company formed our own company and I coined the phrase *entertainment marketing*, because to me, it was not just putting a product into a movie, which obviously was important, but once it was in the movie, there was an opportunity to create a promotion at retail so that the consumer would see the brand and the association with the film. Hopefully, it would induce them to want to see the film and when you went to the movie theater and saw the movie, you'd see the product—so it concluded the circle. To me, that was entertainment marketing.

"I was interviewed by *Advertising Age* in the late Eighties about what we were doing differently than [sic] the product placement companies and the guy that was interviewing me said, 'Well, what do you call this?' and I said, 'Well, I call it *entertainment marketing*,' and I think that from that point forward it has been used as kind of a phrase to identify what we are doing—but to me, it's more than that. It's lifestyle marketing. It's finding ways of getting brands involved with any form of entertainment that involves the consumer. Whether it's at a rock concert, a baseball game, or whether it's at a movie—be someplace where the consumer is involved with some form of entertainment, and let them be subjected to seeing your brand in a favorable light. It's pretty simple how that happens, but sometimes I think you run the risk of stepping over that boundary when you force a product into a scenario that it doesn't belong [in]. As much as everybody loves to watch NASCAR racing, to me NASCAR has gone way beyond the reasonable interpretation of branding because there's too many products, there's too many decals, there's too many signs, and I think they cannibalize each other. Look at their car and tell me, unless it's the main sponsor, with all the insignias on there, who's going to see a little decal on the back pipe of a car going a hundred eighty miles an hour? And what's the emotional connection to the people at the race? They like the driver and they like maybe the sponsor of the car but they don't care about that bumper sticker. And the same goes for other sports marketing. For the release of a _Spiderman_ movie, the studio wanted to buy the bases in baseball parks and there was such a reaction to that and they shot it down. The reason they did that was because all the billboards were in the ballparks with all the messages and the signage and yes, you have fifty thousand people there but they are getting twenty or thirty or forty or fifty or more messages, which at the end of the day, they don't remember any of them—particularly if it's a message that's going to turn them off. I think when you take something as iconic today as _American Idol_—and I've given speeches about it and everyone has raved about the fact that Ford and Coca-Cola are major sponsors of the show—I have a problem with the Coke containers being on the table in front of the judges. That to me is blatant product placement and it has no business being on that show. Because in the judging of a normal competition like that, judges wouldn't have a branded container sitting in front of them. In the real world, that doesn't happen. The consumer looks at that and it looks like it's staged. To further confuse the issue, twice on the show *American Idol* contestants have grabbed the cup that is sitting in front of Simon and have thrown it in his face—and both times, it was water—so they are not even drinking the product, which makes it even more phony. That's not product placement—that's blatant branding and I think as a backlash, the consumer knows one from the other, and I think if you are going to incorporate your brand—whether it's a guitar, or an automobile, or a soft drink—it needs to seem like it's a seamless part of what's going on—and it's not forced. I think when brands find a way to do that, I think the consumer recognizes the brand and is not offended by it and it takes it to a point in my mind, paying for measured media. I think if I were running a major corporation today, I would take the majority of my money and put it into entertainment marketing instead of traditional media. Simply because, if I buy a commercial on television—first I have to spend a lot of money to produce it. I put it on television and it may be on one of the hottest shows on television, but guess what—when my commercial comes up, the consumer has his clicker and they click away to watch some other channel—while the three minutes of commercials are going and then all of a sudden they come back to the show. I've wasted my money on the production of the commercial and of the airing of the commercial and nobody saw it. That's not an effective way of using marketing dollars. A better way is getting the brand involved in the program or the movie, where the brand seems likes it's involved in what going on with the character, and then there's a retail promotion around that. To me, there's a more effective way of spending your advertising dollars where you really reach your target consumer and make them embrace your brand. And when they are out in the marketplace, I think they are at least more apt to try your product. It doesn't mean they are going to keep buying it, because if they buy your guitar, car, or drink your soda—and they don't like the product—all the advertising in the world isn't going to save your product; they are not going to buy it again.

"Once again, I think the infusion on the entertainment properties gets new consumers to try a product, and I think if you can ever accomplish that—then you truly have accomplished something with entertainment marketing. But the key is to associate your brand with something that's fun. I think if the consumer is enjoying what they are watching, enjoying what they are listening to, and they see a brand, then there's a positive association with that. That's why entertainment marketing has grown from when I first started in the business. In twenty years, I've seen it explode from a few thousand dollars to spending hundreds of millions of dollars. More and more corporations are diverting large sums of money to that because they see the results. They see that it's actually working to get the consumer to associate their brand with something that they are enjoying. And I think that is why entertainment marketing has become a far better way to spend your money than traditional measured media—when more and more consumers are turned off by commercials and don't watch it. So if the cost of commercials is higher and the audience is lower, I think you're reaching a diminishing return and you need to find a better way to spend your money, because marketing and advertising is an expense. The best way to get a return on your investment is to try to spend the smallest amount of money in an area that you are going to reach the largest amount of people. To me, today, traditional media is not the answer. To me, it's entertainment marketing, whether is music, movies, television, Internet, or mobile—it's all a factor."

I asked Warren to give some firsthand examples to illustrate his concept of entertainment marketing. I remembered seeing a poster for the movie *The Natural* in his office and at the time he remarked that he was involved in a direct integration between Budweiser Beer and the film's star, Robert Redford.

"It was one of those things—I don't want to call it a fluke—but I was working on the film and at the time I was also working with Budweiser and I'm reading the script. I saw that in the outfield of *The Natural* that they had these old-time billboards that were associated with that era—1920s/early 30s. I did some research on it and found that coincidentally Budweiser was a major advertiser in ballparks, and at the time, they had a very unusual billboard campaign where they had a man in a tuxedo with a bottle of Budweiser on its tray—hardly what you would find in today's world of advertising. By the way, what I enjoyed about it was doing research to make it historically correct. I didn't want to put a Budweiser sign in the outfield that wasn't current of that period and to me, in doing your homework—if you're going to do product placement, in particular if you're working on a period movie—the last thing you want to have happen is somebody in a 1950's present-day movie playing a [2008] present-day Fender guitar. It just looks funny and the consumer is smart enough to know that. I see period movies today and there's products in there and they are using current packaging and it's not period and I think it's a jolt to the system.

"So then I went to the archives and found the ad from Budweiser, went to their production people at the studio, and asked if they could recreate that billboard in the outfield. And they loved it because it was an unusual-looking billboard. They put the billboard up in the movie and there are scenes that Robert Redford is in the outfield and he's standing in front of the billboard. There was also a picture of him from the movie where you see the billboard behind him that ran in a major magazine (I think it was *Sports Illustrated*). We then, in turn, took the picture of him in the outfield and made up a movie poster and gave it out at all major baseball games in association with the promotion; and that luckily happened because one of the senior executives at Budweiser knew Robert Redford personally and was able to call him and convince him to let us use his picture. And to my knowledge, I don't know of another time that Redford has ever been on any kind of movie poster that was branded. As a [matter of] fact, the Budweiser poster is still in my office today because it is such an unusual thing.

"If I had to pick my two favorite placements, the first one was when I worked on a Fox film that was about a young guy taking his driver's test and the scene called for the DMV teacher to get into the car with him and set a cup on coffee on the dash. He said, 'If one drop of that coffee spills, you flunk the test' and with that, he threw his clipboard out the window. The actor looked at him and he proceeded to take his driver's test. When I saw the script, we represented 7-Eleven and I thought this is a great opportunity for product placement. So I went to Fox and I said this will be great for 7-Eleven to be on the coffee cup. And they said, 'Well . . . it might be, but the director will never allow that because he hates product placement because it's too blatant.' I asked if I could meet with the director and they said, 'Well, you could meet him, but it's not going to do you any good.' I went down on their set the day they were shooting—I'm walking across the parking lot and he goes, 'Oh . . . you're that 7-Eleven guy, huh? So what's the deal?' I said, 'Well, I think that a DMV guy coming to work would more than likely be stopping off at 7-Eleven to get a cup of coffee (if he would have walked in with a very expensive cup of coffee, it wouldn't have been believable for a guy that works for the DMV) and it wouldn't be unusual for him to have that sitting on the dash.' He said, 'Yes, but that would just be too obvious of a placement.' So I said, 'I don't want the whole cup facing forward—I want it sideways. All you see is part of the *eleven*—you don't even see the *seven*. You see the green and white cup.' He said, 'Oh, I'll do that—I thought you wanted it facing forward.' I told him that's too obvious—the consumer would look at that and say, 'What is that?' 7-Eleven, in turn, did a major promotion and gave away a car through a sweepstakes—they loved the movie association. So, it was authentic, as it fit into the character in the movie, and I wanted it to be seamless and not blatant, and therefore there was no backlash from the consumer.

"The last example is my favorite placement of all was in [the] *A View to a Kill* James Bond movie. I read in the script that Roger Moore was in a Rolls Royce and he was drugged and submerged under water. He awakens and realizes that he can't surface for fear of being shot. So he gets out of the back of the car and swims over to the back tire, unscrews the cap, and breaths the air out of the tire so he can stay under water. In the real world, that can't happen—but in a James Bond movie, it can happen. I saw that and Michelin Tires was our client, so I went to the studio and asked if we could make it a Michelin tire, and they said, 'Sure' and I asked if it could have (the name) in white letters? They replied, 'Well, most Rolls Royces wouldn't have white letter tires' but I said, 'You're under water in murky water—you'll never see the Michelin name!' Michelin is going to do a major global promotion (which they did) to promote the movie and plus, we gave him and his production company a lot of tires for his vehicles and he agreed to do it. When the movie came out, I was with the executives of Michelin and sure enough, on a big giant movie screen, there's Roger Moore getting out of the car and swimming over to this big Michelin tire and breathing the air. The response we got from Michelin came from all over the world—it was phenomenal. Maybe we took a little trade by making the letters white, but I don't think it concerned anybody. But it worked for the scene and it certainly made people pay attention to the fact that Michelin wouldn't be an odd tire to be on a Rolls Royce. I think if we had a cheaper brand tire, it would not have been believable. But again, I think if you use your imagination finding ways to associate a brand with a movie or a television show (I think it's getting harder to do that—the consumer is getting wiser), and if it doesn't look forced, and it looks like it belongs in that scene, then I think you can do it today and do it seamlessly without offending the public. The worst thing that can happen is somebody sees a scene where somebody opens a refrigerator and they see a carton that says *Milk* and a carton that says *Orange Juice* and people say, 'Mine doesn't say that—mine has a brand name on it.' I think that part of being in the entertainment business is understanding that you can't take too many liberties with the creative process with a brand because you'd begin to turn off the consumer. What swayed the producer to do the deal was the fact that we did a major national promotion in all of the Michelin tire stores, where we had a contest to win a trip to the world premiere, which was in San Francisco. The small amount of money that was paid for the placement plus the tires that we gave him was certainly not a large amount, and I don't think it would have been enough to sway him. I think the back-end promotion to get people to come see his movie (and we also ran TV commercials where we showed clips of the movie in all the markets that Michelin advertised in), and a nice TV and print campaign that helped promote his movie, and he didn't have to pay for it made it worthwhile for him. But to simply take a few thousand dollars and some free tires—I don't think that would have been enough to motivate [him] to make the deal happen."

I told Warren that's one of the things I have been struggling with in writing this book, that there are no set rules. If you're an agency you make your money by product placement, but then you have these fees and the more you talk to people like Warren, who are in the business, sometimes the fees are not really as important as the marketing and promotional value.

Warren continued: "With that being said, the entertainment marketing aspect of the integration is very important for corporations because they are going to look for more ways to be effective, and it has to be effective, because with the money they spent in the past, they knew they were getting diminishing returns. I am currently a partner in a company that is called Cross-Platform Productions. That's exactly what we do—we take a brand and content and marry them together so that they are working together hand-in-hand on television, in movies, on the Internet, on mobile phones, so that there's a synergy between the brand and the entertainment property. And with that infusion, I think the consumer who watches any of these platforms will recognize the brand, want to at least try it, as it makes an impression on them. The average person gets over nine thousand advertising messages a day. How do you differentiate between all those brands? And all those commercials and all those billboards? Maybe if you are able to insert it into some form of entertainment, you're more apt to stand out from the crowd. And to me, I think that's why entertainment marketing not only has made a big leap but I think you're going to see in the next ten to fifteen years, it's going to be the most dominant force in advertising, in my estimation—in the future, in all forms of media."

It seems like both Warren's words, and my experiences in my department were prophetic. According to research recently released by PQ Media, the leading provider of alternative media econometrics, spending on branded entertainment marketing grew 14.7 percent to an all-time high of $22.3 billion in 2007, nearly doubling in size over the previous five years, as brand marketers continue to shift budgets from traditional advertising to alternative marketing strategies, which include:

1. Event sponsorship and marketing
2. Product placement
3. Advergaming and webisodes

This marketing strategy, which integrates products into entertainment venues that provide high engagement and interactivity, represented approximately eight cents of every marketing services dollar spent in 2007. The market for branded entertainment was projected to expand another 13.9% in 2008 to $25.41 billion, despite slowing economic growth overall.

Not very long ago, I had the pleasure of spending time with Gary Arnold, senior entertainment officer for the Best Buy chain. Best Buy had recently test-marketed full-line music departments in a handful of their stores in Southern California and Minneapolis, Minnesota, the site of their corporate head-quarters. According to Gary, sales at those stores met or exceeded the company's initial projections and they plan to have 75 more open by mid-2009. What's interesting to me is that they offer four free lessons when you purchase a guitar—a business model that was the backbone of small mom-and-pop retail music stores in the 1950s, but has somewhat faded for many of our larger retailers today. In fact, the largest music industry chain in the United States, Guitar Center, does not offer lessons at all. It should be noted that when I stopped by one of our local Best Buy locations to inquire about signing up my stepson for guitar lessons, the salesman told me there was a six-week wait.

When Gary came out to visit me at the Fender factory in Corona, California, we casually spoke about our respective responsibilities. I told him that I constantly had my radar turned on, looking for any and all opportunities to promote our brands throughout the entertainment industry. Gary de-scribed his job in a similar fashion, but said that his respon-sibility was to focus on and develop opportunities with the various external industry partners to create unique—and sometimes exclusive—opportunities for sales throughout the Best Buy chain. Not surprisingly, Gary came from the enter-tainment industry, most recently from a stint at the Disney label, Hollywood Records. That experience, along with his love of music, gave him a unique perspective on how Best Buy should position itself in the entertainment industry as a retailer.

"You have to be careful not to lose your way with your core customers," Gary told me. "It's a constant balance between innovation and consumer expectations as to where you can go. Sometimes you go too far and the consumer lets you know, as was the case when we tried selling portable hot tubs, of all things!" He continued, "When we got into the CD business, we didn't get right it at first, but like everything else we do, we learned from our mistakes—and this year we are projected to hit nearly one billion dollars in CD sales in North America." Gary was instrumental in Best Buy's sponsorship of the 2007 Police tour, one of the biggest of the year. He also brought Best Buy into the sponsorship for the showing of *U2 3D* at this year's Sundance Festival, and has fashioned exclusive DVD offerings for Best Buy with such major acts as the Rolling Stones, Christina Aguilera, Mariah Carey, Elton John, Justin Timberlake, Usher, and Tom Petty.

Having the time and resources to devote to my entertainment marketing mission has allowed me to concentrate and develop an incredible array of opportunities for Fender, many of which I document in the following chapters. Instead of embracing the worn-out phrase *thinking outside the box*, I have been focusing on thinking outside of our markets *one box at a time*. For example, ever since I have been in the guitar industry, manufacturers have always been worried about the competition from video games. The conventional wisdom was that for every dollar spent in that market, that was one less for ours. Worse yet, we thought video games would actually replace the desire to play guitar as a leisure-time activity for teens and young adults. It hasn't quite happened that way as both industries are going strong, but we all wondered if there would ever be a way we could partner with the gaming industry to get a little piece of that multibillion-dollar market.[7]

That day came with Activision's launch of the video game *Guitar Hero* in 2005. Instead of incorporating actual guitars into the game, *Guitar Hero* used guitar shaped controls with which the gamer pressed buttons on the neck that triggered corresponding notes on the screen. As the player progressed, the characters on the screen would move up the ladder of success by playing better gigs, getting better gear and transportation, and more—until they hit the top. Even though the gamer wasn't really playing guitar, *Guitar Hero* did give the user a taste of what it would be like to be in a band, and maybe even feel like a rock star because he would be "performing" in front of adoring crowds.

The game was an instant hit, and reached as high as number two on the sales charts for the following year. It's now a billion-dollar franchise. Unfortunately for our company, the *Guitar Hero* franchise used Gibson guitar–shaped controllers, prompting my stepson to remark, "How come Fender doesn't have anything as cool as that?" Ouch.

We got our chance, though, when Harmonix brought the original team behind *Guitar Hero*, who were no longer affiliated with that game—to meet with us in March 2007. My boss, Ritchie, invited only three of us from our department to the meeting that day. Even though I wasn't much of a gamer, I immediately saw what a giant leap forward Harmonix's new game was over *Guitar Hero*. First of all, *Guitar Hero* featured only guitar, while this game was guitar, bass, and drums, just like a real band; hence the name, *Rock Band*. And where *Guitar Hero* mainly used cover songs—hit songs rerecorded to sound like the original, but not by the original artists—*Rock Band* would feature primarily original master recordings by some of the biggest names in rock. Also, the controllers would be much closer in detail to actual guitars; and we had powerful new partners with Boss, with whom we had a great relationship on our partnership with the Roland Corporation, for developing, electrics for some of our new models.[8] We also had one of the best media partners anyone could have wished for, MTV Networks. Ritchie and I used to always say if you can't be the first, be the best; and after that meeting, I knew we had the best.

The game was released in November 2007, and has gone on to surpass *Guitar Hero* on sales charts at the time of this writing. (It should be noted at the same time that Gibson and the original company are countersuing for copyright infringements—so their involvement with *Guitar Hero* may be over.) New songs and artists can be added by downloading off the gaming unit, such as Xbox 360 Live, and we topped thirteen million songs purchased as downloadable content in the first six months of its release.[9] This figure is comparable to one-third of the sales figures for songs sold through iTunes in its first six months. More important for us, the game has opened up a whole new world for partnership marketing with MTV, mass merchants, and the artists featured on the game. It has proven to be a remarkably rewarding relationship—both professionally and personally.

CHAPTER 4

We Will, We Will, Rock You— Marketing to the Big Beat

I talked in chapter 1 about how celebrities like Steve McQueen spent their careers reinforcing their certain brand of coolness by seeking out roles that continually enhanced that image. On the other hand, some companies seem to lose sight of the importance of that fact—even with seemingly unsinkable brands like Cadillac. When I was growing up, we knew that people had achieved a higher level of success when they purchased a Cadillac. It was not just a luxury car, but it was positioned by one of the world's largest auto companies, General Motors, as the absolute top of their line, so it really made a statement when you drove a Cadillac. It's not surprising that many of the early rock pioneers like Elvis, Jerry Lee Lewis, and Chuck Berry proudly showed off their new Caddies—rewards from the labels for their new hit records[1]—in photo ops.

But somewhere along the line, GM started diluting the brand through downsized cars like the Cimarron (discussed in chapter 3), which was introduced during the oil shortage in 1974 to compete with better-mileage-per-gallon cars. The Cimarron was one of Cadillac's least successful models. Automotive writers and critics alike agreed that it served only to tarnish the once prestigious image of the Cadillac brand—and was one in a series of missteps that nearly drove the brand to bankruptcy in the 1980s.[2] Cadillac had clearly lost its way—and its status as one of the most desirable and iconic automotive brands of all time. During the 1990s, the company was losing more and more market share, because its target consumers—Baby Boomers— thought of it as a status symbol for their parents, and therefore, not cool. When that target demo achieved success, they chose other brands, like Lexus, BMW, and Mercedes.

The agency for Cadillac had to do something drastic. Not every brand of car can be a true original like Cadillac, so this gave them a powerful ace in hole. That's why they decided to recapture Cadillac's glory days by going retro. They started by choosing the premier televised event of 2002 for their launching pad, Super Bowl XXXVII. The new ad campaign was titled *Break Through*, and the inaugural ad featured a classic 1960s cherry red convertible, one of the coolest cars of that era. It then showed the Boomer, who had been behind the wheel of that car admiring a new Cadillac (it didn't hurt that the new model was drastically different from your parents' car), as it sped past him. If that wasn't enough to get the consumer's pulse racing, having the commercial set to the soundtrack of Led Zeppelin's "Rock 'n' Roll" would. It was rumored that Cadillac paid a "ridiculous" sum of money for the licensing rights to the song; some insiders quote $7 million. Was it worth it? By combining the heritage of Cadillac's glory years with the nostalgia of the Boomers'—and most everyone else's— favorite heavy metal bands (not to mention one of rock's most ferocious riffs), Cadillac was able to turn things around almost overnight—and achieve a sales increase of 16 percent. In addition, Cadillac moved from third to first in advertising recall among luxury cars, supplanting Lexus and Mercedes.

The use of rock music in advertising has come a long way in the past few decades. When I began working on Budweiser promotions in the 1980s, it was relatively groundbreaking to use this music and these artists to promote major brands from outside the music industry. Around the same time, however, a company named Rockbill was formed to facilitate the relationship between rock 'n' roll and Madison Ave. Once the major artists of the day like the Rolling Stones, Michael Jackson, the Talking Heads, and Hall and Oates had signed on, it signaled that it was acceptable for musical acts to partner with corporations to promote their concerts. In fact, without that financial sponsorship, the production values of a mega tour would have suffered. Today, the widest range of brands—from Best Buy to DKNY Jeans to Vans shoes to Cruzan Rum—are linked to tours and special events through title sponsorships and national ad campaigns.

Major corporations now know the power of using rock and other forms of contemporary music as the soundtrack to promoting their brand's image. The year 2007 marked one of the biggest jumps in major retail brands using popular music in TV commercials. Companies can immediately boost their image by licensing artists' music for their commercials. The days of big ad agencies commissioning jingle writers to create original music for their commercials are waning. Popular jingles that were written specifically for commercials like "See the USA in Your Chevrolet," have been replaced by "Our Country," taken from John Mellencamp's 2007 album, doubling as a pre-promotion launch for the CD.[3] When they were together, the

Beatles never allowed their art to be compromised by permitting their music to be used for advertising products. It wasn't that long ago that Paul McCartney and Yoko One were incensed by the Nike commercial using "Revolution" for their sneaker ad. But today, John Lennon's "Real Love" appears in an ad for JCPenney; the same goes for Paul with Fidelity licensing "Let 'Em In," and "Hello Goodbye" for Target's new "Goodbuy" ad campaign. The incentive of lucrative licensing fees aside, this is merely a prelude for a new generation being exposed to the classic Beatles catalog, which will no doubt greatly enhance the sales of said catalog when it hopefully becomes available on iTunes in the not-too-distant future. Target—a company that sometimes uses hip new music for their ad campaigns— promoted Tony Bennett's 2006 release "Tony Bennett: Duets/ An American Classic," because Tony remains the purveyor of sophisticated cool, even into his eighth decade.

To gain credibility with a certain target market, automotive brands like Cadillac and Mercedes have no problem associating with rap artists to promote their brand. Some rap artists are actually paid a product placement fee from companies to put their brand into a song; and that doesn't stop with the car companies. Teen apparel company, Candies recently paid a reported $4 million for female singer Fergie to write their brand into her next album. Fergie's band, the Black Eyed Peas, struck another kind of gold when the Grammy Award winners inked a multiyear deal with Pepsi and tailored their single, "More," to the "Pepsi More" campaign. Their participation didn't end there. The group also had a prominent role in designing cans, advertising, and "a fan-interactive web site for remixing music." How about reworking an original hit to create an advertising jingle? That's just what such diverse artists as EMF, Devo, and Sir Mix-a-Lot did when they allowed their music to be changed into advertising slogans.

The next stop is personal appearances in ads. A wide range of artists have appeared in commercials and print ads backed by their music—from Sting with Jaguar, Elvis Costello for Lexus, and Avril Lavigne for Visa, to name a chosen few. The reigning queen of the advertising kingdom in 2007 was Beyoncé, who made appearances for American Express, DirecTV, Samsung mobile phones, L'Oreal, and Emporio Armani Diamonds Perfume. (Where does that girl find the time to make music anymore?) Sometimes I wonder when it will all end when I see Bob Dylan appearing in a Victoria's Secret campaign; and Keith Richards recently signing on as the new "old face" for the French maker of luxury handbags and luggage, Louis Vuitton, in a print ad and billboards that show him in a hotel room with a custom-made Vuitton guitar case on the bed behind him. And this trend has gone global as well, with mega brands, Coca-Cola and Pepsi-Cola both incorporating Middle Eastern pop stars into their respective advertising campaigns to win the soft-drink allegiances of the Arab world. Coke's sales already exceed $70 million in the region and both companies are looking forward to the annual double-digit growth to continue.

That is all well and good, since an artist gets the marketing support for a new record and tour, and the brand gets a much-desired association in a much more effective personal way. One thing to watch out for, however, is the *Icarus Syndrome*—getting into bed with a celebrity that can overpower and possibly flame out your brand. Chrysler found out the hard way when they hired Celine Dion to appear in a commercial. They were rumored to have paid $13 million for her appearance and the synchronization fees (music usage)—and the commercial ended up becoming a national ad for her new record. It was a promotional coup for Dion, but as for Chrysler's "advertising recall of the brand? . . . " How about, in my opinion not worth the investment?

Brands that have millions to spend on celebrities and music will be willing to pay whatever the market demands. These will typically be negotiated through the major publishing house for the music, and the major labels for usage of the original masters.

I wanted to investigate how the major labels approached licensing for movies and television in the current climate, so I reached out to Tom Rowland, senior vice president for film and TV music for Universal Music Enterprises.

My initial question was, "Since you have such a strong back catalog of well-known artists and tracks, I assume most music supervisors for movies, TV, and commercials approach you. Is that the case?"

> "The sheer size of our catalog ensures that we are approached by music supervisors on just about every project in development," replied Tom. "We use this opportunity to offer additional suggestions to satisfy their musical needs."

I wondered if there were ever a situation in which Universal would contact a production for a specific track they wanted to place, such as a new artist that they wanted to introduce and promote to a wider audience?

> Tom responded, "We are constantly pitching current artists or catalog tracks that are appropriate for our clients' projects. All of our licensing personnel are responsible for pitching, and additionally, we have dedicated creative people who do nothing but pitch."

I asked, "Is there a situation where you have not licensed a track, even if the fee was acceptable?"

> "In most cases, we are contractually obligated to obtain artist consent for each film or TV placement. If the artist feels the project is not appropriate for any reason, they may deny the request." He went on, "Artists are generally favorable towards film and television projects, but can be more discerning when it comes to advertising requests."

That prompted me to query, "Before you accept or deny a track for licensing, do you have to get the artist's approval before moving forward?"

"In many cases, yes," he answered.

I knew licensing advances can vary, depending on the notoriety of a track or artist, but financially speaking, I wanted to know if Tom could give a general guideline for negotiating the value of platinum artists, as opposed to new, emerging artists.

"A platinum artist will command more money than an emerging artist and a well-known song will command more money than a deep album cut, but there are many factors that enter into a fee negotiation beyond the stature of a particular artist." Tom went on, "We first determine the importance of the recording to the scene or project. If the recording is going to be the main title sequence of a major motion picture, then we would charge more than if it were only going to be used for ten seconds as background source. If the characters in the scene are singing or dancing along with the recording, the use is worth more than a car radio source, et cetera. The term, territory, and media requested for each project also factor into our pricing. Most films require world-wide perpetual rights in all media, since they will exploit the project beyond its theatrical release—either on DVD, television, et cetera. Consequently, a film license is more expensive than a television license since TV producers don't want to pre-pay for rights they may never need. However, more and more television shows are being released on DVD and are available on iTunes, so these rights are being requested more often in that medium."

Thanking Tom, I asked if he had any other comments or background information he felt like adding.

Tom replied, "Film and television placement has become an extremely important facet of any artist's overall marketing strategy. With the shrinking landscape of available radio, retail, and MTV opportunities, a good placement on a hit television show will expose an artist to millions of people. Our job then becomes one of connecting the dots so that viewers can discover more about the artist and turn a positive viewing experience into a CD purchase or a download. We make sure to get a visible mention on the show's web site and request direct links to the artist's home page and online music stores like Amazon or iTunes.

Other major labels have also realized the power of breaking new acts via the soundtracks of popular TV shows. CBS Records was relaunched in 2006 with the goal of specifically signing artists to expose them through placements through television. Nancy Tellam, president of CBS Paramount Network Television Group, CBS Records' parent company, told *Daily Variety*, "The cost of entry is so low that it's a great way of setting up a new model for a record label. If we can lower music costs while gaining an additional revenue stream, it's a win–win."

The benefits are obvious when a label doesn't have the financial risk of recording a complete album for an artist, and then the commitment of several thousands of dollars to advertise and promote it. In 2007, CBS Records was able to place approximately 80 songs into TV shows, a small percentage of the 2,000 or so songs placed the same year in shows, but a promising start nonetheless.

But what if your marketing budget doesn't have that kind of money? Not to worry—there are plenty of young up-and-coming artists looking for wider exposure for their songs that have no problem licensing their music for commercials in the range of $5,000 to $20,000 per track. This gives an advertiser the hipness of being associated with promoting new talent, and the artist receives an introduction to a massive new audience that they could never reach through typical channels, for example, radio, whose formats are becoming tighter and tighter, and are pretty much the domain of major labels. In fact, there are even companies that specialize in finding licensing opportunities for indie bands.

I had the pleasure of working with Art Ford on the "Where Music Meets Film" event at the 2008 Sundance Film Festival and was very impressed with his grasp of the complicated business of music licensing. I wanted his perspective regarding current trends and opportunities in his world, so this is what transpired when we chatted over a few cups of cappuccino at a Hollywood sidewalk café on a balmy Southern California afternoon. I began by asking him to give me a little background on what his company does.

"I come from almost a decade of working as a vice president at BMG publishing in the film and television music department, and in 2001, I left to form my own independent company, Ford Music Services. We represent lots of record labels, music publishers, songwriters, artists' estates, various different content owners, and we market their songs for audio-visual placements in film, TV, commercials, and video games. This is a great time to be an independent because it's like the Wild West as it pertains to distribution. It used to be that distribution of music was for only people that were fortunate enough to get a record deal and have their music released back in the day of phonograph records, and recently CDs. But now the Internet has changed that model, where any artist can have worldwide distribution. They just have to find a way to bring a customer into their artist's brand name and so it's more about marketing now and finding ways to touch a potential buyer. So it's really changed in that sense. As far as the Wild West, I think in the licensing world, with all the new medias (the Internet and now going into all the mobile device cell phones), there's not a lot of precedents set with what is a standard deal and what is not a standard deal. So, in many cases, those rules are yet to be created, so being an independent artist, if you can find a way to have some value and equity to your brand, you can . . . negotiate very favorable deals—even without having a major label or anything behind you as long as you have a valuable brand that will bring eyeballs and ears."

I then asked Art, "So, when someone brings you music and they want you to represent them, do you consult them as well and try to help them? For example, 'I'm a young artist and I don't know anything—I think I'm good and I don't have a record deal, but I have friends on my MySpace page that tell me I'm good.' What do you do to help them or direct them?"

"I do everything I can," replied Art. "A lot of times I try to challenge some of their preconception about having to have a record deal or some other misconception that they may have. In this day and age, it's almost better, in my eyes, for an artist to partner with a PR firm or some sort of marketing partner to help build the equity in that artist brand. If that artist gets the opportunity to get placement in a film or they get a commercial, they're obviously going to want to do follow-up. They're going to want to have people to be directed to that. TV, commercials, video games, and movies are all great ways of finding an audience, because again, it's about the brand being remembered."

I inquired about the parameters for determining the value of a song for licensing.

"It would depend on the media and how long if they are just licensing for television: no Internet [or] radio. If it's a limited media, it would be one price. I would say just in general that an emerging artist should target as far as what we call *synchronization*. . . . Synchronizing their audio to the visuals in television is a great medium, because television licenses a lot of unknown, never-before-heard artists that just sound great and they work right for the show; and in many cases, they will give a "card credit" at the end of the show advertising the artist, and often, their web sites will list hyperlinks that the artists will provide. I know [the] MTV web site does that on their shows, so that the viewer who's heard the song can instantly hyperlink into the artist's site and buy their music."

I told Art I remembered when he and I worked on "Where Music Meets Film" at Sundance and we had singer-songwriter, Tyler Hilton as our MC. I had worked with Tyler for years and when I first met him, he was on "Dawson's Creek" and they put his name and the name of his song at the end of the episode, which led to bigger and better things.

"Film is a little harder for emerging artists just because it's predominantly soundtrack and artist-driven, meaning that a major artist is what the film maker would love to license, because it will help market his film as opposed to an emerging artist—even if the music is equally good.[4] Then, if there is a soundtrack album company (for example, Warner Brothers) and they've paid a lot of money in advances to the film company to get those rights to team up on the film, it's usually those Warner Brothers emerging acts that they want to put in those secondary and tertiary spots in the film. So again, television is a great means and a realistic means of getting placement. Not that you don't get emerging artists in major films, but it's just a harder pitch. Though, if you do—it pays a lot more money than television and commercials. Now, Coca-Cola, various alcohol companies, and even car companies are licensing unknown groups that are just on the edge and right for their campaigns because they can get them for much reduced fees, as opposed to licensing a classic song. And even though that young artist is not known, their sound brings in a kind of edge to their brand in a way that they want. There can be an emotional connection to the song and with the scene itself. Music emotionally charges a picture. You'll see a scene in a movie that will have one different piece of music and the dialogue will mean one thing as the actor rolls it out, and then you'll see that exact same scene with a different piece of music, and the dialogue means something completely different. You mentioned the feather in the movie, *Forrest Gump*, and that dreamy kind of music and if it had been something different or darker or more ominous, the whole movie would have been changed, completely! Just one piece of music. . . . Not everyone thinks of the music; I mean, they hear it and they get the emotion from it, but they're not always paying attention to the delivery of music in that scene. So that's really very key.

That prompted me to ask Art, "Would artists also come to you for hire? In other words, if you knew that there was an opportunity for a TV show or a production that you were working on, you could tell that artist, 'Hey, go and get me something with this kind of lyric or idea' without doing the creative format or direction?"

"Every week that happens and the great thing now for artists is the technology artists have, Pro Tools and Logic, and these recording systems for ten thousand dollars in their bedrooms and houses that ten years ago would have been a million-dollar studio, and now they can instantly jump on a television opportunity. If I had the music supervisor calling me and a song they thought they were going to get for a certain scene is not going to be afford-able because the owners came in too high and the super-visor is going, 'Art, find me something in that same kind of vibe and feel—and I need it by tomorrow at two o'clock,' what I do is I'll [send] an email and make phone calls to various writers, producers, and artists that I think are the appropriate fits and ask them if they want to take a shot at it. It's kind of like a reason for them to write a song. If they don't get it, they wrote a great song and it might be something good for their album. So we take shots at film, commercials, [and] television shows every week—and that's assignment writing, where I assign writers to write and that gets fun because you can get the filmmaker's feedback, and find out what really drives the scene, and what he liked about the song that they can't get and what they didn't like about it, and then you can craft something that has those elements in it. It's not a knockoff or a soundalike, but it has something that has those emotions and elements and next thing you know, twenty-four hours has gone by and you've done a license on a major TV show. And if you get it right (the great thing about film and television placement when the stars align), you did a *great song* and it's in some poignant scene in an episode of a show that has millions of people watching it. And they walk away from it going, 'Who was it that did that song?' and they have to find it; and then they're on the Internet and they're searching it out. It's a great time to be an independent artist!"

I told Art he is like an A&R guy in the classic sense and that it seems like we've come the full circle. For instance, in the old days before it was common for recording artists to write their own songs, the A&R guy for a Frank Sinatra session would be the one saying to the publishers, "Hey, we need a great song in a such-and-such a style for Frank." The publishers would then look to the Cole Porters or Sammy Cahns of the day for that perfect piece of music.

Art agreed, but added, "Most major ad agencies have a musicologist that's on retainer with them so that when they have a music house that calls for a similar jingle or knockoff—a lot of cases, like, say, a back-song, has elements of production (a hip-hop beat, a sitar, and a harmonica) that are very unlikely combinations of instruments—that music house might take that same batch of weird combinations of instruments and do a whole different chord progression (but it's kind of in the same kind of vibe), and then get a singer in a similar style. However, it can't be a soundalike singer because in advertising, there's precedents with legal cases that's unlike television and film. Because of the Bette Midler case, the precedent is set where that an artist cannot have a soundalike singer do their hit song and be in a commercial without paying that artist for their likeness. Because their likeness, even though it's being copied, *is being borrowed*, and it's like taking something out of the store without paying for it. It's not right. The ad agencies get very clever in how they mix it up. Say a Joe Cocker had sung, "With A Little Help From My Friends" and they have a music house write a song that sounds like the same chordal progression, but not the same chords, but maybe the same key and the same tempo and the same kind of vibe and then they *don't* have a Joe Cocker soundalike singer sing it—they would maybe get a Mick Jagger soundalike [to] sing it. So they *mix up* the *likenesses* in a way where that there's no copyright infringement. (You could [have an] exact soundalike for television or film as long as you don't list it in the crawl as the original artist.) It's big business. You remember back to the days where you thought Carly Simon sang, "Anticipation" for Hunt's Ketchup? That was before there was precedents. That was a soundalike Carly Simon singer. It was never Carly Simon that sang that commercial. It was her song, but the owner of her master recording owned it, and she never received a cent for her likeness. She did make money for her composition, but not for the use of her likeness. As I said earlier, most major ad agencies that I'm aware of have musicologists that are either on retainers to check and sign it off on those recordings, and most of these guys are insured by Lloyds of London or other insurers and so they have complete indemnity, indemnification language where that, they take the hit (they protect the agency) if somebody steps up and says, 'You have plagiarized and taken a derivative of my song.'"

I wanted to get more in-depth regarding licensing with major artists, so I asked him, "When we worked on "Where Music Meets Film" together, you were dealing with Josh Groban, Jason Mraz, Michelle Branch, and other established artists. In fact, Groban was the biggest-selling artist of the year; therefore, were there any special circumstances from Warner's you had to deal with, or was everything pretty standard? Also, you were doing synchronization, performance, you had licensed tracks from the live recording; so please explain what that process was."

Art smiled and said, "First of all, Josh was a pleasure to work with and luckily, he controls his own publishing. He loved his performances and even though his songs were co-written by big writers that were with other major publishers, everybody was able to [see] Josh do an amazing performance at [the] "Where Music Meets Film event." Really, with him it was for the master side. We didn't release a CD, first of all. We had the music in the television special and online through the Myspace production, and then we have a download campaign going through our main presenting sponsor, Zone Perfect Nutrition Bars. And they have a campaign going where those certain winning-coupon customers (when they open their candy bar) get a coupon that says, "You've just won a free download." They can go into the Zone Perfect site and download a Josh Groban recording for a period of time. So we had to not only work out licensing for television and through a certain territory, through the U.S. and then we had options for the world, and then we had license for the Internet, as far as exhibition on the Internet through full versions on Myspace, and then we had to license for downloads. Downloads are now being viewed much like as when a record label put a song on a compilation album that included ten other artists. They pay that publisher statutory mechanical royalty for every album that sold. Well, the same thing applies now with downloads. The labels are paying the publishers, the owner of the composition, a mechanical rate. However, those rules are changing now. The publishers are going, 'Wait a minute . . . this isn't a compilation record. You don't have any costs associated with doing this. You're just sitting there collecting money. Why are you, the record label, making all the money and we're just making our small statutory rate?'

"For [the] sake of simplicity, a five-minute song—it's about five cents statutory rate for every record sold—that's what a record label would normally pay a publisher. Well, now, a download, say, is ninety-nine cents and if the net that the record label receives is sixty cents (two thirds percent of that) dollar, they're continuing to pay the publisher only that five cents statutory rate on each download. So the publishers are going 'No, we want to just split it fifty-fifty' and, depending on the record deals that the artists have entered into, some are able to, not allow their publishers to take a position. You have to license that download just as if you were doing a mechanical for a compilation record. So that's a little bit of precedent being set with downloads. I mean, rightfully so. The publishers got screwed over in sense that the writers got the short end of the stick when the film companies were able to lobby Congress in the Seventies, and were able to turn around copyright laws where that, the writers or recording artists don't make a cent any time you rent a DVD of that movie—they don't get a royalty. It's all a buyout up front with film.

"The publishers with all these new medias are being very careful that they don't make the same mistakes that they did when it comes to home video. With movies, they're making sure that they don't make that same mistake when it comes to downloads in music and other rights. There's a change. The old business model worked very well . . . twenty bands are signed—one makes it big and they make enough profit to pay for the [other nineteen] bands. It was a good thing, because it brought in new bands. But now with the Internet, obviously these things have to change. It's not pointing the finger at anyone. Keep in mind that the record labels don't make a performance royalty when their recording plays on the radio. They don't make a cent, but the publisher makes money. So it isn't a one-sided thing. I'm just saying it's a transition and these are some of the areas where the lawyers keep themselves busy."

I asked him how that translated to licensing overseas.

"The international rights laws are different in every country, but the rule of thumb is that if you're licensing out of North America or America and the artist is a writer-signed, EMI-published North America [act] but you're licensing for the world, everybody else, including that artist, just has to go along with whatever the United States agrees to. However, where it gets tricky is, if it's a writer that signs into the U.K. and the U.S. publisher is the subpublisher of the U.K. company, but then the production is being licensed out of the U.S. for the world, then you have to go to the U.K. publisher and get rights that everybody can agree upon. Otherwise, who-ever the original publisher from the territory that the artist has created the content in—they basically set the price. In most cases, they don't have to even ask permis-sion from all the other territories."

We talked about the old days in the 1950s when artists were regularly taken advantage of with regard to their songwriting, as they really didn't understand the ins and outs of publishing. But now, you need pros to do it, because the artists really understand their rights. In a perfect world, the artists create and are given instruction or direction and people like Art Ford to help them secure licensing at terms that won't give away too many of their rights.

"There really is a lot of money to be made for emerging artists, because if they're with a label, there are different laws, but if they aren't with a label, their profit is a big part going to them—it's very profitable. You don't need to sell a million records. In fact, some groups we know that have sold a million records don't make a lot of money because it costs so much to make and promote.

Again, the great thing now about having all these in-house recording systems, you can make incredible recording records for twenty to thirty thousand dollars and it doesn't take many records sold to be profitable. Today, technology doesn't really create talent. All it is, is a translator of talent, and it's happening with film now because of all the digital cameras, and the Macintosh editing programs, and with records, and technology has really opened up. We are in a technology revolution right now. In the last five years, downloads have gone from six to eight percent of the market to some types of music to eighty percent of the market." [*Note*: iTunes is now the number one music retailer in the United States, surpassing Wal-Mart.]

"Everything's changing so fast—it's very exciting."

Where Sunset Blvd meets the 101 freeway, there is a Denny's that, for decades, has been at the crossroads for the Hollywood contingent either on the way to, or returning from, the wild side of Sunset's nightlife just a few miles to the west. It was there that Gael MacGregor and I sat down for an interview over an early dinner. I began by asking Gael what she does.

"I am a music supervisor and I also help place independent artists into film and TV. The company I work with is called MusicSupervisor.com and uses a proprietary program called MS-Pro, which was designed by a music supervisor for music supervisors and it automates all of the paperwork as well as the search for music. We have approximately a thousand labels and independent artists and music libraries all codified in one place, so the music supervisor can do a search for a great punk band, or I need a nineteen-fifties sound like Frank Sinatra, a mid-tempo song, with the word *love* in it . . . and they can find that song, too. One of the things we've done is that we've partnered with a mobile film school. And that's what they are; they are mobile and they go into small towns and such where there's no facilities for kids to learn the art of filmmaking. So they teach them all the basics, but they also want to have music and they want to have quality music for it, so all the artists that are in this, including Styx; Styx is in the system and they own a lot of their own stuff. We have old and gold and former platinum artists, as well as the independent, who's never been heard anywhere. The cool thing is that they have to register; they give us a link to where we can hear their music. We listen to it and decide whether or not the song quality as well as the sound quality fit the criteria and if they basically stack up to anything you hear on the radio in quality—and if that's so, then they get accepted into the system and we go from there. But, there have been many people that we've rejected because the quality isn't there. It's not because we don't like them personally—it's simply the quality standard needs to be met.

"The whole database was built for the music supervisor. To be able to service the music supervisor, you need to be able to have enough music to choose from so they can supervise their entire film from your location, and that's what people are doing now. We started off with maybe three thousand tracks—we've got thirty thousand now and by the summer, because of some bulk uploads from a number of sources and an agreement with the Chinese government to represent the entire catalog of music from China—we'll probably be the second largest music library in the world! Second to only to ABM. How do artists pay for this? It's free. It's free parking. If through the system the artist's music is licensed, we do a fifty-fifty deal with them, with fifty percent of the master use and synchronization licenses we take. We don't end up on a queue sheet anywhere. They maintain all of their publishing. We don't do what libraries do. We think it's a very unethical, but practiced, what many libraries do and that is having the artist rename a song, so that the company can take thirty to fifty percent of the publishing on that song—even though it's the same song that they titled 'Love Me' and they retitle it to 'Love Me Now' for that. We just don't do that. We are all songwriters and artists in our own right and we're not giving away our publishing and we will not allow anybody else to do the same. So, it's fifty-fifty—when we get paid for something that's licensed directly from the site, we don't participate in any of their other things that they do on the outside because, our service is completely free to the supervisor. So they can not only search for and listen to the music, they have the lyrics right in front of them. With a click of the button, they have a place for spotting notes, and based on the criteria they give, the rights they want and how they want to use the music, they get an instant price. So they know if they are going over budget and when they decide to check out, they get their contracts and their invoice—everything . . . boom—it's done! We have automated all the paperwork as well as the listening process. Most of the other online services charge the artists twenty-five dollars to have three songs parked on their system, but when the supervisor wants them, they don't do the licensing for them. They just say, 'Well, here's the contact information for the artist,' and the poor artist is sitting there fending for themselves and not knowing what to do. We come from the standpoint of two worlds: One, we want to represent the artist and be fair to the artist; and two, we want the industry to be using us and most of the major TV stations and film companies are using us regularly and loving it. Because, if for some reason, their supervisor is too backed up and they don't have time to look—we'll look it up for them, as we have three music supervisors on staff and will be looking at their project from a music supervisor's standpoint. We will set up a listening box for them and send them an e-mail saying, 'Your music's ready for you—go listen.' So, we are *not* a song plugger. We don't care whose song it is, as long as it's the theme that we are being asked to place it for. The system is accessible from anywhere in the world and you can share workspace with your team that is scattered around—one could be in Tokyo; one could be in Paris; and so on—and you're all working on the same project going, 'Hey, listen to that one.' This also finds new music that people haven't heard, and maintains the old as well. One of the things that we are starting to do is to help educate the new generation of filmmakers with the Mobile Film School, . . . [because] unfortunately, many of the people don't recognize the power of music in film. They don't understand how expensive it can be. Or, that music really needs to be paid for. It does really need to be paid for if you are making a movie! You can go upwards of a hundred to a hundred and fifty thousand dollars for just the recording of a famous song and then another hundred and fifty thousand dollars for the actual right to use the song. So, if you get the right to the song—you can sing it on screen and you don't have to pay anybody for the actual recording of it. But, if you want Aretha Franklin's version of it, then you're going to pay the same amount that you paid for getting the right to use the song itself. But, the average range for some of the old-but-golds range anywhere from twenty to forty thousand dollars for each side (which means like forty to eighty thousand dollars to use the song and its recording). So, there are a lot of independent artists who will do covers where they can only license their master—they don't represent the publishing side of the song. But they can license their recording to the producer for half the price of the famous recording and still make a lot of money. So a lot of times, when a film has a budget where they know they want this song, but they can't afford to get both sides of it from the major publishing labels, they'll license the synchronization rights—the publishing rights to the song, from the major. And then, they will come to us and say, 'Hey, got anybody who's recorded this?' (laugh). We'll do that too, but it's primarily original material. With the new generation of filmmakers, they don't have money—we can work within their budgets, especially like with the Mobile Film School, they are going in to a lot of areas where kids are just going, 'Wow, I think I'd really like to do this.' . . . So, they make like three-to-four-minute films in the several weeks that they are there (a lot of documentaries and such). They come to us and they license each song (for a dollar!). It gets them using the system. . . . It gets them realizing the importance of music in a film. . . . And that when you do use it— you must pay for it. And so, this our way of giving back to the entertainment community at large so that music retains some sort of importance in the eyes of the film-maker. Because, more and more directors are doing very song-driven soundtracks with source music (for example, *Pulp Fiction*) and the more that happens, the more the filmmakers are coming to the independents because of the price, but at the same time, with our system—the people behind our system are also giving back by educating this new generation of filmmakers. One of the reasons why the industry started going to the inde-pendents was that you couldn't get a phone call returned

from the major publishers and labels. The artists really
need to know if there's a project out there that they
might want to get involved with and feel good about.
They also are very careful to make sure their best interest
is at heart.

Sometimes, this happens the other way around, when an artist is
discovered and then featured in an ad—as in the case of Ingrid
Michaelson. More than 25 million viewers of ABC's *Grey's
Anatomy*'s season finale heard her song "Keep Breathing." She
also benefited from the placement of "The Way I Am" in Old
Navy's Fair Isle sweater commercial in December 2007. Viewers
googled her lyrics and in turn, pushed her self-produced album
"Girls and Boys" to the top of the iTunes charts.[5] Staffers at
Secret Road, a Los Angeles licensing and artist management
company, stumbled upon Michaelson's MySpace page. The
company's founder, Lynn Grossman—who now manages
Michaelson—made good on her promise to get the artist's music
heard. The TV exposure led to 160,000 copies sold to date on
her independent label, Cabin 24 Records.

I knew Julie Shama for years when she worked at Hollywood
Records and always admired her ear for emerging new talent.
She had been telling me about this great new artist she was
managing, Tim Meyers, who was getting his music on TV shows
like *One Tree Hill* and *Grey's Anatomy* and had another song, "It's
a Beautiful World" chosen for a new Target ad campaign—all
without the backing of a major record label. I wanted to know
more about how he accomplished this, so Julie brought Tim to
meet with me in a small coffee shop in the Valley, right down the
street from where Tim was hard at work on his new material. I
began by asking Tim for a little background on himself.

"I grew up in Southern California down in the Orange County area. My dad's a musician and taught me how to play guitar really early on in life. Started taking piano lessons around four. My family is a total musical family and I starting writing songs around thirteen and at seventeen got signed to Interscope. The band I was in was kind of like a Jimmy Eat World and I wrote the songs, played bass, but I didn't sing. That band was on Interscope for about a year and then got dropped. At eighteen, I joined One Republic, writing songs and singing with Ryan Tedder, and wrote about five songs, played bass, played guitar and piano, and then just recently the song that I co-wrote, "Stop and Stare" is like number twenty now [on] MySpace. . . . We became the number one band on MySpace, and we had one or two placements on some different TV shows. With One Republic, it's the first time how I saw you're on the front page of MySpace and we got a bunch of clicks. And then this whole thing started unraveling; you know what I mean? It just became this huge success—we released the record and Timbaland took the single on his record "Apologize," and it went straight to number one. It's the first time I saw how the Internet and being on a few TV shows could really affect getting out there to the world. The success was a combination of being on the front page of MySpace, and having interns at the label on it nine hours a day, and having song placements like *One Tree Hill* and other TV shows playing our music constantly. It was a constant wave of buzz. We played Coachella, did some radio interviews. . . . "

I asked Tim what led to their music getting played on *One Tree Hill*.

Tim chuckled and replied, "It's actually a real funny story how I met up with them. We met up with Zync. I was playing the Viper Room with my band, and the band after me was supposed to go on at nine o'clock and they were really scheduled at ten, so Zync comes in to see them and actually sees my set and they're blown away, and they said, 'This music could be placed on everything, TV shows. . . .' So right away, we sign a contract and our song ends up on the season finale [of] *Grey's Anatomy!* I mean, can you imagine if only one percent of thirty-six million click on your iTunes? It's amazing. They are really good about putting the information on their web site, with links and stuff.[6] [Julie added that *Grey's Anatomy* will place information on the song on their web site in as little as ten minutes after the show ends.] The licensing company takes twenty percent for placement and they did a great job. Instantly, that day, we had a couple of thousand downloads in just a couple of hours.

"Music supervisors love independent artists. My friend Josh Radin was getting way more placements before he signed with Columbia Records. It's funny how my relationship with Zync has evolved, because I'm writing now specifically for movies. I just wrote a song that hopefully will be the title track for this movie *Real Men Cry.* Zync told me they were looking for a song at the beginning of the film that would talk about how life is magic, but they didn't tell anyone at Warner's that I was writing specifically for the movie. So I wrote the song, and when they heard it, they said, 'This is perfect.' The song ended up getting licensed to the Sony film, *Waterhouse: Legend of the Deep.*

I wanted to know how that led to the Target commercial.

"That's another funny story. . . . Well, this movie called *Fred Clause* by Warner Brothers wanted me to write a song about how beautiful life is, how beautiful the world is, and it's gonna be the end of the movie. So I wrote this song and I was really excited, I actually called Julie and she was in Vermont looking at the mountains, and I said, 'You gotta hear this!' I gave it to Warner Brothers and they didn't end up licensing it, and I'm kinda glad 'cuz, Zync sent it over to a few music supervisors and Target just instantly grabbed on to it. Then they played it on *Good Morning America*, and then after that Canon licensed it for their new commercial as well!"

I asked if he gets inspired when the music supervisors or agencies tell him what they're looking for in a specific type of song; in other words, is it a motivator?

"It's been a fun process incorporating the lyrics. In 'It's a Beautiful World,' 'the shapes and patterns of the season make me feel alive; I want to shout it from the rooftop and tell the world that I was blind but now I see what's right in front of me. It's a beautiful world I see.' Just kinda incorporating things about the movie, incorporating my lyrics in the song, being kinda vague, but incorporating the shapes and patterns of the seasons; it's been fun incorporating these things."

I interjected, "What you're talking about is very cutting edge, a new way of building your career. We talk about the older days when you had to have a recording and the band went deep into debt just getting a demo made. I mean they didn't have Pro Tools back then."

Tim responded, "Yeah, artists like Bob Dylan, or John Lennon and Paul McCartney would write a song a day, and I write and record at least one song a day—I'm obsessed with writing and I'm obsessed with recording. I think that's the way you have to do it. I mean, if you think about it this way—if you have a hundred songs and even if just one is a hit you have a bigger chance than if you only wrote twenty."

"Your system is different from the old days where bands built their chops by touring and writing until they were ready to be discovered by the major labels," I replied, "but yours is a great business model for today's world because labels have been forced to cut back on financing artists' careers, but now you can get a bigger piece of the royalty pie."

Julie added, "Basically, *Good Morning America* and Target did for Tim what a label would have done. One play on *GMA* is like 5,000 radio plays. It was our job to make sure when someone heard it that they knew who it was and had a place to find Tim's music, like our web site and iTunes."

That prompted me to ask Tim if he thought companies are going to talk about the promotions he's getting and then not want to pay as much for the song.

"Well, that's it. I'm afraid we're going to be talking about these good ole days someday where an artist could actually make a lot of money placing their songs. Artists have to start saying no to deals because they are desperate to get known and make a bad deal for their future. I was approached by the ad agency for a major cola brand to write a song for a commercial and they had asked maybe ten other bands, some great ones who were very successful, to do the same. I wrote a song and they loved it. They told me it was going to be on the Super Bowl and offered me a deal and it was terrible, and I turned it down because it was a bad deal. They said, 'We're going to make you better known because of the Super Bowl, so take it or leave it,' and I said, 'Well, I'm going to leave it.' I basically set up my corporation with all these people that are in my business circle. I have Julie; I have my lawyer, because I'm doing about five TV shows, commercials, and movies that are asking me for original songs. Out of every ten I do, one will get picked up. I'm paying for studio time and hoping for a return and so we retain the rights to our music. That's why we didn't take the Coke deal for the Super Bowl. It was work for hire and that's a bad deal."

I wanted to know his company handles the retail distribution without a label deal.

"We've been brainstorming and we are thinking about working out a marketing deal through MySpace and thinking about signing up with Starbucks, Target, or Urban Outfitter, and working out a distribution deal because I don't have a record deal. The whole future for me is . . . I can envision all kinds of Internet marketing going and walking into Starbucks or Target and seeing it right there and having them taking a percentage, and maybe using the music in their commercials. I think that's the wave of the future. I have a vision of getting tons of these placements and then having the music available through the Internet and the retail outlets. I also play various shows with different artists who have big draws on their own. Me and Schyler Fisk, another artist who's getting a lot of placements with his music on shows like *Grey's Anatomy*, we team up together and sell out these cafes and we're doing some college shows, House of Blues, and will probably sell out there too. Working hard as an artist you will see a return, but if you sit around smoking pot and chillin' out, you're not going to make money in the music industry; you're not going to be successful. I work every day until one in the morning. If you play with as many people as possible, and write as many songs as possible, and record and network and meet new people, market yourself—you will be successful."

I had an experience similar to that of Tim Meyers's (with original music being written for soundtracks), but it didn't start out in quite the same way. Billy Delbert, who was president of Packy Offield Enterprises (or P.O.E., the backers behind the Fender Catalina Blues Festival—more on that in Chapter 7), had asked me to help out a budding, first-time filmmaker who was working on a documentary charting the history the island's entertainment. His background stories would start at the beginning of the talkies (the first motion pictures with sound), and end with our blues festival. Greg Reitman, the producer and director, asked me for a quick interview regarding our involvement in the Fest. When he showed me the roughs, I was pleasantly surprised. "Wow, you did a great job with clearing the original masters for the soundtrack. The Beatles and Bruce Springsteen almost never allow the original recordings. How much did you have to pay?" Greg's reply, "What do you mean, *pay?*"

Remembering that he was a first-timer, I told him that synchronization rights could cost in the millions for original master recordings from groups like that—if you could even get them at all. Greg obviously didn't have anywhere close to that kind of money; he had actually maxed out his credit cards producing the film. I told him it would be better to use unknowns that could actually write and perform original music. This would then give the movie its own soundtrack, which would be forever be linked to his project whenever anyone heard it. He was hesitant, but he let me approach a couple of independent artists I knew who were extremely talented musicians and singer-songwriters—Omar Torrez and Adriane Leone. Omar was a top flamenco-style guitarist to whom I had given a Fender endorsement, and Adriane had just been added to the cast of the soap opera *General Hospital*.

Both artists were ideal for Greg's film and are the backbone of the soundtrack for *Catalina: Hollywood's Magic Island*. After I secured the support of these two gifted artists, Greg asked me for one more favor. He had a key scene for which he thought only one song would work and that was "Son of a Sailor" by Jimmy Buffet. I told Greg that this song would have been just as hard to clear as "Here Comes The Sun," but he was persistent. I have a friend named Robert Crancer, who lived in San Clemente and surfed the legendary Trestles with a fellow avid surfer—who also happened to be the president of Buffet's clothing company. After Robert spoke to him, the company asked for a copy of the scene in which the song would appear in so Jimmy could have a look. The actual sequence was one of the most dramatic in the film. It depicted a small fishing schooner being bounced around by the stormy seas in the deep channel between Catalina and the mainland. I still thought, however, it was a long shot for the song.

The next day, we received a call from Robert's friend, informing us that Jimmy loved the scene and he was willing to let Greg use his song, and with not as much as a penny up front. Permitting a song like that to be used without any kind of advance was practically unheard of in our industry. The film was purchased by PBS, and Greg's company—Blue Water Entertainment—produced another documentary, *Fields of Fuel*, that was accepted at Sundance and won the Audience Award for U.S. documentaries. In fact, my work with Greg on the Catalina film prompted his father, Bert Davis, to suggest that I write a book. He was the one who advised me on how to prepare an outline and introduced me to John Wiley & Sons. And so another fortuitous—albeit unexpected—partnership was formed.

The Recording Industry—An Endangered Species or Emerging Opportunity for Marketing Partnerships?

O kay, I've put off writing this somewhat painful chapter long enough. To say that the recording industry is in a tailspin would be a gross understatement: Seven years of declining sales with over 5,000 record company employees laid off in the same period; 2,700 record stores closing since 2003;[1] iTunes passing Wal-Mart in 2008 as the top music retailer; widespread piracy (some estimates are that 60 percent of all downloads are illegal); and to make matters worse, major artists from Paul McCartney to Radiohead deciding that they no longer need major labels to get their product to the consumer—Sir Paul through Starbucks and Radiohead's pay-what-you-want bold experiment online. All of these factors signal a less-than-ideal time for this business.

On the flip side, though, customers have purchased over 150 million iPods since its introduction in October 2001; and touring and festivals are still going strong. One bright spot for labels was that 1.2 billion units of albums, singles, music videos, and digital tracks were sold in 2006, up 19.4 percent from the previous year,[2] so we know people haven't lost their taste for music. Industry experts concur, therefore, that it's the modern label business model that is broken. So where did everything go wrong? It's easy to just point to illegal file sharing and downloads as the culprit, but my explanation goes a little deeper.

Back in 2000, label heads sat with Napster CEO Hank Berry to work out a licensing agreement. At that time, Napster had roughly 40 million users who were dedicated music lovers, many of them innovators looking for the hottest up-and-coming new acts—the absolute most important demographic for the labels. Instead of walking away with a deal, the labels ending up suing Napster into oblivion, thereby alienating those 40 million potential customers, and countless more with the hugely negative impact of the fallout. As if that weren't enough, they went after the consumers and sued the very people who had been their most cherished target market. (It should be noted that as of this year, all the major labels now happily sell their music through Napster.) But the seeds of the recording industry's demise were planted years before that.

When I was growing up, we looked to labels to discover new artists, produce them in the best recording studios, introduce them through radio airplay on our favorite stations, and have the records available in the stores when we ran out to buy what we just heard. Some old-time stores like my beloved Pearson's Music in Niles, Illinois, actually had listening booths where we could check out the latest A and B sides of our favorite artists. (Of course, we had to eventually buy something or we were politely asked to leave—thank God for my lawn-cutting jobs in summer and snow shoveling in winter!) Even though a label couldn't be identified as a brand in the traditional sense, we trusted them to give us the best of what was out there.

We knew with our own little garage bands that we had to practice pretty hard, then pay our dues performing for little or no money, build a substantial following, and create a buzz in our area before a major label would even look at us. Becoming lucky enough to be in the minute percentage of bands that were discovered and signed by a label was only the first rung on the ladder to success. Before there was MTV, bands had to tour relentlessly to transform a local following into a national one. And if a band's sales were on a slow upward climb, they had the label backing them with financial tour support, radio interviews, opening slots on bigger tours—all leading up to the big hit.

I remember when my band, Gambler, opened up for REO Speedwagon in front of 23,000 fans after they achieved their first number one hit with "Hi Infidelity,"[3] and realized that they had been on a major label for almost 10 years. When we were signed to EMI America, we had a respected A&R man[4] in Don Grierson, who championed our band. We had another top music guy working with us on the development side, a future president of Capitol Records, Gary Gersh, who was also instrumental in the careers of Nirvana and the Foo Fighters. The point in all of these cases is that the labels had a complete support group of professionals who were passionate about the music and the artists they were responsible for.

At the same time, as in any business, this had to be balanced with the lawyers and accountants, whose responsibility it was to make sure the labels made enough money to keep everyone afloat. The tipping point for the labels' problems came when the balance shifted away from the creative to the business side. Before that time, one successful label could finance several acts that might take a long time to show a profit; or maybe never break even for the label but still bring credibility, which had its own benefits as an attractor for great artists to a label that had that reputation.

It didn't matter if you had franchise acts like the Beatles, the Eagles, Led Zeppelin, Michael Jackson, or Madonna. All those acts were baby acts when they were first signed. Once acts began to get signed based solely on a financial basis instead of a creative one, the industry began its decline. The business model that embraced credibility appears to be gone forever as far as the labels are concerned. With the extreme cuts we have seen in the industry over the past few years, labels can no longer dedicate the financial resources or staffing strength to roll the dice on new, not-yet-proven acts. Because of this, labels are asking new bands to sign "360" deals, where the label will take a percentage of an act's touring and merchandise residuals in exchange for comprehensive tour support. In return, artists will often receive up to double the royalty rate on the sales. Thankfully for the big labels, their franchise acts still support them through what is referred to as *catalog sales*: repackaged greatest hits collections[5] and boxed and collector sets.

Major tour promoters Live Nation, Inc. is betting on that same type of longevity by inking global comprehensive partnership deals with Madonna and U2, rumored to be somewhere in the neighborhood of $100 million each, where Live Nation will now share in profits from touring, merchandise, and in the case of Madonna, long-term recording rights. In the not-too-distant-future, we may see more and more major brands inking these types of deals with artists as well, sometimes with a multi-million "buyout" of an artist's new record, quite possibly making royalty payments obsolete. But how many of today's artists in this world of cookie-cutter *American Idol* instant stars have that type of longevity—for whom the next generation of consumers will be laying out big bucks for their work? Not too many, I fear. The eternal struggle in business will always be between the creative and the financial but a balance between the two is crucial for long-term success in the entertainment world.

The other important ingredient to an artist's success—the supply chain represented by radio and retailers—was transforming itself during this time in a similar fashion. The local mom-and-pop stations and record retailers were long gone, replaced by national programming through conglomerates like Clear Channel and big box stores like Wal-Mart. This proved to be a recipe for disaster, since it caused pressure for labels to produce only the biggest blockbuster hits, and left them with little patience for developing talent. With the boom of popular music during and after World War II, that delivery system (as well as jukeboxes—which were also another important delivery system, especially before the advance of high fidelity, or hi-fi home systems) worked just fine.

When Elvis exploded on the scene in the 1950s, there was an opportunity for separate programming on radio, led by the pioneering efforts of Cleveland's Alan Freed,[6] who is often credited with the coining of the phrase *rock 'n' roll* to describe this exciting new music. Older folks—aka the Baby Boomers' parents—not only did not understand the new music, but for the most part were repulsed by the "jungle beats" of this new genre, which, of course, made it all that more exciting to teenagers. We have all seen those old newsreels of deejays in the Bible Belt smashing rock records. An article in a Boise, Idaho, newspaper happily declared in 1959 that the "fad" of Rock-Roll (sic) was finally dead, "fading into the oblivion from whence it came."[7]

Even though "respectable" deejays like Dick Clark (who had barely escaped the payola scandals that ended Freed's career) kept rock alive with his *American Bandstand* TV show, they did so by promoting a much cleaner, watered-down version that was mostly acceptable to parents.

But a funny thing happened when Ed Sullivan introduced the United States to those moptops from Liverpool—rock exploded to become a creative, social, and sales phenomenon like the world had never seen before. The Beatles led the British Invasion that, once and for all, wiped the Old Guard (except for a handful of major stars like Frank Sinatra, Dean Martin, and Barbra Streisand) off the musical map. They introduced a new era for AM Top 40 radio with the local deejays being at the forefront.

With my transistor radio under my pillow, I imagined those deejays sitting back in a darkened studio illuminated by the muted glow of control console lights, not unlike the deck of some futuristic spaceship. I remember growing up in Chicago and listening to the legendary Dick Biondi on WLS and WCFL's Ron Britain,[8] both of whom transported me to places faraway from my suburban bedroom. Britain in particular let us in on the latest happenings in England ("The Beatles new track, 'Eleanor Rigby' has Paul McCartney backed by a string quartet and no other Beatles. The Who's guitarist, Pete Townshend, just punched vocalist Roger Daltrey in the eye on stage in London, and it looks as if the band has called it quits").

These guys also supported the local bands: the Ides of March, the Shadows of Knight, the American Breed, the Buckinghams, and the New Colony Six, all of whom were catapulted from Chicago-area neighborhoods to the national charts. That was a time when you could organize your friends to call in the request line to get a song played, which is what happened to my very first garage band, the Tobacco Rouges. We actually got our song "Sad Little Girl" spun on WCFL—once.

The rise of albums' importance as a musical art form gave way to the inception and the rise of FM radio, which sounded better than the mono of AM radio because it was in stereo, played cuts longer than the traditional three minutes, and probably most important, it was cheaper to broadcast on. Local FM deejays like Tom Donahue at KSAN in San Francisco; Murray the K, from WINS-AM in New York City (where he achieved fame as the self-proclaimed "fifth Beatle" at the height of Beatlemania); and Jim Ladd[9] at KNAC in Long Beach, California, became legendary in their own markets as they discovered the newest and hippest sounds that their dedicated listeners were craving. The promotion guys from the labels—who were pretty cool in their own right—built strong relationships with the jocks who would play their artists. But distant dark clouds began to loom as radio and labels saw a better business model on the horizon.

Atlanta-based consulting giant Burkhart/Abrams—under the direction of co-founder Lee Abrams—created and built the very first successful national FM format: the album rock format (referred to as AOR, for *A*lbum-*O*riented *R*ock). Eventually, local deejays and programmers were replaced by a one-size-fits-all mentality, so everyone heard the same songs programmed no matter where in the United States they lived. This became the most successful format for every radio station that implemented it.[10] Not surprisingly, it became harder and harder for emerging local artists to build a grassroots following by honing their skills, then expanding regionally, and finally bursting forth on the national scene without that local radio support.

However, the launch of MTV in 1981 presented a contemporary medium that gave a ray of hope to budding artists. This fresh format presented music videos, which were nothing more than minipromotional films for artists and labels. It was another marketing tool that went hand in hand with—and often upstaged—radio to break new songs and bands, particularly in the genre of hard rock. For guitar companies, MTV was one of the most powerful tools in promoting musical gear. Kramer (which briefly became the number one guitar company in the United States, thanks particularly to guitar god Eddie Van Halen's exclusive deal with the Floyd Rose locking tremolo device, which you needed to approximate the fretboard gymnastics of EVH), Hamer, Dean, and Charvel Jackson[11] were all companies that enjoyed a market share increase, thanks to MTV exposure. Due in part to the production values of videos like Michael Jackson's *Thriller*, labels were forced to pour more and more resources into music videos, forcing them to concentrate once again on the sure thing. Baby bands were no longer guaranteed a video, not even a cheap, down-and-dirty one. MTV eventually came to concentrate more on lifestyle programming, reality and game shows, and focused less and less on music videos.

Music had truly become big business, almost all of which was supplied by the large conglomerates. Long gone were the days of popular independent labels like Bang, Swan, Coral, Buddah, Kama Sutra, Imperial, Chess, and VJ. All either went out of business or were bought out by the majors. Even established labels like Geffen and A&M eventually surrendered, getting huge amounts of cash for their roster of name acts. Even though labels had their own in-house promotions departments, it was necessary to hire an independent promotional agency to get a record played on a major station. Many of these were controlled by organizations with dubious backgrounds that harkened back to the pay-for-play scandals of the early days of rock 'n' roll. According to Fredric Dannen's groundbreaking must-read book, *Hit Men*,[12] the record business was paying out an average of $40 million annually to these indies.

Nonetheless, formats were broken down to the smallest demographic, which radio loved because they could deliver their most desirable target market to their advertisers, and prove it by the numbers. It no longer mattered how many listeners they had; it only mattered that their audience skewed to your product. It appeared that labels were afraid to make a move without research consultants, who were everywhere. This business plan cost the labels more and more resources to promote their artists. But that was okay as long as the product made money.

Labels signed less adventurous music because the stakes were so high, so even when a new scene was launched by a cutting-edge band like Nirvana, exploding out of Seattle, major programmers were quick to launch another new format, *alternative*, which morphed into *modern rock*. A typical format like modern rock might have an average of only 12 songs in top rotation with room for maybe only a few new songs added each week. And once Clear Channel was introduced, all bets were off. Here was a huge monopoly that owned stations all across the United States, programmed the music, and even owned and booked the venues in which the artists performed. Pity the poor new artist trying to break through a system that rewards only the ones that can guarantee the biggest success—not creativity or longevity.

Because music had become so profitable, the mass merchant retailers also saw gold in them hills. They offered CDs as loss leaders to get customers into their stores whom they hoped would buy much larger entertainment hardware like stereo systems, headphones, and so on. But real estate in stores doesn't come cheap, and so they could only offer music that had the best chance of selling. So hello to box stores—and goodbye to the little record shop that you could hang out in and browse for new artists. Good-bye as well to another purpose that the corner store served: to build and sustain a community of like-minded and loyal music aficionados that the mass merchants overlooked. In many ways, Starbucks has filled this void with their *Hear Music* customer-centered program, but they can only offer a small sampling of new CDs as compared to a full-line record store. The coffee merchant's digital library of songs for their café visitors, however, boasted up to 150 downloadable titles when it debuted in 2004.[13]

We are fortunate on the West Coast to have the largest independent retail music business with Amoeba Music stores. Collectively, the three locations in Berkeley, San Francisco, and Los Angeles stock 2.5 million titles, representing practically every music genre from rock to Pakistani *qawwalli*. No wonder so many producers and music coordinators for movies and TV hang out at the Los Angeles location, looking to the knowledgeable staff for recommendations of new music and little-known artists that would be ideal for their latest production. Unfortunately, co-founder Marc Weinstein has no immediate plans for expansion beyond the three stores.[14]

Today's business plan for the popular music would make sense—if you assumed that people liked only one type of music and listened to it all day and night. This is the mythical consumer in whom every advertising and marketing exec would like their clients to believe. First of all, advertising rates are based on the demographic you can deliver for your client, not the total number reached (unless you are looking for a massive audience like the one that watches the Super Bowl or *American Idol*—and these are much too few and far between). Therefore, the more you can break down that consumer to the nth degree, the more easily you can justify the cost. But when it comes to music, this type of "traditional" marketing thinking just doesn't fly.

I don't need to offer any backup research to support this other than to ask you to look at the music that's on your favorite MP3 player. I may be in the mood for a certain type of music from one of my favorite artists, but most often, I just hit *shuffle* and I am taken on a journey through all different types of musical styles from different eras. As I write these words, I hear my iPod in the background through a speaker dock—U2 followed by Neil Young, Spoon, and the Foo Fighters, then a left turn to Aaron Copland directing his own "Appalachian Spring" with the New York Philharmonic, rudely awoken by the Ramones, then lifted by Ol' Blue Eyes with "Fly Me to the Moon" and the Beach Boys' "God Only Knows," "Crash Landing" with Hendrix, and finally settling in with Jeff Beck's exquisite "Where Were You?." The Beatles, Mozart, Gram Parsons, Ryan Adams, Los Lobos, John Mayer, Mana, Marvin Gaye, Joni Mitchell, Bob Marley, Billie Holliday, Django Reinhardt, Jaco, Miles, the Left Banke, Merle Haggard, James Brown, Nat King Cole, Buddy Holly, Muddy Waters, the Who, and Radiohead—just a sample portion of the massive list of songs from my iPod that defies any attempt to categorize by genre, era, style, or demographic—and a marketing researcher's worst nightmare.

Fender used to have weekly updates from different departments that would end with our providing a list of what our top 10 favorites from our MP3 players were for that week. I was amazed that no one ever had the same song show up. As members of the music industry, a wide variety of songs and artists would be expected, but my friends and family who were not in the biz had just as wide a range—sometimes even wider. Whatever contributes to our tastes in music, the end result is that we are selecting from an infinite list of classic and new music—much to the chagrin of the marketers who are trying to squeeze us into a smaller and more manageable box. No wonder that the launch of the Internet and the iPod opened the door to a whole new supply system to meet the demand. The numbers don't lie: Sales of digital tracks were up from 352.7 million in 2005 to 581.9 million in 2006 and it's worth mentioning again, 150 million iPods sold since October 2001. Now—back to the future.

If in 2000, the labels that met with Napster had let creativity drive the interaction, they would have ended up using the principles of embracing your most important customer and could have possibly protected themselves against illegal downloading. They could have utilized the Internet as a means to provide a free download to introduce new artists to those innovators (which, by the way, they have begun to do now; even Nine Inch Nails, a successful and respected band, just released their new record with free downloads). This would have worked even in the business model of the day, because it would have been a cost-effective way to promote new talent—by utilizing the creative side of the labels to discover these artists and thereby using an almost-free delivery system. Obviously, if people liked what they heard, and a licensing agreement was in place, they would pay for more of the same and that would create demand from radio stations and retailers. Can anyone say "win squared?"

But I didn't intend to pick on the labels, because they are some of my best partners. And the creative, passionate side is still there today. The label execs who looked into the future and embraced the Internet and new technology, like Mastertones, for mobile phones (a program that utilizes the artist's original master recordings, as opposed to ring tones, which are simply rerecordings of famous riffs), which favors the major labels' well-known songs from their catalog, are the ones now in the top positions. The creative A&R directors are still there—albeit in much smaller numbers—but they are still there looking for the next franchise artist. That's precisely why I feel there are currently more partnership opportunities than ever for brands to partner with the record industry.

As I discussed in the last chapter, major and independent artists have struck gold by licensing their music to advertising campaigns for major brands, and for movie and TV soundtracks. Even though artists like Tim Meyers have had success without record company backing, it still helps if you can have the staff at a major label behind you, who are still masters at promoting their artists and their music. That is, of course, if you can't find other methods, like independent licensing companies; or simply exploring other means to get noticed, with or without a major label.

The Chicago band OK Go created an amazingly cost-effective video (just $5!) to promote its first single, "A Million Ways," from their 2005 album, "Oh No," without the knowledge or consent of Capitol Records. Due in part to their unique fashions and creative dance routines (choreographed by Trish Sie, the sister of lead singer Damian Kulash), the video became the most downloaded of all time—over 9 million. Their next video, for the song "Here it Goes Again" has been viewed over 31 million times and won a Grammy in 2007 for "Best Short-Form Music Video."

Fledging artist, Ashley Alexandra Dupré, found another creative way (albeit inadvertently) to drive her MySpace views from a handful to virtually over 2 million in one day, by being the call girl in the scandal that brought down former New York governor, Elliot Spitzer.[15] I wouldn't recommend the latter of these methods as a surefire bet for fame, but it is certainly worth noting to demonstrate that there are different ways of utilizing new media to build a career.

That being said, record labels still provide the most solid foundation in many ways. In my introduction to this book, I explained that you couldn't possibly listen to all the music released over the Internet. Without taking sides, that's why I recommend at least considering working with labels to promote your music or brand to take advantage of all the powerful media outlets with which they partner. The timing couldn't be better, since one of my friends in the record biz recently told me that labels no longer say they are in the *information age*, but rather the *recommendation age*. This is meant to convey their desire for partners to recommend and thus promote their music. This could represent everything from iTunes links on company web sites to MySpace friends and bloggers. In fact, this concept works equally well for promoting any brand or product.

A current example is Taylor Swift. In an interview with *Billboard* magazine,[16] the teen country star and Grammy nominee revealed that she was all of 12 when she secured taylorswift.com. Swift comes from a generation that grew up on the Web, so by the time she signed with Sony/ATV Tree Publishing at 14, and released her self-titled CD on Big Machine at 16, she was already a pro at promoting herself and her music through the Internet. And the majors still have the one thing that is the backbone of their sales, and that is catalog. These are the master recordings owned by major labels that cover just about every popular artist from Abba to ZZ Top, the Beatles to the Beach Boys, Jimi Hendrix to Led Zeppelin, the Eagles to Pink Floyd, the Stones to the Who, and from the biggest names today all the way back to the classical recordings from the dawn of recorded music. And as Karl T. Bruhn told me in Chapter 2 during our interview: "A marketing department didn't create the Beatles and Stones; the people did." That's some pretty powerful equity to have at your command.

Back in the old days of the early 1990s, it was fairly straightforward to conduct promotions with radio stations. I remember when beepers were the new technology and manufacturers or retailers would run their ads and many would give away a beeper as part of the campaign. Pretty boring, right? Guitar companies knew that the models signed by their artists were in great demand by labels promoting those same artists; therefore, we, as an industry, sold thousands of dollars worth of instruments to the labels, which, in turn, would trade them out as part of their ad buys. Radio stations would regularly inflate their value of a

30- or 60-second spot, and the labels could use the retail value of the guitar (which no one paid in stores) as a trade. If the guitar featured a logo with an event or corporate brand outside the music industry (such as Budweiser), and it was autographed by an artist, the value increased dramatically.

I want to add that I started doing these types of promotions with Dean Guitars in the mid-1980s, which was relatively ground-breaking at the time, and the autographed and logoed guitars have showed no sign of diminishing as a promotional tool, because their collectability has remained high. Guitar companies' opportunities for their brand to be hyped by excited deejays is an example of what we called *breakthrough* in the 1980s: having your product mentioned without it sounding like an ad.

When I worked with Anheuser-Busch on their music marketing, they would actually pay radio and TV personalities an annual fee as part of a personal services contract for live appearances. The deejays, in return, were expected to casually mention Bud when on-air and in public appearances. When popular Chicago Cubs announcer and Bud pitchman, Harry Carey, returned to the broadcast booth after recovering from a heart attack, the Cubs' organization hosted a major welcome home party for Harry on the Wrigley Field diamond before the game. The party was hosted by none other than the governor of Illinois, Big Jim Thompson, and when he went to the mike, he toasted Harry and the cheering Cubs fans with "This Bud's for You!"—the company's catchphrase at the time. The epitome of breakthrough.

The third part of this equation was the win-and-fly trip to see an artist in an exotic location (like balmy Los Angeles, which had nationwide appeal, particularly in the middle of winter). Major corporations began to sponsor these trips, with the labels bringing in additional co-sponsors like hotels and airlines, which were more than happy for the in-kind trade-outs. Add a signed guitar and you had the makings of a great sweepstakes package.

Today, most of these promotions usually happen with the morning drive on-air team because so many radio stations have replaced local personalities with nationally syndicated shows. We have come a long way since then with our promotions, and, as I mentioned, signed guitars are still popular prizes, and radio stations have moved on to even more elaborate packages. In fact, in my department, we rarely partner with stations that often ask for the guitars as in-kind unless we have a third major partner like a label or another corporate sponsor.

By the way, this concept is not limited to the record business. When *That '70s Show* was in its prime, we created a promotion with the Fox Network and the Subway sandwich chain. Since Fender has several classic models representing certain eras, we came up with a grand prize of a 1970s Stratocaster guitar that was signed by the cast of the TV series. The sweepstakes was launched on the season premiere with a special ad that Fox produced and was backed up throughout the Subway chain with counter cards announcing the contest. The promotion was such a hit that Fox came back to me to duplicate it for the following season.

With the demise of national record retailer Tower Records at the end of 2006, we lost a great promotional partner. Not only was Tower an aggressive marketer, but the famed Sunset Strip location in Hollywood in particular hosted many artist appearances and performances in support of new releases and tours. I personally worked on several record label national campaigns with Tower. My good friend and associate at the biggest label, Universal Music Enterprises, Director of Pop Promotion, Elliot Kendall, brought many opportunities our way. Elliot is one of those passionate label guys who still spends his weekends scouring the bins at record conventions and flea markets looking for the one "Holy Grail" vinyl his collection is still missing. He is also a lover of surf music, and he and I had worked on the same project without knowing it: the 2000 made-for-TV movie, *The*

Beach Boys: An American Family. Once we learned this, along with our common tastes in music, we became fast friends. In 2004, Elliot was looking for promotional partners for the three-disc compilation, *The British Invasion 1963–1967*. He wanted to offer a unique sweepstakes prize he could bring to Tower for a national in-store campaign. The cover art featured a large guitar pick emblazoned with the iconic British Union Jack flag. Elliot thought it would be cool to have a Fender Telecaster guitar with the face covered with the flag art, so we created a handful for the promotion. Tower set up displays announcing the sweepstakes to win the very collectible guitar, since it didn't exist in Fender's regular line. Stores had their own internal competition for the best display so the coveted "real estate" we were able to obtain for the release was astounding (particularly since a catalog release like this wouldn't normally receive this type of attention from a retailer).

An offshoot of this promotion was created for our clothing licensee, Defiance, for a national sweepstakes with clothing retailer Nordstrom's. Timing was everything, since Defiance was meeting with Nordstrom's at their corporate offices in Schaumberg, Illinois. When they called me about their idea for the campaign, which had a distinctive British element, I only had to send them down the block to see the British Invasion guitar on display in the flagship location. We ended up creating 17 Union Jack Teles that were purchased by Nordstrom's as grand prizes. Once again, we were able to get considerable real estate with displays in designated boutiques chainwide. We also helped to showcase our Fender-branded clothing, although Elliot and I were disappointed that we didn't have the time to develop a tie-in to the CD package, which would have made it a perfect promotion as far as we were both concerned.

I was involved in another label campaign with Tower, which proved to be the last one before the chain closed its doors for good. Warner's Reprise was looking for a blockbuster campaign for the release of Eric Clapton's *Crossroads* DVD, because they knew that this was going to be a major seller. It had been recorded live at the Cotton Bowl in Dallas to benefit Clapton's Crossroads Centre, a world-class addiction-treatment center, located on the Caribbean island of Antigua. The festival was a who's who of great guitarists—Buddy Guy, B.B. King, Carlos Santana, John Mayer, Doyle Bramhall II, John McLaughlin, Joe Walsh, Jonny Lang, Vince Gill, Jimmie Vaughan, David "Honeyboy" Edwards, Steve Vai, Robert Cray, and Billy F. Gibbons with ZZ Top and more.

Working with Paul DeGooyer and Liz Ermin and their staff at Warner's, we developed a campaign that featured life-sized standees of Clapton's legendary "Blackie" Stratocaster guitar, displayed at Tower locations across the United States. The guitar was instantly recognizable by anyone remotely familiar with Clapton, as it had appeared on several album covers and also on the back-cover art of the *Crossroads* DVD. As part of the fund-raising, Clapton auctioned the original guitar, which was purchased by Guitar Center for a record price of just under one million dollars. Indecently, a year later, Fender replicated 100 of the original, called "Tribute Models,"[17] which were authentic recreations right down to every scratch and chip, and were sold through the Guitar Center for $23,000 each. People waited in line the day the guitars went on sale, and each and every one was sold within minutes.

We had one hurdle for the Tower promotion, which was that Clapton had stopped signing guitars because he apparently felt they were conflicting with his fund-raising efforts in auctioning his guitars, by bringing big bucks on eBay that didn't go to Crossroads. He was right in this assumption, since, the fewer collectible guitars that are out there in the market, the more people are willing to spend for them. We decided that the grand prize should be only one guitar, the Fender Blackie edition Stratocaster guitar from our regular production line, valued at $2,000. Since it wouldn't be autographed, we laser-etched the

Crossroads logo and date on a special black anodized pickguard. This guitar was featured in all promotional slicks for the DVD (which Clapton did agree to sign), which went 8X platinum (and still counting). I think this would have been a huge success with or without our promotion, but for my efforts in the Tower campaign, I have a nice Platinum Award commemorating the sales hanging on my office wall sent to me by the staff at Warner's.

For 2007's *Crossroads II*, I worked with Liz Ermin again, as Paul DeGooyer had moved on to MTV Networks (where I continue to work on campaigns with him for *Rock Band*); Warner's recreated the Stratocaster standees, this time featuring the special Sun graphic designed and hand-drawn by Clapton himself, which also appeared on the DVD packaging.[18] Fender's vice president of marketing services, Paul Jernigan, created a special program to allow 100 percent of the money generated to go directly to the Crossroads Centre. One hundred of the guitars were produced and sold directly to the public over the Fender web site. The Platinum Package featured 50 of them with replicated 1957 Twin Amps that displayed Sun art and a commemorative badge on the amp. They featured an autographed plaque by Eric and were priced at $30,000 each; the Gold Package was the guitar alone, priced at $20,000. We worked directly with Warner's on several radio networks and used our production line model, Clapton Blackie Signature Stratocaster guitar, along with other signature models from artists who appeared at the second festival, which included Robert Cray, Jimmie Vaughan, John Mayer, and Jeff Beck.

One potential area of worry when working with artists is that there will be circumstances beyond your control. I have seen many artists I thought were destined for greatness, for whom only one unforeseen obstacle arose that was severe enough to sidetrack a promising career. It can be anything from a bad management decision, to a change in personnel or direction at the label, to the wrong tour.[19]

That last was the twist of fate that sidetracked a very strong promotion in 2007 for a promising young artist on New Door (which was at the time a subsidiary of Universal Music Enterprises). William Tell had experienced some success with his former band, Something Corporate. Tell was branching out on his own and had everything going for him at the label, including the Executive Vice President and Head of New Door, Richie Gallo, a respected record man who had been instrumental in the careers of such stars as Peter Frampton (and who I had known when he was at A&M Records before its purchase by Universal). Elliot Kendall would be on the radio team, and driving the train was the Vice President of Marketing, Jeff Moskow, whose staff was totally committed to breaking Tell. Elliot invited me to meet with William to potentially bring him into the Fender family, and perhaps turn him into a promotional partner. At our initial meeting, William told me that he grew up not far from the original Fender factory in Fullerton, California, and that he and his boyhood friends would cruise by the garbage bins at the back of the factory on their bikes looking for guitars. (The rumor at the time was that Fender threw out guitars that didn't meet the company's standards.) It didn't hurt that William was managed by Andy Gould, who also handled such major acts as Rob Zombie and Linkin Park. After seeing William live, I brought him to artist relations, and we were on our way.

Elliot and I were still disappointed that we missed the opportunity for the British Invasion CD promotion with Nordstrom's. Jeff Moskow was encouraging his staff to think outside that dreaded box, so we began to investigate another retailer to bring in as a partner for this promotion. Entertainment marketing was also looking for opportunities to promote not only the FMIC family of products, but also our extended family of licensees for their co-branded products. Fender Watches' licensee was City Life, and their Head of U.S. Sales, Ed Walton, came out for a William Tell marketing meeting at Universal.

Ed was ecstatic about the idea of offering one free download of a track from his CD "You Can Hold Me Down," with the purchase of a Fender watch. The download card would be inside the packaging and would give purchasers a code and direct them to the web site—all paid for by City Life. Ed found the perfect retail partner in Dillard's, which was having strong sales with Fender watches. Ed had previously worked with Fender in creating in-store displays for Dillard's that were "dummy" amps that showcased the watches where the speakers would normally be. An actual Fender Stratocaster guitar was mounted on the side of the amp to create a truly striking visual. We had a famous-in-his-own-right rock star photographer, Neil Zlozower (with whom I had worked on ad campaigns all the way back to my days at Washburn), shoot William for a feature ad in *Blender* magazine, which would announce the sales campaign at Dillard's. Through the efforts of Universal's licensing department, William's track "Sing Your Own Song" was being featured on the promotional spots for the new season of *American Idol*. William himself also appeared on promotional spots for ABC Family.

At the time of the campaign, Fender was working on artists for our sponsorship of the annual Tempe Music Festival just outside of Phoenix, Arizona. The year before, Fender's Vice President of Artist Relations, Bill Cummiskey, contributed immensely to the festival by coordinating a celebration of Fender's sixtieth anniversary with the coup of booking John Mayer and Jeff Beck, among others. As part of the promotion, MySpace ran a national competition to find bands to place on their sub stage at Tempe; one lucky band would get to open for John Mayer in front of 10,000 fans.

Thanks to Bill's efforts, I felt that we owned the festival that year. Bill came through yet again the following year with a featured slot for William on the Fender "Frontline Live" stage, which was streamed to millions of viewers on the Internet through YouTube. We also found out that a sponsor of the festival—none other than Dillard's—was going to have an on-site retail store, so we quickly coordinated meet-and-greets with William at the space. More good news came our way when Bill was able to get another spot for William at the festival—this time on the main stage—and a showcase at the opening night's sponsor's party. If my boss, Ritchie, hadn't permanently banned the clichéd word *synergy* in marketing meetings, I would undoubtedly have used it at that very moment to describe what was transpiring.

William came to rock the house at the sponsor party, and the Fender gang was pretty impressed with our new discovery. With his usual efficiency, Elliot booked William for an appearance on *Good Morning Arizona*, one of the area's top-rated news shows. William was phenomenal at the festival each night, and Dillard's loved the fact that they got to throw T-shirts into the crowd after William's performance. Additionally, the line for his meet-and-greet with fans was filled to its hour-long capacity.

For me, William was—not unlike Nuno Bettencourt and "Dimebag" Darrell Lance (discussed more in Chapter 10)— another ideal artist for this type of event, because he truly enjoyed interacting with his fans. He also possessed a charismatic boyishness that was appealing to his female followers, and could rock until he dropped, which appealed to the guys as well. Dillard's regional marketing director for Arizona even sent an e-mail to owner, Todd Dillard, recognizing the *cool factor* that William brought to the retailer's presence at the festival. I recall thinking to myself, "This was almost *too* easy." That was until . . .

Before the release of his CD, William had toured with another Fender artist, Teddy Geiger, and found the perfect audience for his music. We anticipated that he would be booked on another, similar tour to promote the CD. With William's success at Tempe, Dillard's was ready to present as many meet-

and-greets in their stores as he could do, coordinated around the tour. Unfortunately, William was hastily booked on a packaged tour of colleges that also featured rap artists—a genre that I considered to be a totally wrong audience. To make matters worse, the shows were restricted to the students at the school, and so there was no way for Dillard's to participate to promote ticket sales, and therefore no reason to present the meet-and-greets at their stores. Like the proverbial house of cards, the campaign completely collapsed.

I was heart-broken for William, because he had been so accommodating. He did everything possible to promote our watches and Fender—featuring one of our brands, a Grestch guitar on the cover of his CD, and using Fender products exclusively in his shows. At the end of 2007, Richie Gallo left Universal and went to Rhino and New Door folded, but I have faith in William and truly believe that he will soon get another chance because of his talent and drive.

Despite the difficulties that can arise, I've had some of the best experiences of my career working with the majors. One instance in particular involved a 2007 project with Universal. I met with Adam Star, senior head of product at Universal, to discuss the launch for the complete Elvis Costello catalog that iTunes was rolling out. I was a big fan of Elvis's, once getting to open for him and his band, the Attractions, at his first Chicago appearance, in support of his groundbreaking album "My Aim is True." More important, ever since that particular album cover featured Costello playing his Fender Jazzmaster guitar, he has been associated with this uniquely shaped model. It didn't hurt that 2008 would mark the fiftieth anniversary of that model and its sister, Jaguar, and that we were looking for a marketing tie-in.

Adam had laid all the groundwork for the campaign by bringing in Visa and House of Blues Concerts. The idea was to send fans to a web landing page through the Visa site and have them answer a marketing survey that each company could contribute to for data capture. For their effort, fans were entered to win tickets to see Elvis in a special acoustic performance, and receive a Costello-autographed Jazzmaster. The contest garnered thousands of responses, and we were surprised by how widely in age Elvis's fan base ranged (17 percent of the respondents were between 18 and 24). As a bonus, we also were able to work out an agreement with Elvis's management to produce an Elvis Costello Signature Model Jazzmaster guitar for the model's fiftieth anniversary in 2008.

Following the success of the Elvis–Visa campaign, Adam introduced us to the team at Primary Wave Music, which handled licensing for several major artists. Justin Norvell, Fender's electric guitar marketing manager, and I met with Primary Wave in New York to work out an agreement to launch another signature model for the fiftieth anniversary, this one for the late artist Kurt Cobain. Fender had introduced several years before a Kurt-designed guitar called the Jagstang, which was a morphing of the two models he regularly played: the Fender Jaguar and the Mustang. Kurt's tragic death had occurred right around the time when the model was to be launched and even though we did well with it, we never had the chance to recreate his original guitars as a tribute. Primary Wave had access to his personal guitars, owned by his widow, Courtney Love. Because of our new relationship with them, we had the chance to use the guitars again, and both models are now in the works for release in the near future. This was an instance when working with a major label granted us some great opportunities; not only to come with new projects, but (in the case of Cobain's guiters), to revisit and complete one that we were extremely pleased to get a second chance to work on again.

CHAPTER 6

Product Placement—The Inside Story of Getting Your Brand into Movies and Television

I t was predicted that in 2008, estimates for product placement in movies and TV would top an astounding five billion dollars![1] That's up from just over one billion in 2001, an almost un-precedented growth factor by industry standards. It's no secret that when you see a well-known brand in a movie or on TV these days, the company probably paid a substantial amount of money for the placement. We refer to it as an *integrated placement* if the program takes it one step further, and works the product into the story line. If the brand is specifically mentioned, it's called *text placement*, and will cost even more money. How much? It was rumored that Pepsi paid the agency for *The Apprentice* over \$3 million for Donald Trump's team to design a new Pepsi product as a project. When Trump mentioned that Pepsi was his favorite drink, the company had to shell out an additional \$1 million, which eventually caused a rift between Trump and the producers, who wanted their cut.[2] The show could make such a demand because of its high ratings and the choice demographic it reached. Placement fees are negotiable, but it's what companies are willing to pay for star power and promotional tie-ins that ultimately determine the price.

But why can producers demand so much for these types of placements? If it's TV, isn't running ads enough exposure for your brand? The problem, with the expanding *TiVo effect*, is that viewers using the service, or their own Digital Video Recorders (DVRs), can skip the ads altogether. Even when they see an ad, they engage in what we refer to as a *one-way transactional focus*, the old-fashioned twentieth-century way of pushing ads at consumers that results in little emotional interplay.

And that's where product placement excels. It goes back to the dawn of the film industry by using an integration of recognizable brands that lend authenticity and realism to the production. It also helps to actually set the tone for the character and action by tapping into the collective experience and emotional attachment that an audience has to a particular brand. For example, a filmmaker who wants his star to be recognized as an anti-hero, need only to place him or her on a Harley-Davidson motorcycle. There are a lot of street bikes on the market that have the look of a Harley, but only the HD has the rebel vibe. Ducati—a brand that's noticeably different from a Harley street bike—has recently committed their resources to branding their high performance sport bikes to a new generation through placements and tie-ins with movies like *Freaky Friday*. They went so far as to produce two limited-edition models, the 998 and Monster 620, inspired by the Matrix trilogy, and featured in *The Matrix Reloaded*.[3]

One of the earliest documented, integrated product placements I could research for the purpose of this book was in *The African Queen*, filmed way back in 1951. The producers needed a recognizable brand of alcohol for Humphrey Bogart to drown his sorrows in, and they needed cases of it donated for the right visual effect. Gordon's Gin came to the rescue with those several cases that were placed on the dock behind Bogie. Then something unexpected happened—Gordon's Gin sales increased by 35 percent. Even with those convincing numbers, decades later, when Steven Spielberg wanted M&Ms for his blockbuster *ET*, Hershey's was reluctant to participate because they thought the alien might be too frightening for younger viewers. So Reese's Pieces, a much less recognized brand, stepped in, and as a result, increased sales 50 percent in the first six weeks after the movie's release. That's the thing about product placement—viewers need to see a familiar brand in a movie or TV show for it to garner credibility, so the established brands have an edge. But conversely, producers know that a hit movie or TV series can increase a product's sales by its appearance onscreen alongside stars with whom consumers identify, to whom they aspire to be, and whose lifestyles they want to emulate. Therefore, producers can put a price tag on that kind of exposure to the point where product placement has become an integral part of the production budget.

My experience in product placement for Fender happened almost by accident. I had originally been hired by Fender to be their director of artist relations, where I was to work with major and emerging artists to bring them into the endorsement program. I had been in that position for less than two years when the prop master, Will Blount, who was working on a new Tom Hanks movie, *That Thing You Do!*, needed an expert to assist in documenting and supplying Fender products from a certain era,

1964, to be exact, the same year as the Beatles' emergence. Lucky for me, I knew it all too well as that was also the year that was pivotal in my determination to make a career in music. A prop master's primary responsibilities are to seek out and provide the correct products for each scene in a movie or TV show. Since they are also looking for products that will lend credibility to or enhance the projects they are working on, prop masters are the key players between the production and the brands.

Over the years, I have been able to build close working relationships with prop masters who will contact us whenever a script calls for a musical instrument. Unless they are lucky enough to hook up with a long-running hit TV series, most prop masters are independent contractors who are constantly moving from project to project—as one ends, they are already setting up their next job. Therefore, a prop master can be your company's best friend and your best source for finding placement opportunities for your trademark brand.

Will had contacted our corporate offices in Scottsdale, Arizona, and they said, "Oh yeah, we've got a guy on the West Coast that does that kind of thing." They meant me, and even though I had no experience with product placement at the time, I went out to meet the prop master and lo and behold, Tom Hanks[4] was there to discuss some of the product. This wasn't just any ordinary movie for Hanks; it was a movie that he had written, produced, and starred in; therefore, an absolute labor of love for him. I learned so much from Hanks and his prop master on accepting nothing short of perfection with the placements, not only for the year 1964, the time in which the movie was set, but also for the appropriate instruments for the age and experience of the many players in the movie. These actors were also expected to play their instruments "live" to the soundtrack while filming the concert scenes, so for the ones who didn't have any experience, Hanks brought in a music instructor. My assistant at the time, Alex Perez, was also on hand for those scenes to make sure the guitars were set up and broken strings were replaced.

This was the first time a production had put that much effort to making sure that all the products that appeared—guitars, amps, radios, TVs, refrigerators, and so on, were historically correct. If fact, the movie became so revered in the industry that there was even a web site devoted to the dissecting of all the placements. Not bad for my first experience in product placement!

I was contacted by many prop masters after that because I became known as the guitar guy who worked on *That Thing You Do!* It's funny to me, because just a decade before that, most prop masters were not aware—or simply didn't care—if musical instruments were authentic for a certain era. In an otherwise very good movie, *The Buddy Holly Story*, the Fender Stratocaster guitars played by Gary Busey as Holly were totally wrong for the era. Yes, they were Stratocaster guitars, but they were current models with colors and hardware that didn't exist in the 1950s. It was obvious to almost anyone who knew anything about Fender that these were way off. Even today, prop masters will ask me, "Say, you aren't the guy who was responsible for putting those guitars in *The Buddy Holly Story*, are you?" Thankfully, that was before my time at Fender.

Because of our reputation and the strength of the Fender brand coupled with its historical significance, we are often asked to participate in placements without having to pay. In fact, I have never solicited a placement on behalf of Fender products other than simply letting a producer or prop master know that we are available for their support. That is atypical in our industry, but it does illustrate the power of a uniquely recognizable brand. When you walk through a major music retailer's store, you may see guitars that resemble Fenders except for the variations that make them instantly recognizable as limitations, because our trademarks on the headstock and body designs are unique to our models. If a prop master doesn't know the difference, it could be a noticeable mistake to place a Fender lookalike in a scene that requires the real thing. And, as in *The Buddy Holly Story*, missing the authenticity on a product from a specific era, or placing a knockoff, could be downright embarrassing.

One of the best projects I had the pleasure to work on was the Johnny Cash biopic, *Walk the Line*. Not only were we asked to provide products for a precise era, we were depicting the exact instruments that were used by famous artists in specific perform-ances. I was fortunate to have two prop masters for *Walk the Line* who really did their homework before our initial production meeting. Brandon Boyle and Chris Peck came out to our manufacturing facility in Corona, California, armed with several actual concert scenes from Johnny's performances that were to be recreated for the movie. Just to give you an idea of how deep the director, James Mangold, was into this, they were planning on shooting the concert scene where Johnny played with Elvis Presley in the actual venue in Memphis. Talk about authenticity! That put the pressure on us to make sure we were up to that level, and so I asked one of our senior master builders from the custom shop, Mark Kendrick, to attend.

Mark used to be my builder when the top artists came to Fender for their dream guitars, and I knew that his uncle had worked at Fender in the 1960s, so Mark knew a lot of the history of that era firsthand. It also didn't hurt that Mark was a major Cash fan. That served me well when Brandon and Chris produced photos of one of Luther Perkins's Telecaster guitars. Luther was the legendary guitarist who is credited with creating the distinctive guitar style heard on hits like "Walk the Line" and "Folsom Prison Blues" and this movie would finally show his influence on Cash's signature sound. Because the shots were so grainy, even the prop masters were not sure about the details of Luther's guitar. Mark took one glance at the guitar and remarked that not only did he recognize the exact model, but had actually done some work on it for Marty Stuart, who acquired it after Luther's untimely death in 1968.[5] That locked the deal right then and there.

Furthermore, we had to do some additional detective work on another grainy black and white shot of an amp used by Elvis's guitarist, Scotty Moore. It was based on a Fender Bassman of the era, and called an EchoSonic, custom built by Ray Butts. Not too many were ever made, but Scotty had one, and it was important to get it right, even if it wasn't one of ours.

To do so, we visited Mike Eldred, who was the marketing manager of the Custom Shop and had played with Scotty. Mike gave him a call, and we were amazed when Scotty said he still had his original amp. He sent us 360-degree color shots of the amp and we were able to supply the correct covering, grill cloth, and tone controls from our vintage line for Brandon and Chris to replicate. When the film was completed, Scotty called Brandon to compliment him on nailing the amp. (Unfortunately, Brandon was driving in the typically heavy traffic of Los Angeles and told me that he almost drove off the road when he realized who was on the phone!)

Fox ordered the same instruments that were depicted on the screen with which to record the soundtrack so that even the tones would be authentic. The film garnered both critical and financial success, which included several Academy Award nominations, a Best Actress Award for Reese Witherspoon, several Golden Globe wins, and a hit soundtrack. The great Johnny Cash was introduced to another generation and we had another watermark to which to aspire in product placement authenticity.[6]

But music instruments are only a small part of authenticity in product placement. Any movie or TV show depicting a bygone era has to make certain everything on camera is historically correct. Take a closer look at *Walk the Line* and you will notice cars, clothing, fishing poles, airplanes, and even the sink that "Johnny" rips out of the wall in his dressing room. The prop masters had to make sure each and every one of these items were as close to authentic as possible.

There are prop houses in Southern California that specialize in vintage pieces for television and film productions. History for Hire and The Hand Prop Room are just two that cater to the industry by acquiring and categorizing tens of thousands of items from different decades. They do their research, but they also rely on manufacturers for information and support. Jim Hayes, with whom I worked on placements through The Hand Prop Room, now has his own prop house—LA House of Props—in another new emerging film locale, Shreveport, Louisiana. Jim told me many times that brand names will get on camera if they have the historical significance for the era depicted in the film. This is an ideal way for any company that has been around for at least a decade or so to place their products without incurring substantial costs. Prop houses will seek out and acquire products from different time periods to build up their stock, and often work directly with the manufacturers for their guidance. I once visited History for Hire in Los Angeles. It is a huge structure that houses row after row of every type of product, including a substantial musical instrument collection. I thought to myself that this was like walking through a major museum in any part of the country. It was a truly fascinating experience.

We have been involved in very many film productions—*Ray; Dreamgirls; Rock Star; I'm Not There; Shake, Rattle and Roll; The Beach Boys: An American Family*; and even a flashback episode of the TV series *JAG*—all of which required authenticity to depict an era or specific scene. If we didn't have the guitars and amps available from our vintage or classic series, we would custom build them. But there are not enough productions requiring historically correct products to keep a full-time department like mine running year round, so the bulk of our placements come from two types: the cachet of the FMIC brands led by Fender, and what I call "one-stop shopping."

FMIC has several recognizable brands, which can also represent a wide range of music styles and certain looks that will bring authenticity—or simply the "right look"—to a given scene. The Fender Stratocaster guitar, Telecaster guitar, and Precision Bass are most representative of the iconic instruments for which Fender is known. They also come in a wide range of colors. When Rick Young, the prop master for Disney's hit, *Freaky Friday*, was looking for a classic instrument that Lindsey Lohan's character's late father has willed to her, he chose a Fender Telesonic guitar that had the classic look, but that also had a bit of a custom look in a unique burgundy red. This was chosen as the *hero* (the most prime placement a brand can get as the main star handles it) guitar, which appeared in the poster and major billboards promoting the movie—a much-coveted hat trick in our business. When the movie came out, we heard from many of our dealers that young girls were coming into their stores with their parents to inquire about the model played by Lohan. It didn't matter that the Telesonic guitar was almost $2,000, which is probably out of a beginning guitar player's price range. That's the beauty of having your brand on camera; it doesn't necessarily have to be product-specific to get the point across. Consumers will spend what they can afford as long as they recognize the brand and look as something that is comparable to the one they remember seeing onscreen.

Another red Fender—this time a Stratocaster guitar—ended up as the hero guitar for actress Saffron Burrows in Amy Redford's 2008 movie, *The Guitar*. The guitar is the focal point of the mystical healing powers of music (as documented in Chapter 2). It's featured in the exquisite poster for the film, placed against the back of a sitting nude Burrows, with the guitar's feminine shape mirroring hers.[7] To the young "half man," Angus, on the hit series *Two and a Half Men*, we supplied our Squier® by Fender value brand, when he was a preteen and had just started playing guitar. We then progressed him to a Classic series Fender Stratocaster guitar when he became a teenager. In the 2008 movie *Wonderful World*, we were alerted by Jim Hayes of the L.A. House of

Props that the prop master wanted a classic-looking acoustic in a specific red tint for Matthew Broderick's character to purchase from a small Southern music store owner (James Burton, the legendary guitarist with Ricky Nelson and Elvis Presley, who appears in a perfect cameo role); so we were able to supply a custom-painted one-off acoustic guitar from our Guild® line, since that brand has established its classic looks over the past 60 years. In addition, using Jim as our on-site consultant, we provided the prop masters with enough products from our various brands to equip the music store set. For a rockabilly artist like Brian Setzer, we have the Grestch® line, the ultimate cool cat's guitar from a line that has been around for more than 100 years. For heavy metal with imagery such as skull graphics, we have Jackson®, the cornerstone of 1980s metal. We just acquired Kaman Music, which gives us new opportunities with recognized guitar brands Takamine® and Ovation®, plus the formally missing part of our Gretsch line, Gretsch Drums. And it goes on and on.

Very few companies can offer a full line of equipment with several brands in the same scene like FMIC. Whether it be a full retail-store reproduction, or several band performances, it's no problem for us. Most companies will specialize in one or two products that are the cornerstone of their brand. For instance, Gibson is known for electric and acoustic guitars; Martin, Washburn, and Taylor for acoustics; Ibanez and Dean for electrics; and Marshall and Crate for amps. They may try occasional brand extensions, but these products are the bulk of their business.

When the movie *Stranger than Fiction* decided that it wasn't cost-effective to shoot in a music store in Chicago, we were able to step in and create a very believable-looking full-range store. The added benefit was that we also captured the hero placement guitar that Will Ferrell's character was lusting after, which was also mentioned in the voiceover in the scene.

We've been able to create a variety of different-looking stores—like the mom-and-pop store in the aforementioned *Wonderful World*, the suburban mall store in the made-for-cable movie *American Mall*, and the Greenwich Village collectors' shop in an episode of *CSI: New York*. The same goes for full band sets, because a real band would rarely play all the same brand of equipment, whether they were just beginning or were superstars.

For the 2008 movie, *The Rocker*, we had two distinctive types of band—the heavy metal Vesuvius, and the angst pop ADD. For an episode of *Vegas*, we supplied three completely different band scenes without repeating a duplicate instrument. For the VH1 series, *Rock of Love I & II*, we were able to provide Bret Michaels' bachelor pad with almost 30 different-looking guitars, many of which we used again for a commercial for Time-Life featuring Bret.

Speaking of commercials, other companies will use our products for authenticity and variety in their own spots: Hewlett-Packard featured a depiction of kids all over the world playing the riff from "Smoke on the Water"; Pepsi's "Little Jimi" featured an 11-year-old "Jimi Hendrix"; Nissan showed the king of the surf guitar sound, Dick Dale; Aamco displayed race car driver Danika Patrick serenaded by country artists Whiskey Falls; clothing retailer, Ross portrayed a preteen rock band; and FreeCredit Report.com[8] has run a series of hilarious commercials featuring down-and-out musicians performing on our gear.

Now with the addition of Gretsch Drums, we have a whole new set of placement opportunities. The only product we don't manufacture is electronic keyboards, but since we have a partnership with Roland for some of our high-tech electronics, we have access to their full line as well—truly one-stop shopping.

If your brand does not have this type of cachet, variety, or historical significance, however, you will most likely have to pay a fee, or trade in-kind for placements. That doesn't mean it will cost you millions right off the bat, but there are other ways to participate with such practices as product trade-out, promotional and advertising tie-ins (think BMW with a dealer's 007 plates—but didn't James Bond drive an Aston-Martin in the original novels?[9]), and through third-party placements. Plus, indie films will cost you much less than Hollywood blockbusters, and many times, they will have a cool factor that big budget movies don't have—which can be better for your product's association. Even though it's rare, a brand can actually command a fee to lend authenticity to a film. Twentieth-Century Fox ponied up $550,000 to the Smithsonian for usage of the museum's moniker in the title of the sequel to *Night at the Museum* (due out in May 2009). Talk about reverse engineering!

A word of warning: sometimes, your brand can lose credibility by going overboard with too blatant of a placement. How many times have you seen an actor pick up a bottle of beer and hold its label to the camera in a very unnatural manner? It might be funny when Mike Myers's "Wayne" spoofs it, but it's often offensive to the viewer. Sometimes, particularly on TV, you will also notice that a product's logo is enlarged so that it will show up better. For a placement to work, it needs to be credible and organic and cannot interfere with the flow of the production. In the "How low are you willing to go?" file, as exposed in the *Los Angeles Times*, companies are putting product placement into snack foods masquerading as learning guides. Oreos, Hershey's Skittles, and Keebler Grahams' Bug Bites all pretended to be teaching kids to count and read, but were truly doing nothing more than marketing to kids to want their brands.

The first step to credible and effective placements would be to hire a reliable agency, which usually takes a monthly retainer of several thousand dollars to place your products in front of prop masters and producers. Agenices have an inside track to what the productions are looking for, and can do research for demographics, exposure, and so forth on your behalf. Once they have secured a placement, they will negotiate a fee for the placement or an in-kind trade-out agreement. Sometimes, for an initial placement, they will throw you a *solid* by placing your product in a major TV series or movie to demonstrate their capabilities.

Recently, I was working on a co-promotion with the British motorcycle company, Triumph. The company was well known for movie appearances in the 1950s and 1960s (Brando, riding one in the *The Wild One* and Steve McQueen atop a few painted to look like authentic World War II German Army motorcycles in *The Great Escape*). Triumph was also the bike of choice for such notable musicians as Buddy Holly, Bob Dylan (who sports a Triumph shirt on the cover of his seminal album "Highway 61 Revisited"), and the king himself, Elvis Presley. The company had hit hard times and went under, just to resurface about 10 years ago, still respectful of the look and history of their classic bikes. I introduced them to an agency with which I had worked for several years, Pier 3 Entertainment. They immediately saw an opportunity for prime placements with two of the hit series they regularly worked on, *Grey's Anatomy*[10] and *Ugly Betty*.

When I first started working in placing Fender products into movies and TV, I was pretty fortunate to be introduced to Pier 3 Entertainment, one of the companies that was in on the ground floor of this relatively new industry. They are still going strong today and therefore have a unique perspective on how the industry has grown and changed. The company was founded by brothers John and Joe Tache—identical twins, better known as the Jetsyns. For this interview, I visited their beautiful oceanfront offices not far from the famous pier in Redondo Beach (hence the name of their company). I began by asking John for a little history of their company.

"We started Pier 3 Entertainment back in June of 1996 and at the time in *product placement*, that's what it was

called back then. There were a lot of guerilla marketers
or guerilla product placement agencies and when I say
guerilla, there were maybe fifteen to twenty doing serious
business with the production themselves to save money off
of the end budgets of each of the productions. So, in other
words, you had people who had relationships who knew
people on the set and they'd go to the set and if the set
needed a particular prop or a particular wardrobe, or
particular car, or particular guitar for any weekly given
shoot, the product placement agencies would provide the
goods at no cost to the production. The production would
thus save money, as they wouldn't have to go out and buy a
Fender guitar; they wouldn't have to buy a Volkswagen.
They could get these from the promotion house or the
placement company for no charge at all. So we started
back in 1996, when there were a handful of product
placement companies doing it, and everybody knew
everybody else, and the way it ran is, if you came through
with your promotion or product for the TV show or the
movie, then you were looked upon as dependable and
they would keep coming back to you. But if you ever
promised a production or a movie or a TV show with
something that you didn't come through with, then they
would know that they couldn't depend on you, so you got
to wear out your welcome in the business real quick,
because there weren't as many product placement companies around so the cream always rose to the top."

It seemed like such a cottage industry back then so I wanted
to know if they had a business plan to actually make money
doing it as a full-time business.

"What was fascinating to me at first, because I came here
to be a writer, and, you know, a struggling writer doesn't

make much money, but it was a fascinating way for me to go in to the business and go onto the stage and meet people I hadn't been able to meet. I was selling Hollywood. The thing that was very surprising to me was about the amount of money you could make off of this industry, and how much the corporate people would pay to get on to the venues I was selling, and that I had at my disposal. In other words, it's easier to sell John Travolta in a feature film as opposed to selling a gym membership at Gold's Gym. A John Travolta feature one week then turns into a Bruce Willis feature the next week, which will turn into a Julia Roberts feature the next. The sale is always different and interesting, and I think that's the difference of the product placement compared to selling anything else.

I was curious about one thing. "Since you were there at the forefront of it, I was reading research that's available and they said that in the year 2001 it had grown to one billion dollars, and in 2007, it's close to five billion dollars. Do you feel like it has grown like that?"

John Jetsyn replied, "I think the biggest difference now is that with the advent of TiVo and when TiVo came into play, all the backroom deals and all the mom-and-pop type of deals we had with production got transferred to the studio system. And the studio and all the producers and all the suits in the office were looking for a way to make more money off of something that had been established ten years earlier. No longer were the ads being watched on TV because of TiVo, so there was a transference of getting the brand . . . into the content or into the program itself, thus alerting all the studio higher-ups to be the police and the gatekeepers. And when that happened, there were a lot more gates and a lot more processes to get into and the costs increased. The great thing about the suits getting involved in the prices did go up because back in the day you would get very little money for product placement. You make a nice deal for promotion and you make a nice deal for ten or fifteen placements throughout the course of the season and you took your money and ran. It was very short money. It wasn't anything astronomical unless you fell into a good promotion. Nowadays, because it's a quantifiable thing and there are a lot of different entities involved, being the studio, corporations, and product placement companies, people are accepting the fact that they have to pay more money to get onto these mediums, whereas before, they were just donating product."

I asked John that if an average company (let's say it wasn't Fender) approached Pier 3 wanting to get their product into a movie or television production, could he give some of the steps they would go through.

"The first thing I like to do when someone comes and approaches me is I ask myself, 'Can I do a good job for these people?' Fender? Going to a set with Fender is like driving an entertainment stake through the heart (laughs). I mean, when somebody needs music or musical instruments or anything that has to do with music, you go to Fender and you get the number one guy and it buys you a lot of leverage with other things and so when you go in with a Fender, it's a means to an end. When I go in with Fender, I can say, 'Well, you can take my Fender, but I would like you to take product A, B, and C from my other companies that are not as desirable to you' but you leverage them in. When you have a good client list or a good client base, Fender's always been a great thing because everybody needs it and you can always leverage other clients in with the Fender brand.

"Getting back to your question, which was, if a company doesn't have that kind of cachet or recognized brand, but they are a player, they have distribution either nationally or worldwide, and they look to film and TV to promote that brand, and they look to us and say, 'We don't have that kind of cachet but we want to get on a show,' you would first look at the brand. If it's a competitive brand, you can do something for it. That's the first thing. Number two, I always want to ask the company, 'Where [do] you want to be?' Do they want to be on *Desperate Housewives?* Do they want to be on feature film? Do they want to attack the cable market? One of my clients, Kitchen-Aire, bought Bosch, and the first year we had them, they wanted to be on all the TV shows. We got them all the Bosch kitchen appliances and dishwashers—they're all over the *Desperate Housewives* set. We put that on *Desperate Housewives* when that was just a pilot. But Bosch wasn't happy with their logo just being on *Desperate Housewives.* They were only happy getting verbal mentions, so . . . we transferred them over from their refrigerators just being on TV shows over to cable shows, where you have the HGTVs [Home and Garden], the Food Network, the Home Shopping networks, the home fixer-upper shows, where they were not only getting seen but they were also being mentioned verbally, endorsed by the construction guys building the house or building the kitchen. So it was more bang for their buck on cable than what they were paying on network TV.

"So, after you identify a client and you think you can do a good job [for] them and you identify where they want to be and if the places that they want to be aren't charging a lot of money or you can make a backroom deal or go in the back way, more power to them. But if it's something like a urinal cake? How many places can you put a urinal cake and be seen without being too risqué, so, you're *not* going to take money off of the company and say, 'I'll give you thirty placements.'"

We talked about the importance of relationships in this tight-knit community.

"Fortunately for Pier 3, we've got a great TV department and we make friends with everybody from the writer to the celebrity to the producer to the prop guy to the set decorator to the wardrobe. And those are all the blue collar people that come to work every day—they don't deal with the corporations, they don't deal with the studio suits, they just come in and they make sure the shot's ready to be shot and they get their stuff in there and [at] the end of the day, if it doesn't last fifteen days, they go home and they start all over again. They are totally isolated from the studio world where you have the suits dealing with the office stuff and they are trying to quantify product placement and the suits by charging money there. Whereas, the people on the set and the relationships you make on the set gets you ten times further than you would by dealing with a suit in the studio. Because, number one is, they, the suits, don't have control of what's going on in the set. Number two is, they can only charge money, and number three, at the end of the day, they aren't the people who are really going to push for you to be on the show."

Knowing John Tache started as a writer, I asked, "What about an integrated placement where companies are asking for their brands to be written into the script? We know we talked about examples like *Knight Rider*, where it's really almost like an infomercial for Ford Mustang, but how does that work?"

"I'll give you a good case. We were representing Volkswagen, back maybe [in] 2000 and 2001 and what happened was Mike Myers was doing the second of the Austin Powers movies, and at the time, they wanted a Volkswagen to be a time machine that Mike Myers would get in and go back to the Sixties. So, we had a big production meeting with all the suits and what production wanted was a lot of money out of Volkswagen to be Mike Myers's car. But we, on the other hand, knew that no matter what kind of money they got out of Volkswagen that they were *still* going to use a Volkswagen—okay? So, we brought Volkswagen into the production of Mike Myers and all the producers, and they drew us some pictures of what the time machine would look like. They said they were going to cut off the top of the Volkswagen, which was a no-no at the time because there were no Volkswagen convertibles, so the Volkswagen people were kind of up in arms about that but eventually knew that they would be making a convertible. Anyway, Volkswagen kept their mouth shut; the studio offered them all this great exposure; and at the end of the day, we walked out of the office and we said, 'Your car is going to be in the movie. There's no reason why you should pay,' and Volkswagen took that stance and they said the reason why they weren't paying was because they didn't want to alter the Beetle—because there was no convertible Beetle out yet. Obviously, they had a good out and they also knew that it was written in to the film so, the integration at the time with Mike Myers was a perfect thing of getting it [in] to the movie and not paying. But the other end of it, you have the *Matrix*, where Cadillac paid fifteen million dollars to be in the second *Matrix* movie, and they had, like, twenty Cadillac Escalades in there, and that was the structure with Cadillac. Cadillac paid a lot of money, but at the time they could have used Lexus instead of Cadillac, so Cadillac didn't have a big negotiation hand. They just took the deal and went with what they could get out of it because unlike a Volkswagen Beetle, it's more generic than that."

I told him I thought that was a great story that put it all into perspective. I wanted him to elaborate more about a new business plan that they had discussed for product placement, where there would actually be an escrow account set up by corporations for their brands that could be accessed by prop masters, set decorators, and so on for placements on an ongoing basis, instead of negotiating with the suits on a placement-by-placement basis.

"That's an idea that my brother, Joe, came up with. I don't think it will ever come to fruition because the main crisis in the industry is you have the creative versus the corporate side. Corporate side is always going to want the money. Volkswagen made a deal a couple of years ago with NBC Universal where they were paying like two hundred million dollars in escrow and for that Volkswagen got first look at all the car parts in TV shows and feature films. Basically, what Universal was doing, was any car that they had, they would go to Volkswagen and say, 'Hey, we got a car opportunity. Do you want to be it?' If Volkswagen said yes, they tapped into that escrow account. On the other end of the street, Volkswagen, at approximately that same time, was paying our company not even one-fifth of that and they gave us six cars. We took those six cars and we put them on *CSI, Alias*, and *Malcolm in the Middle, JAG, NCIS*, and *Ghost Whisperer*, anything that could be used on them, and we got over two to three hundred million viewer impressions for a fraction of what they had in escrow over in NBC Universal, and they had more choice of what they were doing with us. We just took the cars and moved them around to different sets and we were more flexible. Whereas the deal they had to sign with NBC Universal, only limited VW to Universal projects. Either way, they are always going to want to integrate the corporate brand into something that is an art form, a creative art form, and you are basically telling Francis Ford Coppola that you are going to pay him ten million dollars to put a Big Mac in Don Corleone's hands. And with Don Corleone, that's not always going to work. We have a client, Google, who likes to be in "contextually." If it doesn't fit—and we mentioned this earlier—if it's not a contextual fit, it will irritate the viewer, and it will piss them off and make them think, 'What do you think, that I'm stupid?' So with a contextual integration, if it's seamless and if it's a part of the story and it goes along, it works. Take *The Bourne Ultimatum*. We had a scene where Matt Damon goes into an Internet café, on the run, and he types in *Google* and he finds out the people he wants to look for and he goes on his way. That's a contextual integration."

I wanted to know, "Will you help a company to kind of navigate that? In other words, would you advise a company to say, 'Look, we know you want the placement, but if it's not contextual—if it's not right, it's going to be diminishing returns.

It's not going to be the right look or people are not going to accept it.' Can you do that for your clients?"

"We know up front if an entertainment marketing company or a product placement company is doing their job, they are going to know exactly what their clients want at all times. And they are going to know exactly where. If somebody comes to me and asks me for a Fender guitar and they want it for a questionable scene that Fender might not like and I know they don't like it, it's not going to happen. But if the guy on the guitar is Matthew McConaughey, and he's playing in a romantic comedy and he's going to be seen by a lot of people, I will put that on the client's table and say, 'What do you want to do?' Here's another story: We did a movie, *Bedazzled*, and we did a great scene with Brendan Fraser, and it was probably one-fifth of the show, and after all that work we put into it, it [hit] the cutting room floor. But it made the DVD, so at the end of the day, it could be a great fit, but it won't show up. On another day, it could be a great fit, but it will show up and show up in every other scene—think FedEx in *Castaway*. Nowadays, they call product placement *integration* now. So it's more exact [if] you can buy your way in and if they have an opportunity, they will tell you what the opportunity is, and they will stipulate what the opportunity is, and let you give it to your client. But, the client won't always take it, so the problem with our industry is, it's always a quick match-maker and you always have to do it quickly, because it's always got to be done yesterday."

I wanted to know if it was strictly about the numbers, that is, impressions, or were there other factors at work to make a client pleased with the results.

"This is an interesting story. When I first started selling product placement, I called up a diaper company, Drypers—disposable diapers were big on shows—and I made a deal with this lady and asked, 'Which show do would like to be on?' She said, "I'd love to be on *ER*, and I'll tell you what. If you can get Drypers on *ER*, I'll sign a deal with you and you can put me on everything.' So I said, 'Fine.' I had worked [it] into a show on that season, and *ER*'s on late, so I kind of dozed off on the couch, but I remember waking up and seeing the main character, Jeanie Boulet, who was about to have a baby, walking down this store aisle with two walls of Drypers. I did the deal pro bono to gain faith with the client, and the next morning I got call from the lady at the company and I signed them up. They knew what they wanted, they gave me a challenge, and it took me two months to do it, but after that, I was in good with them and I had a deal with them."

I added, "You guys are a full-service agency, so if they missed it, you still would been able to capture it for them."

Tache nodded in agreement. "Yes, we have a great IT department, and Andrea (Rawlings) will have it up the next morning. If it shows up on Thursday night, it will be on the client's web site on Friday morning with a video capture, all the ratings, the time the product was on the air, all the info a client wants to know in a running log so the client can check it out any time on their own personal, private web site."

With that, we were joined by Joe Jetsyn Tache to pick up where his twin brother left off.

"I want to go more in-depth on the *Vertical Solution*, which will revolutionize the product integration avenues of entertainment simply because it would tie corporate into the creative unions that run all of Hollywood. . . . Somebody's grandfather and father before them was the prop master on some movie and the job was given to them, as it's all legacies in Hollywood—set decorators, wardrobe, property masters, transportation coordinators, are all Teamsters; they're all union people and their affiliation is all with production and getting the production done and in the can. They don't have any dealings with NBC, ABC, CBS, as they are just regular people who live paycheck to paycheck. One week at a time, and don't get any of the residuals but are ninety-nine percent responsible for the end product that's put in the can for TV and movies. The producers are the ones that deal with the networks and are told what they can and cannot do. When corporate America tries to buy advertising space on any of these individual shows, the networks will in turn take these demands to the creative producers who are putting together the shows, and ninety percent of the time, the creative producers have nothing to do with what the networks are trying to get integrated on their shows. If it fits in the creative end of the show, they'll put it in, but if it doesn't, they won't, because they are not receiving any supplemental budget from the networks on a week-to-week basis. The check they receive each week to produce the shows is relatively the same for twenty-four weeks. If they have a car chase, an explosion, or a guest star that's costing them extra money, they have to find creative ways to get that money to support that one week's show.

"With the Vertical Solution, what that would basically do is take all the corporations at the upfronts, set aside a budget in escrow for all the shows they want to be integrated on, and go to a company like Pier 3. I can only think of one other company besides us that has those types of relationship with all the unions in Hollywood, that would actually successfully integrate their products on a show, and includes pictures and information for the corporate web sites. Unless the networks would hire us to individually execute their target lists that they would get at the upfronts with what shows they need to be integrated into through the escrow budgets, I don't think it would ever work because TV moves too fast. It's a week-to-week production, and they wouldn't be able to handle the time line at the fast pace it takes to integrate the product on the show. By the time they got clearance from corporate America to get the placement done, the show would already be in the can for that week. Currently, there is no special program to set aside the budget for the escrow for the creative integration. If creative production would share from that budget, they would have the incentive to integrate product because when they did, they would know that they could withdraw money from the corporate escrow budget to help out the production. We pitched this to NBC two years ago and they took a part of it from us for *The Office*. Reveille Productions was handling that but after a while it overwhelmed them, and they stopped doing it, and the person at NBC who initiated it is no longer there. I still think it should be implemented, but the greed of the network to the individual production companies, whether it be Touchstone, Dozier, Bruckheimer, all these independent companies that are cut off from the networks from getting any external budget for any individual show."

At that point, I wanted to talk more about the relationships needed to get on the set so an agency could get to speak one-on-one with creative production. My experience is that after

September 11th, security became so tight at the studios that it's virtually impossible to gain entry to a set unless you have clearance and to do that, you need to know the right person. Yet, time after time, I was able to walk right onto a set when accompanied by Joe Jetsyn, who was greeted as a friend and an associate on major shows that included *ER, Grey's Anatomy, Scrubs,* and *Two and a Half Men.*

> As my dad said, "If you are around the game for a long time and you have character and integrity, and you are punctual and get the product there on time, and you're eliminating budget concerns by supplying promotional product at no charge, you are always going to make friends." Pre-9/11 was a good point because there was a lot more competition in product placement, with companies trying to do what we do. But my brother had tremendous skills as a salesperson, who had the ability to get to corporate America, so the strength of our client list pre-9/11 enabled us to have strong relationships with property masters, transportation coordinators, et cetera. The things that cost the most money for individual productions are cars, kitchens, electronics, and musical equipment, so if you have a client list that includes those, independent productions will look at that and say, 'Wow, if we can get them to promo Thermador, we just saved ourselves eighty thousand dollars!' If that same production has a stage that needs musical equipment, and we can supply Fender products, we just saved the production another thirty thousand dollars in just one week. But after the planes hit the towers in New York, agencies that didn't have a strong client list were basically pushed to the side, and it was impossible for them to get on major lots like Warner Brothers, Universal, Paramount, Sony—I mean the lots had dogs, mirrors to look underneath the

cars, and you had to have three forms of identification, so at that time, a lot of companies went out of business. Pier 3 kept going right along, and then the product placement wave came in where corporate America thought that they could make a lot of money on product integration. So then you have all these upstart companies on the fringe who have no relationships with the unions, creative, et cetera, but they call the networks offering all these clients, and so the networks decide to squeeze money [out] of those clients. But when it comes to fulfillment, the networks had no control, so these agencies were just throwing away the money their clients paid. Production didn't care what the networks said because they had total creative rein over their shows, because that's the agreement they had going in. The only way that would work [is] if the corporation is dealing directly with creative to get promises before they get to the network. The way it really works is that production has an agency's client list, and when the script calls for something, they have two to three weeks lead time, which is plenty of time to call Pier 3 so they can get the client's approval to proceed. Agencies that don't have their act together will wait until the last minute, hoping to get something into a scene, and it just won't happen that way."

As you can see, there are no "established" rules for any type of placement. Necessity is just as important as what a client is willing to pay. I was contacted by the prop master on the TV series *The Bachelor*, who needed any acoustic guitar for a campfire scene. The bachelor had apparently forgotten his guitar and the shoot was the next day. The prop master informed me, as an afterthought, that there would also be a fee of $300,000! When I told her we weren't interested, she said, 'Okay, forget the three hundred grand; just make sure the guitar is on set tomorrow.' She added that they wouldn't be showing the Fender headstock logo because we didn't pay (no worries there, as the Resonator acoustic I sent had the characteristic backward Fender *F* (also depicted as the *F* on the word *Factor* for this book's cover art) as the body cutouts—instantly recognizable to anyone who would have cared). The point is that someone must have been willing to pay the going rate of $300,000 to get exposure for their brand on the series. Either way, companies are willing to pay big bucks for brand integration.

The NBC made-for-TV movie, *Knight Rider*, a remake of the 1980s crime-fighting series that originally starred David Hassel-hoff and his Pontiac Trans Am, now features a muscle-bound Ford Mustang. Due to the not-so-subtle product integration by Ford, *Los Angeles Times* critic Mary McNamara described the program as a "two-hour(!) movie/pilot/extended Ford commercial." (The show may become a full series again.) And it's not enough that Simon Cowell has the big red Coke glass in front of him each week on *American Idol*; he commented on a recent episode after taking a long swig about how much he enjoys the soft drink.

Just in case you missed the placement of anything from a car to an article of clothing, there's SeenOn, a division of the California-based company Delivery Agent Inc., which "brokered deals with Television networks, movie studios and other media outlets to provide a link between thousands of products characters use on-screen and consumers eager to buy them."[11] Once products appear, they almost immediately go up on the Web, orders are taken and processed by Delivery Agent, and everyone involved—the production company, the broadcaster and, of course Delivery Agent, gets a cut of the profits. Even the stars sometimes share in the profits.

I recall reading a story that Ray-Ban paid a monster placement fee of $10 million to have their glasses integrated into

Mission Impossible 2. For that, they received the hero placement with Tom Cruise. I suspected that they didn't pay a cent, but rather Sunglass Hut footed the bill for a national tie-in through their retail outlets that featured Cruise in point-of-purchase displays.

The explosive boom of reality shows, most recently helped along even further by the prolonged writers' strike of 2007–2008, has also been a windfall for product placements. Reality shows, love 'em or hate 'em, are cheaper to produce, don't use writers (although they do hire *script consultants*), and don't have high-salaried stars, so placement fees can generally become gravy for the producers.

I was approached by the producers of the TV series, *Rock Star* for its inaugural season in 2005. They were looking for a major guitar company to sponsor a giant guitar-shaped stage for $700,000. (For us, it would have been a Stratocaster shape.) Not only did we feel that that was an exorbitant request for a new and unproven show, I personally felt that that type of blatant placement was so over the top that it would have diminishing returns for a respected brand like Fender because it was the antithesis of organic.

I would rather not have our name in the credits at the end of a production because that is usually reserved for brands or companies that pay a fee for the placements. If a producer wants to thank us in the credits for our efforts in delivering the right product on time for their shoots, that's okay by me, but I would never solicit that. If you are not paying a fee, some productions even have a policy that you need to provide a certain amount of product—usually a minimum of $75,000 worth—to get mentioned in the credits. Our main competitor, Gibson, did sign on for *Rock Star* for an undisclosed fee in the same neighborhood, but without the giant stage. Even though we declined to pay, our gear made it into the broadcast because I had given one of the house band members, Jim McGorman, an endorsement with

Fender back in 1998 with his band, the New Radicals. To the credit of the producers, they let the band choose the gear they required to guarantee the right sound for each song.

According to data posted by iTVX.net,[12] the top 10 network shows for product placement—22,046 occurrences of them—were all reality shows. That amounts to far-reaching opportunities for brands looking to network TV. ABC's *Fast Cars and Superstars* led the pack with *Extreme Makeover: Home Edition* coming in second. I saw the power of the latter when Fender was contacted to participate in the first season's finale. I spoke directly with host Ty Pennington, who wanted to make a very special "reveal" at the end for the one older brother who was faced with the responsibility of raising his eight sisters after their parents both died. We rocked out his room with guitars, amps, a wall of speakers, and—thanks to help from Universal Music and Experience Hendrix—a poster for Jimi Hendrix's *Blue Wild Angel* DVD. Ty even led his own group of designers and contractors in a special local fund-raising concert for the siblings. What's so attractive about this program is that major corporations like Sears and their suppliers can tap into the good karma atmosphere of an entertaining and popular show and also receive the personal endorsement of the show's very cool star, Ty Pennington.

Of course, the big daddy of them all is *American Idol*, which boasts weekly 30-million-plus viewers per episode. With those types of numbers, Coca-Cola didn't blink at the reported $3 million per show sponsorship fee to have those big red Coke glasses from which judges Randy, Paula, and Simon incessantly sip to make sure the camera doesn't miss the placement. And it's no surprise that *American Idol* had the top number of placements of network shows—4,349 occurrences, of which 3,111 were the Coca-Cola brand.[13] But when you play in the big leagues of top-rated shows like *American Idol*, and top-rated sports spectaculars like the Super Bowl, you will get what you pay for if you are willing to shell out $1 million for a 30-second spot on *AI*[14] and a whopping

$2.7 million for the same on the last Super Bowl.[15] We have been very fortunate to have our brands showing up on *American Idol* with artists like Jeff Beck and Maroon 5 in 2007, and in 2008 with ZZ Top in the finale. For 2008, the producers have let the contestants use instruments if they so chose and we've lent the show guitars and amps for the backing band. Winner David Cook has used a Fender Telecaster guitar and Takamine acoustic. When he wheeled out an Eddie Van Halen amp rig from our EVH line, we even received an unsolicited on-air comment from judge Randy Jackson, whom we consider part of the Fender family for all of his dedication to our gear over the years, as a world-class bassist and top record producer.

Cable TV is one step down from network TV, and it witnessed a 15 percent drop in placements last year to 136,078. The leader of that pack was *American Chopper*, which had 41,657 occurrences.[16] I had some experience with their fees when they contacted me in 2006 to ask whether Fender wanted to have them design a Custom Stratocaster bike on one of the episodes. The price to FMIC would have been $90,000, which *American Chopper* claimed our competitor Peavey was willing to pay. Peavey is another American guitar manufacturer, which, despite being a quality company, has, in my opinion, based most of their designs on Fender guitars and amplifiers. We politely declined to participate and Peavey went forward. They built a pretty nice bike, although I feel that *American Chopper* would have received considerably more than $90,000 worth of exposure if they waived their fee to go with us.

A new trend in online advertising that seems to be gaining steam is Consumer Generated Marketing (CGM). The idea consists of companies empowering communities of citizen marketeers and brand loyalists; in other words, finding people interested in promoting information on the brands they love and giving them the video-sharing tools to do it. But unlike with YouTube, marketers have control of what gets posted. According to Owen Mack on mediapost.com, "On platforms like Ning and

Kickapps, marketers are building spaces where niche audiences of brand lovers post video content about their lives, their creative endeavors, and their brands." CGM is managed by the marketers and is another form of placement that can take on the best aspects of peer marketing—geographic, demographic, and use-based targeting. Doritos took this humble concept all the way up to the big game with their "Crash the Super Bowl" contest.

As I have shown in this chapter, the first rule of getting your product placed is that there are no rules other than a certain amount of resourcefulness. That's what makes it so challenging, yet rewarding, because we know what companies are willing to devote to product integrations because of their powerful and emotional impact on the consumer.

CHAPTER 7

Event Marketing— Reaching Your Core Demo One- on-One

One of the most straightforward ways I know to reach a key market for your company is through event marketing. This simply means placing your brand in front of hundreds to thousands of potential consumers who are attending a particular event. Whether it's sporting, racing, or a concert, you will be in the midst of people who have chosen to participate in a shared entertainment experience. Some will be casual attendees, but many are passionate about why they are there. For you to put your support into this type of event casts your brand as passionate in their world as well.

There's another important reason that marketers see an advantage in event marketing, according to Robert Silverman, founder of SFX Concerts (who sold this company in 2000 to Clear Channel for $4.4 billion): "If you go to see Tom Petty or the Spice Girls, you've chosen to do it. You're excited. You're not doing this passively—like watching TV at home. You're spending money, and you're very receptive to hear direct or subliminal messages."[1]

Every time I go a major league baseball or pro football game, I am amazed at all the ads plastered throughout the stadium because I find it hard to believe that any message is getting through to the fans attending. It's no wonder that MLB Properties, Columbia Pictures, and Marvel Studios formed a marketing alliance and actually tried to have the webbed logo from the movie *SpiderMan 2* imprinted on the bases and on-deck circles of 15 stadiums; a deal that would reputedly be worth $3.6 million, with large-market teams like the Yankees and the Red Sox receiving $100,000 for their share.[2] Thankfully, the idea was canned just before the campaign would have been launched; otherwise, the next step might have been promotional tie-ins on the players' uniforms! It's one thing to have an athlete showcase a sporting goods company's logo on his uniform or clothing that the company manufactures and sponsors the athlete with (think Tiger Woods's Nike *swoosh* emblem on his collar—totally acceptable in today's sports world) but over-the-top tie-ins similar to the doomed *SpiderMan 2* and MLB concept would be just too insidious and could actually alienate the fans.

The same clutter is found in the countless brands plastered all over the NASCAR racers—to the point that you can barely tell what color their cars are. As entertainment marketing specialist Warren Weideman remarked to me in his interview for this book, "When you are sitting in the stands with a hundred thousand other fans, how are you going to notice a little decal on the back pipe of a car going a hundred eighty miles an hour?" I myself have a hard time picking out more than a few of the dozens of logos adorning the drivers' racing jumpsuits.

So why would a company take a chance on potentially estranging the fans? In a word: money, and lots of it. Even though NASCAR owners won't divulge specifics, it has been reported that a team can get anywhere from $10 million to $20 million for a primary sponsorship on the car, with associates sponsors paying $500,000 to $1 million for a secondary spot. Of course, for their investment, sponsors can receive uniforms, transportation, and drivers who will appear for marketing purposes.[3]

North American companies were projected to spend a whopping $14.9 billion on sponsorships in 2008, which is an increase of 11 percent over the year before. Anheuser-Busch leads in spending once again with a budget of $330 million-plus, followed by PepsiCo, General Motors, Coke, and Nike. It should come as no surprise that the athletics industry leads the pack with 66 percent of the total expenditures, followed by entertainment tours with 11 percent, and festivals, fairs, and annual events at 5 percent. Arts, causes, and association and membership organizations combined make up the remaining 18 percent.[4]

Another avenue for brand sponsorship is naming rights for the venue. This is done most often for large stadiums, because the cost can be prohibitive to anyone but major corporations. For instance, FedEx paid $205 million to rename the Washington Redskins home "FedEx Field." Brands, however, can also purchase naming rights to smaller venues. In our industry, our closest competitor, Gibson Guitars, signed a 10-year contract at $1 million annually to rename the 6,000-seat Universal Amphitheatre the Gibson Amphitheatre. Since Gibson is based in Nashville, Tennessee, they probably determined that making a splash in the heart of the entertainment industry would enhance their initiatives to position themselves as not *just* a guitar company, but as an *entertainment* company. Whatever the cost, naming rights include the benefit of having your brand mentioned and attached to hundreds of high profile events every year.

Even if your company doesn't have millions of dollars earmarked for large-scale sponsorships to promote its brands, there are many other sponsorship opportunities that can be cost-effective—if tailored to suit your brand's needs. They can also give your brand face time with your consumers.

Event marketing can work with any size budget, from the title sponsorship all the way down to a simple on-site booth. Sponsorships can be broken down based on several levels that all have their own sponsorship fee. For the biggest brands, nothing shy of the prestigious title or presenting sponsor moniker will do when their brand stands alone at the top, and for a major tour, this can run into the tens of millions of dollars.

Don't forget that whatever level your brand is at, you may be able to recoup some of your investment with on-site sales. For food and beverage, it's equal parts branding and necessity (beer and hot dogs for the hungry masses). There are hundreds of desirable products that can be sold or given away that have your company's logo prominently displayed as a co-branded souvenir of the event. And that's not just with the typical consumer.

If there is one thing I've learned in the music industry, it's that no matter how big the star or executive, they always love free stuff, or the rock slang version of it—*swag*. Once during a meeting with Mattel regarding a co-branded program with Hot Wheels, the head of boys' marketing commented that she was surprised I didn't bring any cool products from Fender; this was after she gave me several collectibles for my stepson from their Hot Wheels collection. When I replied that I thought that perhaps swag at her level was maybe not appropriate, she replied, "Del, let me tell you something—swag is always appropriate."

Even as a freebie, brand awareness is the key to true value in having your brand taken home from the event. If it's a

T-shirt proudly worn by an attendee who wants to show off his memento ("Hey, I was there. Don't you wish you were as lucky as me?"), you have a branding opportunity that can go on and on. I have always felt that the event tie-in is a much stronger incentive for someone to promote your brand on a shirt or product than just simply advertising your brand as a stand-alone, (unless it's cool enough to stand alone). But even the *cool enough* brands will sometimes clamor to get their products into the celebrity gift bags given away to participants at such high profile events as the Oscar and Grammy awards. The fees alone—not including the price of the posh gifts—can be substantial, and drive the value of these bags into the tens of thousands of dollars. Just recently, because the IRS has forced recipients to claim these gifts as income on their tax returns, many celebs have chosen to donate theirs to charity. Even so, all of this is worth it if just one celebrity is caught on camera displaying your logo.

A company with which my wife, Bettina, partners on promotional items recently developed a unique concept that we utilized for the 2008 Sundance Festival—logoed T-shirts shrink-wrapped to appear as though they were mini-guitars. What's more, the shirts could be packaged with download cards that send a customer to a web landing page to find more information on the brand's events, download free music, and how to register for a sweepstakes to win cool prizes (like autographed guitars, maybe?). The download cards could be fashioned in the shape of just about anything, including guitars, cars, or any other form relative to the brand's products. And for the green crowd, they can even be made recyclable by including seeds in the manufacturing process so the cards can be "planted" once they've served their purpose, Once a consumer is directed to the landing page, the registration works well for data capture and building consumer lists.

Speaking of green, Bettina also works with a company called Earth Friendly Apparel, which specializes in manufacturing 100 percent organic logoed clothing printed with nonpolluting soy-based ink. This comes in handy when you want to *truly* be green, since even though cotton is organic, most of the printing dyes are not. This is, quite clearly, an urgent concern for many companies and individuals. Earth-Friendly Apparel allows brands to garner support for themselves while showing that they are aware of environmental issues (and hopefully persuading their customers to be so also).

My first real experience in creating a major event was a long time coming. When I performed in bands, each gig was like a mini-event in itself because we had to create our own promotional materials and distribute them to reach out to our following and potential new followers—all to guarantee that we would draw enough paying customers that the venue would make money and therefore book us to come back. Our very survival depended on this; otherwise, we would have to go back to working our dreaded day jobs to support our music habit. There is nothing better than being able to support yourself doing what you want to do, but that is pretty rare in most careers especially in the entertainment business. Even though I was going to college on a music scholarship, and playing enough shows to (barely) support myself, my relatives used to tease me by saying, "Cut your hair and get a job." Just to prove them wrong, my band, Buster (which also included my brother, Bruce, on keyboards) and I would work harder and harder at promoting ourselves.

At that time, as we were endlessly promoting Buster, we began to notice another local band, from Rockford, Illinois, called Cheap Trick, that was starting to draw huge crowds and generate a ton of publicity. Even before we got a chance to see them when we opened a show for them, we knew these guys had taken street marketing to a new level. They were a great band; you knew upon seeing them perform in a club that they were destined for bigger and better things. If you drove any of the toll roads in Illinois and the neighboring states during that time, you couldn't miss their clever logo (a descending repeat of the *Cheap Trick* moniker appearing as if it were typed on a dysfunctional ancient typewriter) on stickers plastered on virtually every toll basket. I can only think of the millions of travelers who had that logo indelibly etched in their brains. Those tactics became legendary once the band hit it big with their "At Budokan" album.[5] I didn't realize it at the time, but this was the precursor to the viral street-marketing teams that record labels employ regularly today, using fans to promote their artist's concerts, appearances, and new records.

When I entered the guitar business with Dean Guitars in the 1980s, my promotional chops got even better when I had the chance to create special concert events during our big industry show, the National Association of Music Merchants (NAMM). Then, when I got to Washburn in 1990, I worked on creating even bigger NAMM concert events for thousands of attendees by presenting some of our biggest artists. I was even able to bring in co-sponsors to enhance the events, such as Budweiser, which provided enough brew to guarantee a full-blown party.

When I was hired by Fender in 1995 as artist relations director, I was responsible for maintaining our relationships with existing artists, and building new ones with up-and-coming artists. This was a slight comedown from my previous position in marketing, but I determined that it was well worth it to get in the door at the most prestigious brand in our industry. Dick Shelton—the head of marketing, who hired me and became my boss—wanted someone with my background because he felt that Fender needed some new ideas in promotions. It didn't take long for me to get my opportunity.

Fender's fiftieth anniversary was coming up in a few months, and NAMM was in January, so Dick decided that we would pull out all the stops with a major event to kick off the anniversary year.

He had already launched a program with Bonnie Raitt to sponsor music education for young girls through the Boys and Girls Clubs of America.[6] Bonnie agreed to perform a fund-raising benefit concert at NAMM, and it fell on my shoulders to coordinate it and to work with Bonnie to get other Fender artists to perform. I had the earlier-mentioned experience on these types of concerts, but I'd never worked on a fund-raiser and never with so much pressure—I needed to prove myself in my new job.

I reached out to such diverse artists as Richie Sambora from Bon Jovi (Richie is wonderful about donating his time; he has never turned me down for any type of large or small charity event), Marty Stuart, and Kim Wilson from the Fabulous Thunderbirds. I drew upon the relationship I had formed with actor Steven Seagal (by finding the best builders from our Custom Shop to build his dream guitars). As a Chicago boy myself, I was a big fan of the Chi-town-based movie that launched his career, *Above the Law*. Steven was riding high on the success of his most recent movie, *Under Siege II*, and he was all too happy to host the concert and even did a respectable job playing some mean blues guitar with Sambora.

I was working with the band the Ventures on their Signature models when Joey Carducci, the marketing manager for guitars, suggested that we have them open the show. If you grew up playing guitars in the 1960s like I did, you absolutely worshipped the Ventures since there was a pretty good chance that the first song you ever learned with your band was one of their big instrumental hits like "Diamond Head," "Hawaii Five-O," or their biggest hit of all, "Walk, Don't Run." I didn't want to put my boyhood idols in an uncomfortable situation because I wasn't sure how they would go over with all of the other contemporary stars, but their legendary drummer, Mel Taylor, assured me they would be fine.[7]

The show was sold out; our dealers and employees (no comps) each paid $100 per ticket. We were able to raise $160,000 before the first note was played. We also auctioned a nice array of top-end guitars autographed by such stars as Bob Dylan, the Rolling Stones, the Eagles, Eric Clapton, and, of course, Bonnie and the gang. Keep in mind that most NAMM events at the time were not intended to be fund-raisers—just industry parties. The evening couldn't have gone better and the Ventures blew the doors off. Bonnie and friends played their hearts out to show their gratitude for the many people who were willing to pay for what normally is a free NAMM event.

Following the success of the concert, John Wooler from Point Blank/Virgin Records approached us and asked us to create a fiftieth-anniversary CD compilation of Fender greats, led by Bonnie Raitt, with the proceeds—once again—going to the Boys and Girls Clubs. Thanks to Bonnie's and Fender's friends and associates, and John and his staff's diligent efforts, we were able to secure well-known tracks from artists who included Eric Clapton, Keith Richards, the Beach Boys, Vince Gill, and Bonnie herself. Coupled with the sales of the CD and the NAMM event, we were able to provide funding for instruments and instruction for more than 100 clubs around the country. I had finally gotten my education in organizing and promoting a successful large-scale event which, little did I know at the time, would be the precursor to bigger and better things.

It was just over a year later when the head of sales and marketing for the Wrigley family's large venues on Catalina Island, Bettina Hiniker, (if the uncommon first name sounds familiar—you're right, I ended up marrying her!) contacted me to inquire whether Fender was interested in lending our name to a new event they wanted to create. The event would be a blues festival, and the Wrigley family—who owned and developed much of the island—would put up money and supply the venue in order to bolster tourism and awareness for the island, which had drifted away from event marketing. Even though I had a lot of confidence in my abilities after the NAMM event, this was a totally new challenge and way out of Fender's comfort zone.

Our CEO, Bill Shultz, the person responsible for bringing Fender back from near bankruptcy under CBS in the 1980s, had never lent the company name to anything other than guitars. At the time, my office was next to Vice President John Page's in Fender's Custom Shop. John was immensely talented in marketing the Custom Shop he had co-founded with Bill's blessings. Bringing back Fender was not enough for Bill; he wanted to show the world that Fender could create a world-class custom instrument worthy of the top guitarists. John assembled the top builders he could find, many of whom had established themselves as custom builders to the stars, and who managed to bring these stars with them to Fender.

Not sure if I was taking too far of a leap, I asked John for his help, and with Fender president Kurt Hemrich's approval, John and I headed over to Catalina on an exploratory mission. Keep in mind that I had never been to Catalina (although I was intrigued when Bettina lured me by informing me that my beloved Chicago Cubs used to have their spring training camp there); most of what I knew about the island was gleaned from the song "26 Miles" by the Four Preps. Sitting in the historic Casino Ballroom, built in 1929, with its lovely Art Deco furnishings, we knew we had something worthy of the Fender name for our first non-industry event. Because the island has such a rich history of entertainment, from the big bands like Glenn Miller and Woody Herman, who used to broadcast radio concerts from there, to the movie stars like John Wayne and Humphrey Bogart, who made it their playground (Ronald Reagan was discovered on the island while announcing Cubs games), to the many film premieres that were held there, we knew we would have to make it a celebrity event as well.

One more facet was added to all of this: a charitable cause. Packy Offield—who was a member of the Wrigley family and also owned Packy Offield Enterprises (P.O.E.), the company that administered the casino and other venues we would use—was planning to finance the festival, and was also on the board of the island's conservancy. John Page therefore determined that we would create a one-of-a-kind commemorative guitar that would be auctioned to benefit the conservancy. Bettina had sent us a rendition for the poster featuring the stunning mermaid from the artwork on the front of the casino building playing a Fender Stratocaster guitar—the perfect icon for the festival. John commissioned our longtime artist for the Custom Shop, Pamelina H, to officially design the poster and the guitar, which was to be hand carved by George Amicay, one of John's in-house artists. John officially christened it the "Regina de Mare"—"Queen of the Sea."

For the artists, we booked Jimmy Vaughan, who had just released his own signature model Stratocaster guitar with us, and, representing the Hollywood celebrity connection, we had Jim Belushi and his Sacred Heart Band, which was made up of top blues musicians.

I remember being at the back of the line with our volunteers from the Custom Shop on the day of the festival. I was waiting to board the ferry, enjoying the lovely day and a few brews, when I was summoned to the front of the line by Bill Shultz. He was first in line with an entourage of Fender vice presidents for support and he was visibly uncomfortable standing in the hot sun (I later found out that he thought the boarding process for the ferry was like boarding a plane, and had arrived an hour early). It didn't help that he was probably second-guessing his decision to allow us to brand an unproven event—on an island, no less! In spite of the event not yet being sold out, I assured him that everything would be fine, although down deep I was thinking my resume wouldn't look too good surviving less than two years at Fender.

Thankfully, just before the doors opened, Bettina was able to place a sign on the box office window that proclaimed: "This event is SOLD OUT"—no small accomplishment when you consider that attendees had to take a boat to get there, and book hotel rooms to stay in after the concert. Jim Belushi was thoroughly entertaining and Jimmie Vaughan brought the crowd to its feet with several encores. In the dressing room after the show, Bill Shultz and Jim Belushi donned Blues Brothers' glasses and black fedoras for publicity photos. The next morning, Bill called a meeting to express his excitement for the event, stating that in his opinion, "This could be one of the premier blues festivals in the country." If that wasn't enough, the Conservancy guitar was auctioned for $70,000—to Packy Offield of the Wrigleys!

We had committed to the festival for five years[8] and each one got bigger and better, attracting nationwide attention and virtually selling out every venue we used on the island, from picturesque Descanso Beach, to the historic movie theater and ballroom in the casino, to the country club building, the converted Cubs' locker room. We created a template for the modern blues festival by combining legendary artists like Buddy Guy, Taj Mahal, Honeyboy Edwards, and Robert Jr. Lockwood, and top young artists like Kenny Wayne Shepherd, Jonny Lang, and Susan Tedeschi, with rock artists who were heavily influenced by the blues such as Edgar Winter, Paul Rodgers, and Savoy Brown. When one festival would end, fans would book their hotel rooms for the next year. Tickets would be purchased as soon as they went on sale—even without a firm lineup of artists—because we had created a sense of trust in our fans by supporting and bringing together so many wonderful acts. The island embraced the festival, as local merchants gave their encouragement, and major brands like JVC took note and joined in with sponsors' booths. The last year we presented the concert, we unfortunately had to turn away hundreds of distraught fans for the final event on Descanso Beach, featuring Double Trouble and friends, even though we had increased the capacity by 30 percent over the previous year.

In keeping with the charitable element, each year a new version of the Regina de Mare was auctioned. The second year, it was for the Kids Rock Free music education program at the newly founded Fender Museum, just down the street from the Fender manufacturing plant in Corona, California. The guitar brought in between $27,000 and $50,000 for the program in each of its five years. The Four Preps lyrics, "The Island of Romance" turned out to be prophetic for me, as Bettina and I were married in 2003.[9]

The Catalina festival was a pivotal event in my career at Fender. Bob Heinrich—our chief operating officer at the time, and who negotiated the agreement with the island—saw it as a great opportunity for branding the Fender name beyond guitars. With his support, I was able to create a new department under him, Market Development, which moved me away from the Artist Relations department and into my present position in entertainment marketing (as detailed in Chapter 3). John Page eventually left Fender to donate his full time to the Fender Museum and its education program. After Bettina and I were married, she founded Plan B Events, a company that specializes in creating concert events for local and regional charities.

Wanting firsthand experience on how sponsorship packages worked for live events, I had to look no further than my lovely wife, Bettina. I began by asking what's the difference between a presenting sponsor and a title sponsor.

"Every event that I've had a part in creating, marketing, or promoting has been different in so many ways. Even before attempting to put a value on sponsorships for an event, there has to be a vision of the event in its entirety—the big picture. By this I mean every event has a certain feel to it, which then needs to be packaged for sponsorship opportunities. I've always looked to the presenting sponsor as a cash sponsor—the one that means the event is funded, whereas the title sponsors might have the value in their name being associated in the title of the event. For example, the 'Fender Catalina Island Blues Festival' . . . it's still music to my ears!

"When we created the template to continue the blues festival, this is how we laid out the overall sponsor's benefits:

- Alliance with an established brand name festival with a five-year proven track record
- Co-branding with the musical industry's top manufacturer and the most recognizable and respected name in guitars, amplifiers, and related products
- Media attention on both a national and local level through advertising, sweepstakes, promotions, and general coverage
- Goodwill through a festival that has previously generated almost a quarter of a million dollars to benefit music education and other nonprofit organizations
- Based on the wide range of talent in a musical genre that is not limited by narrow demographics, direct access to a key target market of affluent buyers and their families

"To illustrate how a typical event breaks down into real dollars, I'd like to use another event I created on Catalina Island. This was a one-day event that was put together as a concert for 'Friends of Avalon Bay' (FAB), to benefit the City of Avalon, a nonprofit, for research on the purity of the water, and to take steps in educating and preventing pollution into the bay by manmade causes. We were fortunate to have Donovan Frankenrieter, a world-class surfer and recording artist, donate his performance for the concert. We also had a beautiful concert poster designed and donated by John Van Hammersveld, a legendary artist who created the famous poster for the seminal surf film *Endless Summer*, which set the tone for countless surf posters and albums covers that followed. To follow is the breakdown we presented to potential sponsors:"

SPONSORSHIP CATEGORIES AVAILABLE*

Presenting Sponsor (exclusive): Five thousand dollars
• ID primary placement on event poster (five hundred)
• ID primary placement on event postcard (five thousand)
• ID on Catalina chamber web site within event listing
• ID on event banner on Front Street (up for one week)
• ID on main stage event banner
• ID on PA announcement from main stage during concert
• ID on Catalina Island cable TV (available in all island hotel rooms)
• Ticket package (twenty-five general admission)

*Corporate hospitality packages are available that could include transportation, lodging, and other activities while on Catalina Island (additional cost based on requirements)

Associate Sponsor (two available): Two thousand, five hundred dollars
• ID secondary placement on event poster (five hundred)
• ID secondary placement on event postcard (five thousand)
• ID on event banner on Front Street (up for one week)
• ID on banner placed at event site (sponsor provided)
• ID on PA announcement from main stage during concert
• Ticket package (fifteen general admission)

*Corporate hospitality packages are available that could include transportation, lodging, and other activities while on Catalina Island (additional cost based on requirements).

"Friends of Avalon Bay"—PLATINUM LEVEL: One thousand dollars
• ID or individual name on event poster (five hundred)
• Ticket package (six general admission)

"Friends of Avalon Bay"—GOLD LEVEL: Five hundred dollars
• ID or individual name on event poster
• Ticket package (two general admission)

"The event occurred on August twenty-seventh, two thousand six, at the Descanso Beach Club on Catalina Island, and netted FAB over ten thousand dollars after all expenses were covered, which is pretty good for a first-time event of this size. We brought on AbTech Pacific, a company that manufactures filters and catch basins for storm drains, as our presenting sponsor. To follow is our post-concert review we supplied to them."

Review of Sponsorship Benefits Provided to Sponsor:

- ID primary placement on event poster (Five hundred)
  - Printed quantity was actually one thousand—posters were distributed throughout Southern California coastal communities and sold at the event as part of the event merchandise.
- ID primary placement on event postcard (Five thousand)
  - Printed quantity was actually fifteen thousand—posters were distributed throughout Southern California communities and used in a variety of promotions to help with event awareness.
- *ID on Catalina Chamber web site within event listing*
  - Logo added August eighth to Chamber web site
- ID on event banner on Front Street (up for one week)
  - Main banner was actually up for two weeks. In addition, banners were also printed and displayed in Catalina Express boat terminals for the week prior to the event and on [a] display table near the Wrigley Stage on Front Street, which was staffed by volunteers selling tickets and providing event information.
- ID on banner placed at event site (sponsor provided)
  - No banners provided, however, sponsor logo [was] included on both sides of main stage banners printed by event

---

(*Continued*)

- ID on PA announcement from main stage during concert
  - Sponsor mentioned prior to opening act, intermission, before [the] headline act, and after the show prior to final event raffle announcements.
- ID on Catalina Island cable TV (available in all island hotel rooms)
  - Logo added August tenth, ran continuously through event
- ADDED—ID on paid advertisement in local Catalina Island newspaper
  - Weekly ads placed for month prior to event
- Ticket package (Twenty-five general admission)
  - Tickets were mailed to sponsor prior to event to be used and distributed at its discretion
- On-site space for sampling at the event
  - Space was available, however, [the] sponsor determined prior to event that on-site sampling and promotion was not feasible for this year
- Use of festival name for cross-promotions
- First right of refusal for next year's sponsorship at associate level
- No conflicting sponsor (only one presenting sponsor available)

"The money spent by [the] presenting sponsor AbTech Pacific (now Hydrophix) fits well inside the guidelines (where applicable) as set forth by the company IEG, Inc., who has created a methodology for valuing tangible benefits."

Sponsor ID in nonmeasured media
- Signage
- Public address announcements
- Collateral materials

Value range equals two and a half cents to five cents per impression

Sponsor ID in nonmeasured media
• Web site

Value range equals two and a half cents to ten cents per unique visitor

Sponsor ID in measured media
• Media Buy
• Broadcast exposure

Value range equals five percent to ten percent rate card value

Sampling and Display
Value range equals four cents to fifteen cents per person sampled

Database Access
Value range equals seven and a half cents to fifteen cents per name

Tickets and Hospitality
Value equals face value

"Keep in mind that merchandising rights for co-branded apparel and items are a separate fee, and fees will vary if it's a charity event, and it also depends on who is making the charitable donation. For the concerts we promoted for Crossroads Christian Church, it was the church that was making donations to local charities but the artists were still getting their fees. Some artists donate their performance but the band, travel, accommodations, production, and per diems need to be paid. So fees do vary for a charity but someone is picking up the ticket along the way. For example, Plan B Events donated services for the FAB concert but covered some basic expenses. We don't always donate services for charitable causes—we'd be out of business—so we find creative ways to raise funds for the charities."

Established festivals that have become entertainment events for company sponsorships include the Sundance International Film Festival, and its looser, yet much larger, counterpart in regard to movies and artist showcases, South by Southwest in Austin, Texas. I give more details on Fender's involvement in Sundance in Chapter 12; here, I focus on SXSW.

The festival started over 20 years ago as a music conference and showcase for unknown and unsigned bands. When I used to attend in the late 1990s, major label bands started showcasing their new music to gain street-level credibility and sometimes even revive their careers. Today, SXSW presents 1,500 bands (500 of which are international) and has attached a very respected film festival for independents the week leading into the music showcases. For the most recent SXSW festival, Fender partnered with Red Gorilla Musicfest, one of the other free music festivals that is held at the same time to take advantage of the crowds at SXSW. Fender supplied full back-line (amps and bass amps) for the more than 600 bands Red Gorilla presented during their series; none of the bands were charged an entry fee to perform. With the number of bands performing, plus the number of attendees, SXSW offers a multitude of different image-enhancing sponsorship opportunities that can be tailored to any budget.

As detailed in this chapter, successful event marketing can cost millions of dollars. However, with a little creative thinking, a company without that level of resources can attain similar favorable publicity for a fraction of the cost by showcasing its brand as an active participant in front of legions of excited attendees whose passion brought them there, and, with a little more positive energy, have that passion transferred to the company's products.

CHAPTER 8

Charitable Causes—Doing Good Things for the Right Reasons

It has been said that the definition of philanthropy is "doing good by doing well." I have worked on Fender's behalf over the years supporting such causes as Nordoff-Robbins for autistic children; St. Jude's Hospital for Children (a favorite of country artists); the Susan G. Komen Foundation for Breast Cancer Research; the MusicCares Foundation, which provides assistance to musicians, including those who suffer from addiction; Amnesty International, whose fund-raising programs are supported by some of the biggest names in music; the Surfrider Foundation and Heal the Bay, which both deal with keeping beaches and ocean waters clean; and Borders for Breast Cancer, a surfer-driven charity.

In 1999, I was asked by Fender to be the corporate recruitment chairman for the Riverside chapter of the Juvenile Diabetes Foundation. Even though I was like the proverbial fish out of water speaking in front of many of the business community leaders in my area, I've learned how dedicated many of these leaders are, and how much they want to give something back to the community that was responsible for their livelihoods. We were able to raise $220,000 with our walkathon for the foundation, an amount that was enhanced by some of the artists we called, who gladly donated their talents to entertain the walkers.

I think one of the reasons that I have become such a staunch believer in the importance of philanthropy is because of my wife's company, Plan B Events. Plan B has put together many celebrity-driven fund-raising events so I have witnessed firsthand how getting behind the right causes can galvanize an audience to often bring a good concert experience soaring to new heights. As a member of the entertainment industry, I am aware that there is no shortage of celebrities who have their own causes—or who are willing to donate their time, energy, and name to guarantee the success of a fund-raiser.

Roree Krevolin, a good friend of mine who formerly ran Amnesty International's Music for Human Rights program, a nonprofit that I have supported through Fender, told me of a wonderful conversation that took place between Bob Geldof, the founder of Live Aid (a single, internationally broadcasted concert whose purpose was to help relieve a famine in Ethiopia), and Sting. Bob was running short on finances, so he asked Sting to donate funds to keep it going. Sting replied, "You can never send enough money. You have to give of yourself." That conversation was taken directly from Bob Geldof's book, *Is That It?*[1]

While we're on the subject of artists and causes, I also recommend the powerful *Stand and Be Counted: Making Music, Making History* by legendary artist David Crosby and author David Bender.[2] The book chronicles artist-driven fund-raising events like Live Aid and what David considers to be the foundation of them all—George Harrison's Concert for Bangladesh. But regardless of whether it's a mega-event like Live Aid, or simply a local charity, star power greatly increases the chances of a successful fund-raiser.

Through all of the charitable causes in which I have been involved, I always felt that I could approach artists with whom I had a relationship. I worked directly with such notables as Steve Miller and Joe Walsh, who graciously donated their time in concerts for music education, and greats like Bruce Springsteen, the Rolling Stones, and Eric Clapton, who signed instruments for nonprofits. The Rolling Stones autographed a custom-made Stratocaster that brought in $100,000 for the nonprofit Fender Center for the Performing Arts, which offers free and low-cost music education to children in Southern California. Other fund-raisers included the sale of large, 10-foot, hand-painted Stratocasters throughout Cleveland in conjunction with the Rock 'n' Roll Hall of Fame in 2002, which benefited the United Way. We donated auction guitars for a concert in Portland for refugees in Darfur, put on by Amnesty International that was spearheaded by Rage Against The Machine's guitarist Tom Morello and Oscar and Emmy award–winning actress Mira Sorvino. We donated several Fender guitars for a concert recognized by Don Felder that raised $150,000 for Katrina Victims. We helped St. Jude's Hospital with a banjo signed by the Oak Ridge Boys, along with tickets to their concert; and the five years of the Fender Catalina Island Blues Festival has benefited music education and the nature conservancy on Catalina Island.

Throughout all of this, Fender's late chairman of the board, Bill Shultz, the man responsible for bringing Fender back to prominence over the last few decades, always instilled in us that Fender was to take a back seat to the cause and never try to place our brand above the charity. In fact, he wanted our involvement to be downplayed as much as possible to ensure that we were "doing it for the right reasons." Words to live by, because you don't have to be famous, or in the music industry, for that matter, to follow that interpretation. I recently heard of a billionaire philanthropist named Chuck Feeney, who declined to even name his foundation, Atlantic Philanthropies, after himself, and has anonymously given over $4 billion to charity. He laid the road map followed by Bill Gates and Warren Buffet in what he refers to as "giving while living."[3]

It's funny to me that when I told my family about putting my efforts into this book, my fourteen-year-old stepson Kjell told me to make sure I included a few paragraphs on *karma*. I guess he heard that old karma lecture enough times from his "old hippie" step-dad, so here it goes. No matter how much of my own time I have to devote, I have always enjoyed working on charitable causes because it really is the gauge of the passion of the human spirit. There is something uplifting for the soul in seeing people come together to do something for the common good—once again for the right reasons, which is the definition of selflessness. It seems that whatever my wife and I have given, it always comes back magnified—not immediately, or even directly, but always in some form or another. I know that the good that you (and your company) can put into the world always has a powerfully positive effect.

The Fender Center in Corona was started by John Page, vice president of Fender's Custom Shop, as a museum (which I mentioned in Chapter 7 in the section about the Catalina Island Blues Festival). John had the idea when he was still at Fender to have a nonprofit facility that used the Fender name to promote music education through a curriculum that he developed called *Kids Rock Free*. He felt it would be a great asset to Fender's manufacturing home in the Inland Empire to have thousands of children taking advantage of the program. Once John established a facility for the program in Corona, he ended up leaving Fender to devote himself full-time into administrating and directing the Fender Center. He did so with Fender's blessing, since Bill Schultz firmly believed in music education and was willing to give both financial support and the support of Fender employees as volunteers.

I personally volunteered for several events there because I felt the music education program was absolutely fantastic. When I was growing up, I was fortunate enough to have parents who gave me the opportunity to take music lessons—and it clearly made a *big* difference in my life. In addition to laying out the path that my career would eventually take, it paid for my college education when I received a scholarship for music. So many schools today—in Southern California and across the country—however, have suffered budget cuts. Unless the school is privately financed, most of them all too often are forced to make music and the arts the first things to go.

In 2006, Fender's sixtieth anniversary, the company decided that it wanted to do a major fund-raiser for the Fender Center, using our artists and our abilities to make promotional instruments—high quality, limited edition Custom Shop instruments upon which people could bid. The idea was that if we could get to ask the biggest-name artists to autograph them—and possibly one of them to come perform, perhaps we would be able to raise some pretty significant funds. My boss, Ritchie Fliegler, and our Head of Marketing Services, Paul Jernigan, brought me into the program. We then enlisted our County Supervisor, John Tavaglione, who was based in Riverside, California, and was a very supportive Fender Center board member. We felt that he could get the right constituents there to participate in the auction. Working with Debbie Shuck, the director of operations at the Fender Center, we put the plan into motion. Since all of this took place in October and the event was in January, I didn't have much time to find an artist to perform and some big names to autograph the guitars.

Ritchie decided to make the fundraiser a commemorative event—a celebration of the fact that Fender was 60 years old. This would be reflected in the instruments that we were creating—ten pearl white Stratocaster guitars displaying a little diamond in the inlay, with the characteristic Custom Shop *V* at the headstock.

The first signing opportunity came with a publishing company in New York called Music Sales, with which I had worked on a book project when I was with Washburn Guitars. Since I had negotiated this history of Washburn coffee table book with them, I had remained friends with the people there, including the Vice President of Marketing, Steve Wilson. Steve called to tell me they had recently signed Tom Petty to distribute his book, *Conversations with Tom Petty.* Fender didn't have a formal relationship with Petty, but we knew he sometimes played a Custom Shop Fender Telecaster onstage, so Music Sales decided they wanted him to sign 12 Fenders for promotions with book stores.

Autographing the pickguards is acceptable, but we knew from experience that signing the bodies makes the guitars even more collectible. Sending Tom the 12 guitars would have been difficult for him—having to open the boxes, take the guitars out, sign them and rewrap them and send them back again. So I volunteered to personally deliver them to Tom's house and take care of the unpacking and repacking. This arrangement had worked well in a similar situation involving Joe Walsh and a promotion with Miller Beer that required 20 signed guitars.

Petty's management representative told me, "Come at three P.M., not one minute early and not one minute late." So I drove out to his home in Malibu, and sat right out in front of the gates, and precisely at three o'clock, the gates magically opened. His manager greeted me and I took the guitars through a beautiful, long hallway lined with Buddha statues (which I was pretty sure was influenced by his close friend and Wilbury brother, George Harrison, which was confirmed at the end of the hallway by a Traveling Wilburys poster). Just when I got all the guitars laid out on the dining room table, I see Tom pass through the kitchen with a cup of coffee or tea. His manager says, "Oh, there he is. Go talk to Tom." So here am I, a stranger walking unannounced into Tom Petty's kitchen and suddenly he turns around and just about pulls a "Danny Thomas" on me (spitting the coffee out). I said, "Tom, it's okay, it's okay. . . . I'm Del—I'm with Fender."

Relieved that I wasn't a stalker, Tom signed the instruments as I told him about the charity that we were doing for music education. Upon hearing about our fund-raising efforts, he was more than happy to autograph the guitars and some books as well. Once I had Tom's signature, it seemed that all the others fell into place. His was the one that really started the program.

In the weeks to follow, more of the folks with whom I had been in touch came through—Tom Hanks, and then Eric Clapton (who we know doesn't normally sign guitars because it competes with his Crossroads Centre fund-raising guitars) ended up signing one. Bruce Springsteen signed, Sheryl Crow signed—and we're getting close to all 10 being finished.

What happened next is a very interesting story. Billy Gibbons of ZZ Top had just had a book come out on his hot rod cars and guitars. So when I saw Billy at his signing event at the Petersen Automotive Museum, I asked him if he would autograph one of the 10 guitars and maybe come out to the Fender Center, not to perform, but for a book signing. His publisher agreed to supply books that Billy said he would sign and 50 percent of the money raised would go to the event that evening. So I had one celebrity. The second celebrity I reached out to was Joe Walsh, whom I also asked about performing with the kids' band. Since he was getting ready to tour with the Eagles, he agreed to get the whole band to sign a guitar. Unfortunately, because of the holidays, I lost touch with him and did not have a firm commitment on the performance part. It just so happened that around this same time, Billy Gibbons had gotten married and was in Las Vegas for his honeymoon. As luck would have it, he ran into Joe. "Hey, you're doing that thing at the Fender Center; that's pretty cool." And, Joe, caught somewhat off guard replies, "Yeah, I'm gonna do it." Celebrity number two locked!

Now the only problem was we were down to the last week— and I still didn't have the final guitar signed, which was MIA with the Rolling Stones.

I had gone to the Rolling Stones concert months before, when they were performing at nearby Anaheim Stadium, to get the guitar signed. There were 80,000 people expected at the concert, so I went to the sound check and spoke to Pierre de Beauport, who was Keith Richards's guitar tech, who agreed to let me leave the guitar with him to have it signed at sound check. The full band never appeared together at the sound check, and although I did get to see a phenomenal show, it was the last time I saw the guitar that night because it ended up getting packed up with the rest of their gear for the road.

Fast forward to the Friday before our event. I called one of the guitar techs, JD, with whom I used to work when he was at Fender, and asked, "Whatever happened to that guitar?" He said, "It's still with us on the bus, but they haven't signed it yet. By the way, when's the event?" and I said, "Oh, it's like, next week."

So, the next time the whole band would be together would be for a date in Boston, which was also the last date before our event. We couldn't have cut it much closer, but thankfully, a few days later I showed up at work in the morning and up against my door was this box with the guitar, signed by Mick, Keith, Charlie, Ronnie, and Daryl, just lying there. Also included in the box was the set list from that night showing what songs they played with a hand-printed list from JD of the names of who signed the guitar on the back. It just blew me away that I was able to get the Stones' autographs, and of course, the last and one of the most important guitars I needed for the event.

The night before the event, Joe's Walsh road manager, Smokey, called to tell me that Joe was a little nervous because he wasn't sure the kids could nail his songs, particularly "Rocky Mountain Way," because it has some tough parts, even for pro players. I told him that I had just watched them rehearse it, that the kids are amazing, and that Joe's gonna love it because it's going to sound just like the record. I wasn't hyping him because they really sounded that good. When I arrived at the Fender Center for the event the next day, I found out that Joe had spent the whole afternoon rehearsing with the kids. When I went in to the stage area, I saw the signature "talk box" that he uses on "Rocky Mountain Way." Right then I knew that the kids had proven themselves to Joe.

The event sold so many tickets that it had to be moved to an outside tent because in winter, nights can be quite chilly in Southern California. The auction couldn't have gone any better, as the Rolling Stones guitar brought in an unbelievable $100,000 by itself. When we auctioned the Eagles guitar, Joe Walsh ran up on stage with me to help the auctioneer. I began by telling the stories about how these instruments got signed, and Joe said, "Hey, the Stones got a hundred grand, so we have to get the same." So, thanks to Joe's prodding, we actually got that much for the Eagles' signed guitar as well. But the best moment by far was when the Kids Rock Free band played with Joe. The looks on the kids' faces and the reaction from the crowd—along with Joe's acknowledgment of how great they played, said it all. I remember thinking that it was just one of the best nights of my life, and certainly a high point for any kind of fund-raising that I had ever been involved with.

The following week, my wife and I were on a much-needed vacation in Hawaii when my boss called to tell me that the event raised over $450,000. This was really spectacular to hear, because with any kind of fund-raising, you can work so hard just to raise ten or twenty thousand dollars on a local event. That much money in a small community like Corona was practically unheard of and it was an amazing accomplishment for us.

Following the success of the fund-raiser with Joe Walsh and the sixtieth anniversary, Debbie, John, and myself partnered again on a concert event for the center. This one would also have a fund-raising element through the sales of the tickets and this time, just one guitar auction—which we would do with the legendary Steve Miller.

Steve Miller had donated the proceeds from two previous performance events at the Fender Center, but one of the persons responsible for securing these events had left, causing us to lose touch with Steve. And even though Steve was a Fender guy all his life, we never really had a formal relationship with him. But as good karma would have it, I had helped the Thornton School of Music at the University of Southern California with one of their groups, the Los Angeles Guitar Quartet, a great jazz band that was going to tour Japan. Their songwriting instructor, Chris Sampson, called me and asked if we could assist with Fender Twins amps once they arrived there. It was no problem to set them up with Fender promotions in Japan, and they did a stellar job.

Chris called me when they got back to tell me that they couldn't have pulled it off without Fender's help and wanted to return the favor. "Steve Miller is coming to our department to do a clinic on songwriting and I'd like to invite you." Wow—what an opportunity! I asked if I could bring Deb and John along and told Chris that we were going to talk to Steve about doing another fund-raiser. Steve gave a wonderful presentation and we went up to him afterward and introduced ourselves. Steve then told the music department that "the Fender Center has the best music education program for kids in the country." Debbie then asked him about coming back to do another event, to which he responded, "Absolutely. Not only will I do the event, but I'll give you a date." Scott Boorey, Steve's manager, whom I found out I knew from previous years (he'd worked with Journey and a group called the Storm when I was at Washburn) gave us the date of August 6. We left feeling empowered with our ability to make it a great event.

Having a set date for the event along with Steve's commitment allowed John to go out of his way—yet again—to get the right people to attend. Debbie put together a fantastic presentation and even got artwork for a guitar donated by a gifted local artist, Carson Grier. But the beauty of the guitar was its face, which was designed as a replica of the album cover from "Book of Dreams." It featured a winged horse that had been reproduced brilliantly—except that when you looked closely, each one of the lines was drawn with song lyrics from a selection of Steve's songs. This truly made it a one-of-a-kind stunning piece.

At the sound check before the show, we showed Steve the guitar—and he was just floored. He said that he had some wealthy friends who were going to come and bid on it, to which my wife responded, "Well, they would like to have the guitar bring in about a hundred thousand dollars, as we need three hundred and fifty thousand dollars to pay off the loan on the Center. One more thing—we'd like the guitar donated back to the Fender Center so that it can be displayed, because it's such a rare and beautiful piece." Even though Steve said he understood, Bettina was pretty relentless—so he finally laughed and told her, "We heard you about the tenth time. We're gonna work on it."

John Tavaglione and I hosted the auction, and when it stalled out at $25,000, my wife came out of the crowd and bid $30,000. I said, "No, no, that's my wife. We can't take that bid!" John disagreed and said yes, it was a good bid. Later on, I asked my wife, "Why did you do that?" She said, "You were doing such a miserable job up there that I thought I would inspire you." And she did—because soon after her appearance, we got the bidding up to about $85,000. Just as we were about to say, "Going once, going twice . . . " a voice from behind me rang out, "NINETY-FIVE THOUSAND DOLLARS." I turned around and Steve's manager, Scott, was standing next to a gentleman giving me a thumbs-up sign. Scott said, "It's a good bid—take it." So I turned back around and told the crowd that we just did $95,000. When I went back to shake the guy's hand, he passed me his cell phone— and none other than Steve Miller is on the other end, calling from the loft above. He was in the Green Room, saying that he bought the guitar and he was donating it back. He knew all along he was going to buy it and give it back to the Fender Center, but he wanted me to go back and get the last bid of $85,000!

So I went back to the microphone and said, "Stop the presses." . . . and filled the audience in on the story. The crowd's cheering, and the gentleman who had the last bid stands up and says, "Del, I'm going to give you eighty-five thousand dollars for the guitar and I'm going to donate it back to the Fender Center as well." If that wasn't enough—there was one extra Fender guitar that we had there. Another person stood up and said, "I don't have a hundred thousand dollars to bid on a guitar, but I did bring twenty-five grand to spend. Can I get something for that?" So Steve was kind enough to sign a Fender Stratocaster guitar, and added some of his own personal artwork, for which the second gentleman paid his $25,000.

Steve followed the auction with a tremendous performance for the SRO crowd. In the middle of the concert, he said that he understood that we had raised the complete $350,000 during the evening (the auction and the performance). He gave a marvelous presentation, and invited a couple of the Kids Rock Free band members who opened the show to be up on stage with him. It was just another very special night, and as Sting had said, Steve Miller not only gave money that evening—he truly gave of himself.[4]

For another point of view on this program, I asked Tony Frankin, who was so eloquent with his comments on the spiritualism of music in Chapter 2, to present his firsthand experiences in fund-raising at the Fender Center. The event he hosted was a much more intimate gathering than the major outdoor events I have described, but relatively speaking, just as successful, as you will learn.

"I was recently conducting an auction at the Fender Center for the Performing Arts in Corona, California. We were auctioning a medium-priced instrument that was signed by Paul Rodgers of the band Bad Company, who also attended the auction. (I was in a band called The Firm with Paul Rodgers and Jimmy Page for a couple of years, back in the Eighties). The money raised from the auction would benefit the Kids Rock Free program at the Fender Center—a year-round program that provides low cost and free music lessons to students aged seven to seventeen in Riverside County. The waiting list for free lessons is a year, and the students simply love the classes.

"Now, Corona is not like being in L.A., so our expectations for the auction were not super high. The bidding started at two thousand dollars and we were hoping to achieve somewhere in the region of ten thousand dollars. I knew that I had to appeal to the bidders on a deeper, more personal level. If they felt they were bidding on *just* a guitar, we wouldn't get very far. I wanted them to realize that the money raised would be contributing directly to the quality of these young student's lives, giving them a lasting gift of music, creativity and a connection with other aspiring musicians. The instrument would simply be a symbol of that gift.

"I conveyed some of my thoughts about the spiritual power of music. It is one thing to be touched by listening to good music, but to be part of the process of *creating* the music that touches and inspires others, takes it to a whole new level.

"And it doesn't mean that we have to have hit songs being played on the radio, or be performing on the big stages; we can touch and move people by performing for our friends, or at a wedding, a graduation, or a hospital, or a retirement home. I see playing music for others as an incredible privilege, a rare blessing. I've heard it said that music is one of the highest callings, and I really believe that this is the case.

"For myself, and musicians like Paul Rodgers, Jimmy Page, and others, *playing gigs* was our musical education. This was where we learned to master our instruments, how to put on a great show, how to communicate with fellow musicians, how to write songs. It was often a harsh learning environment, but we learned! And we forged a bond and cultivated a deep respect for each other that never goes away. Even if you have disagreements musically or personally, the connection and camaraderie between you is undeniable. I see that connection between the students on the Kids Rock Free program, even from a very young age, and it warms my heart.

"There are not so many gigs for the upcoming musicians to play these days, and this is where the Kids Rock Free program fills a void, teaching the students those invaluable 'gig' skills, led by some of the finest and most passionate music teachers around. World-class musicians like Paul Rodgers, Brian May of Queen, Steve Miller, and numerous others, have selflessly given their time to the program."

"There are numerous statistics available on the Internet about music education. (Do a search for 'the benefits of music education'—the pages go on and on . . .). Here's an impressive statistic: Schools that have music programs have significantly higher graduation rates—ninety point two percent opposed to seventy-two point nine percent. And the higher the quality of the music program, the higher the graduation rate! Kids Rock Free is one of the highest quality music programs available, certainly in this region.

"And so these people were not bidding on *just* a guitar, albeit a very nice guitar signed by a rock and roll superstar. The money would be directly enriching the musical education, the quality of life, and the future of these children and students. And it wouldn't stop there, because the music that the students created would go on to enrich and touch the lives of all who heard it. It is a gift that just keeps on giving!

"The bidding started at two thousand dollars, and was quickly moving up. When we reached nine thousand, Paul Rodgers's wife, Cynthia, added a little 'incentive' by contributing a beautiful silver necklace that Paul had been wearing. The necklace was hung over the neck of the guitar and the bids edged up to eleven thousand dollars. At this point, there was a phone call from an anonymous bidder, who said he would contribute twelve thousand dollars, but only if someone else matched the bid, and agreed to let the guitar stay in the Fender Center as an exhibit. A deal was struck, and the instrument sold for twenty-four thousand dollars! I'd never said, 'Going once, going twice, sold' before. It felt good right at that moment."

The moral of this chapter is that whether it's your company, or just you by yourself—get involved for the right reasons and you will make a difference.

CHAPTER 9

The Celebrity Quotient—How to Wrangle It, and How to Deal With It When You Do

What exactly is it that attracts us to celebrity? In *This is Your Brain on Music*, Daniel J. Levitin compares the flamboyance of a male rock star performer to a peacock spreading its golden tail to show off to attract the opposite sex. Whatever the explanation, we know celebrities are different from the rest of us, and the adulation that their fans give them shows that we aspire to be like them—or at least get some of that adulation. One could write a series of books that could fill a complete department at a major bookstore analyzing why someone would want to be a celebrity; (and many people have already done this), but the old cliché works the best—whether it be through politics, money, sports, or entertainment, power is the ultimate aphrodisiac.

When I was writing the music column for my school news-paper, Ron Oberman,[1] who was a public relations executive at Mercury Records, which had offices in Chicago at that time, had taken a liking to me. Maybe it was out of pity, or that he was formerly a pop writer for the *Washington Star*, but nonetheless, he wanted to help me as the fledgling reporter I was at the time. He was excited because one of his fastest-rising stars, Rod Stewart, would be performing with his band, the Faces, in nearby Milwaukee. Both solo Rod and the Faces Rod were breaking on the charts, and the solo version had released what would prove to be the singer's breakthrough hit, "Maggie May."

My girlfriend at the time and I drove 90 miles north to meet with Ron, not knowing he had set up a private dinner with Rod. Even though Rod was not extremely outgoing in person (which is a complete 180-degree difference from his stage persona), I couldn't help but look at him as if he was so far above my station in life. After that dinner, I was hanging with Rod's guitarist—and future Rolling Stone, Ronnie Wood—and then I got to witness one of the loosest, yet most dynamic rock concerts I have ever been to. I had been a fan of Rod's vocalizing as part of the Jeff Beck Group (which my band modeled itself after) through their album "Truth," but now I wanted to dress like him, and of course, create the "rooster" look of his wild hair. My grade school graduation pictures attest that I was born with hair that can't be tamed, so Rod's look worked perfectly (as I have said "Thank God for Rod"), and it still kind of works for both of us today.

You might think that after all the years of meeting famous artists during my music career that the luster would have worn off. Even my wife thinks I should be over it. (She has never been into celebrity worship. Although I do remember her going on and on about talking with Brad Pitt at a movie premiere we attended. Or meeting Peter Frampton with me. Well, I totally understand that one because her first concert experience, at age 14, was to see Frampton.) But nothing could have prepared me for the day in 1997 that I was contacted to pick up some guitars upon which the Rolling Stones wanted some work done in our Custom Shop.

I had been at Fender only a few years and the only contact I'd had with the band was through Keith Richards's guitar tech and confidant, Pierre du Beauport. When I arrived at the studio in Los Angeles, the security guard told me "the boys" wanted to talk to me; I assumed that he meant the crew. I walked in to the studio to see Mick, while Keith and the rest of the big bad Stones were working with producer Don Was on their "Bridges to Babylon" record. Mick took a break, led the others into the control room and remarked, "Oh look, it's the Fender guy!" I wanted to tell Mick how much I loved the band when I first saw them on the Ed Sullivan Show, and even though my parents thought they were surly, that didn't matter to me and . . . but I just replied, "Pleased to meet you."

After spending some time joking with the band (joking with *the Rolling Stones!*), they told me they were using only *all Fender* guitars and amps that night because they knew I was coming; otherwise, it would have been our competitors' guitars. Mick said they were going back for a run-through and told me to go in to the kitchen and take whatever I wanted. All I could find in there was a big round clear plastic bin of Twizzlers, like the ones you see at Staples checkouts, and large gallon pumps of vodka. So there I was, back in the control room, with a Twizzler in one hand (which to me will forever be referred to as "Stones food") and a cup of vodka in the other. The studio engineer glances up at me and says, "Can you believe this? You and I are watching the Stones rehearse. Pretty cool!" Indeed.

We hear marketers refer to a *celebrity quotient*, as a measure of the equity or value of a celebrity. That equity can be immediately transferred to your brand through endorsements. According to *Entrepreneur* magazine, "Seventy-two percent of children between the ages of ten and thirteen say that seeing their favorite celebrity use a brand makes them want to use it as well." Older teens and adults are also fed a steady diet of celebrity activity through tabloids like *People, Star, In Touch*, and TV gossip shows like *Entertainment Tonight, Extra*, and *Inside Edition*—all of which reach audiences in the tens of millions. Like anything else in today's popular culture, celebrities can run hot and cold. While Rupert Boneham remains popular, and still draws large crowds to his personal appearances years after he was on *Survivor*, former *American Idol* contestants Taylor Hicks, Ruben Studdard, and Katherine McPhee have already been dropped from their record label, Sony BMG, because of flagging sales.[2] But this shouldn't stop a brand from investigating what celebrity may be right for the brand at that time, and seize the moment.

Soccer superstar and celebrity David Beckham, who brought his international fame to the Los Angeles Galaxy soccer team in an effort to boost the sport's appeal in the United States, recently posed in a sexy ad for Emporio Armani underwear. According to Sky News, demand for the entire Armani range has risen 30 percent, with some stores in London showing an astonishing sales increase of between 100 and 150 percent for the brand.[3]

The most straightforward way to tap into a celebrity's equity is to hire one as an official spokesperson for your brand. Fees for such positions, which can total thousands or hundreds of thousands of dollars, are based on such factors as the popularity of the celebrity, the number of ads in which they are appearing, the set number of personal appearances, and so forth. Obviously, this takes you to the big leagues of promotional fees, so if that's not in your company's immediate budget, there are a few other tricks of the trade. There are many web sites for companies—celebrityendorsements.com, for example, that promise everything from celebrity appearances to full endorsements. For the budget conscious, they offer celebrity gift bags at major TV events and trade-outs for product placement. Because my department at Fender allows me the opportunity to interact with celebrities on a regular basis, I don't have much need for companies like that. Although some make the promise that, "It's not as expensive as you might think," I suggest that you do your own research before committing to their programs.

Everyone, however, celebrities included, has a special cause that's close to his or her heart. Maybe you have an employee who has an illness in the family, or who has simply run into a string of bad luck—it happens to most everyone sooner or later. That's when people need the support of friends, family, and co-workers (their extended family) the most. Respected fund-raising organizations like the Susan G. Komen Foundation for Breast Cancer and the Elizabeth Glaser Foundation for Pediatric AIDS are named after real people because they personally experienced these setbacks. The point is that whether it is on a local, national, or international level, you can make a difference with your company's involvement.

If you live in New York or Los Angeles—or any other major cities with professional sports teams, you have direct access to celebrities through charitable and promotional events. On behalf of Fender, I have worked with former Yankee centerfielder Bernie Williams when he released his top-selling jazz record, "The Journey Within." My good friend and associate, Lauren Harriett, who specializes in fund-raising campaigns with Major League Baseball featuring musical elements, brought me into the promotion. For Bernie's campaign, we built a handful of Telecaster guitars airbrushed with the Yankees' top hat and bat logo, Yankee pinstripes, and Bernie's number, which were auctioned for MLB charities along with a portion of the sales of his CD. We delivered one guitar to Bernie, which he used during a performance in Chicago as part of the All-Star game, which turned into an Emmy-winning documentary on the making of the record.

Lauren and I also worked on campaigns with former Boston Red Sox pitcher Bronson Arroyo, the estate of Pittsburgh Pirate Hall of Famer Roberto Clemente, and my boyhood idol, "Mr. Cub," Hall of Famer Ernie Banks.

Other than sports stars and local personalities like musicians, the most likely place to find celebrities would be trade show events, many of which are not open to the public unless your business is registered in that industry, or fan-based events like collectibles shows. Either way, celebrities are more approachable if you share a passion with them, or if you are supporting a charitable cause that's close to their heart. Celebrities can be ardent fans themselves of many pastimes, some of which can include sports, music, or racing cars or motorcycles. Most often, their passion reflects something unrelated to what made them famous.

At Fender, for example, we have been able to attract several actors and athletes who want to feel like rock stars by playing guitar, even though they are worshipped by millions of fans for their day jobs. My boss, Ritchie Fliegler, referred to these types of guitarists as "civilian guitar players" and he felt that they had a very positive effect on promoting the brand to nonplayers. Time and time again, these celebrities benefited from their association with us as well because they want to publicize this additional talent to the general public. Dennis Quaid, Stephen Collins (who wrote a complete episode of his TV series "Seventh Heaven" around his Fender guitar), Steven Seagal, Jim Belushi, Adrian Grainer, Kevin Costner, and Will Ferrell are just a few of the actors I have worked with on behalf of Fender, who incorporated their music into their film or TV gigs and charitable events.

WARNING: Never, under any circumstances, should you approach a celebrity when they are not attending an official function. This will almost always turn him off to anything that you may have to offer, and you may even be mistaken as a stalker. You must be willing to go through the manager, agent, or PR person (which can bring its own difficulties). Even though celebrities may be passionate about something, their managers or agents will also have to get involved so they can justify their paychecks. I don't begrudge them that—everyone has to make a living—but sometimes the management is so protective of their clients that they will actually get in the way of what the celebrity wants to do. Some of these people are such control freaks that they can actually do harm to their clients by blowing opportunities that could have benefited their clients' careers. I know of a few artists whose manager burned so many bridges while the star was on his way up, that even when they ended up firing the manager, the people who could have helped the star get another chance on the way down were still smarting years later—and therefore refused to help.

The first step in garnering a specific celebrity's support would be to research what that celebrity's passion is. You can then reach out to her through an organization that she supports. Then, if you have access to a major celebrity, and you also have an event or cause you think she may be interested in backing, it's totally appropriate to open the door without putting the celeb in a position where she is forced to commit on the spot. If she is generally interested, she will have you call her agent or manager. If you get the brush-off from management, you can still request a signed script or personal artifact that can be used as an auction item. If it's a charitable cause, expect this to be donated at no charge. Many times, in the placement industry, products are placed on the set or into the hands of the star, and the star will request to keep it—to which the producers are all too happy to oblige. At that point, it's okay for you to ask a celebrity to support your brand, even with a simple testimonial that can be used as a sales tool (make sure at this time that you have written approval to use any photos or testimonials that will be officially used for your brand). In my experience, this type of authentic support is a much stronger breakthrough than one that was obviously paid for.

I thought the best way to illustrate this concept was to sit down with Gael MacGregor, who was on the ground floor of hooking up celebrities with the right charities with her company Celebrity Connect.

While interviewing her regarding her expertise in music licensing, I found out some interesting background information when I asked her how she got started in the entertainment business.

"Actually, I started out as a concert cellist and played a lot of different instruments and discovered that the best instrument I had was my voice. I went around the world singing with different groups and such and been to many places that I thought I'd never see. All on someone else's nickel, which was nice. Then, I came back and even though we were big stars overseas, nobody knew who we were back here. But I also had a taste of what it was like being famous, so to speak; you know, with people out running after you, standing for hours getting photographed and signing autographs and I went, 'Ya know, maybe I don't want this!' (chuckle)

"When I came back, I thought, 'I want to be able to pick out my own tomatoes at the grocery store.' So, I had done a lot of musical theater and dinner theater and such across the country, before I had gotten into doing just the bands and everything, and when I came back from working this one tour, I kinda got diverted. I had worked a part-time job for a guy for a pharmacist and a real estate guy, and a friend of his son's wanted to start a business that was a matchmaker between celebrities and charities. And so, I barely had even gotten off the plane, jet-lagging from an 22 hour overseas flight, when I got this frantic call saying, 'I'm getting ready to start the business . . . come help me!' (Laughing). This was in 1985 and using computers for your business was still relatively in its infancy. They had the really big five-inch floppies, you know, and nothing that looked like anything unless it happened to be a Macintosh, and of course, he had PCs. So I not only had to learn how to get this industry going, but also how to access the data through dBase III and Ashton-Tate's Framework for word processing. So, it was very, very primitive and such. But his goal was to be able to set up a clearinghouse for celebrities who had causes, to align themselves with the charities that they believed in, and for the charities who felt that a certain celebrity would be more to the demographic that they were trying to bring in to help their charities, and such. So, we had to create a questionnaire for the celebrities to fill out. Well, of course, you never want to go to a celebrity via their agent or their manager because great big dollar signs go off in their eyes. Whereas, [when] you . . . go to their PR people, they go, 'Oh, he's going to look really cool if he does this!' (chuckle) We started making friends with the big PR firms (not dropping the names, but some of the biggest), and we had various celebrities who already had causes that they wanted to be involved with. We helped Victoria Principal get aligned with the Arthritis Foundation—and she was their spokesperson for five years because they agreed to allow her in her public service announcements to talk about Lupus—a disease that hit home for her family and often includes arthritic symptoms—and she was able to address both in the PSA. We worked with Ray Bolger in his last years. In fact, some of us in the company actually took him to his chemotherapy appointments during the last times he was with us. But he got involved in a reading program in a small school and the children gave back to him with hundreds of 'get well' letters which really touched Mr. Bolger. And we helped bring all these different people together, and part of it was through designing a questionnaire in such a way that we found out what we needed to know, such as: What are the organizations that you believe in? What are the diseases that are more important [to] you, that have possibly touched your family (rate them one to five)?

"So we put all this stuff in and created this database that had all this information about all these different celebrities. It was a big task getting to all the people. There were some people who didn't get it and were going, 'What?' And we were fortunate enough, actually, to be one of the first people to align various celebrities with the first AIDS benefit done . . . that Dr. Chen Sam and Liz Taylor organized. And we helped because we figured, well, she's mega-famous and she was having trouble, sometimes even with her friends, getting people to come out, because there was very little known about the disease at the time. People on the A List were afraid that if they got aligned, it would ruin their reputation. . . . The people on the B List thought that it might keep them from getting on the A List, and the people on the C List were just scared of everything. . . . So we got things going through developing a rapport with the PR firms in the industry. Unfortunately, the founder of the company didn't have great business sense and he ended up going on and selling it to someone who actually continues to run the company. It is called Celebrity Connection, and it's still going strong some twenty-three years later. The company was a really good idea because a lot of the celebrities didn't know how to get in touch with the right contacts at various charities. So, with the questionnaire information from the celebrities, we contacted charities and matched them up. Once the word got out that we were doing that, we had more and more charities coming to us asking for specific specifications (gender, age, background, et cetera). All this information was in the database and we put in a string and ran a list of who matched their criteria. At times, there were organizations that were shortsighted about what that celebrity could do for them because they didn't think they were big enough and time went on and the celebrity grew big and the celebrity had aligned him- or herself with another charity meanwhile. But, some of the celebrities eventually ended up helping these charities. But, part of what we did was, we went after the people who were curmudgeons—and the ones that nobody could get to do anything, because they didn't want to be involved with all the famous charitable organizations because they figured they had enough star power or somehow or another. I made nice with Ed Asner's secretary, which goes to prove that secretaries rule the world, and she got him to fill out the questionnaire and he ended up doing a half-a-dozen things for us, all for various things. The celebrities all donated their time and the one thing that was constant and consistent, was that the charity always supplied round-trip first-class accommodations up and down the line, from the hotel, airfare, food, ground transportation, et cetera for two: the celebrity and their companion, and it was always top-notch and they received no compensation. The celebrities would agree that they would do certain things. We put up a contract saying for 'good and valuable consideration' type of thing. We would lay out [what] the responsibilities of the charity were. Lay out the responsibilities for the celebrity. We helped with public service announcements, et cetera. What we did was, we really identified what were celebs pet causes and identify why or what in your life made you want to sponsor this? Some of them did it deeply from the heart and others did it to make themselves look good, so that they could get more work. Other people felt it was the thing to do. Kim Fields as a child was working with us. Every time you turned around, she was doing something and it was really out of the goodness of her heart. Even as a kid she was very socially responsible. We were essentially a clearinghouse, taking the database of one group *charities* and taking the database of another *celebrities* and playing matchmaker. Identifying what the charities' goals are (Type of events? . . . Are you trying to raise awareness? . . . Are you trying to raise money? . . . et cetera.) And we would just put all that criteria together, spit it out of the computer and then start talking to the people and try to get them involved. Especially if there was a charity coming to us saying that there was a specific celebrity they were interested in. We didn't so much advertise the company. We really just went to the public relations people who saw the absolute win. I hate to use the win-win phrase for their celebrity, but their whole thing was to get their celebrity into the public's eye in a really favorable fashion and what better way than someone giving back to the world at large. So, for the PR person, it was their bread and butter to keep their celebrity in the public eye and for the celebrity, someone like Victoria Principal saying well, 'My parents suffer from Lupus and Arthritis and I really want to get the word out,' and of course she was very big at that time because of *Dallas*, so she was in the public eye all the time and everybody wanted her. And she chose to do this because it had affected her personally.

"During this time in the 1980s, it also created a change in the way musicians were viewed in that it became a very positive thing, from rock and roll, it was always considered 'scary and the rebel guy' and all of a sudden, these musicians were the ones doing Live Aid and other major fund-rasing concerts on a global scale. The most valuable commodity is your time and they gave it. My grandmother was a Salvation Army officer and one of the things that she said was, 'The most valuable thing you can give to anyone is your time.' And, she [also] said, 'the mark of a true friend is someone who will give you their time when it's the least convenient for them.' So, she said, 'If it's easy for you, great! But, really go out of your way . . . *really* go out of your way to make a difference and make a change and do something for someone when they ask.' She had the whole concept of 'pay it forward' way before it became fashionable. So I grew up ringing the bell with the Salvation officers. I don't think it was an accident of the universe that I ended up there. Because I was able to give a different perspective to the people who were looking to 'Well, we're going to get money from the organization' who we were doing the matchmaking for. Because that's where the money came from. It was the charitable organizations that gave the money to the matchmakers and they also had to pay for the celebrity's expenses so I always did my best to get both sides on the same page, working on the same goals."

One thing to be careful about, whether you are approaching a celebrity for a charitable event, or hiring him to promote your brand, is to make sure that this particular person is appropriate for your brand. You can delve into a celebrity's background to make sure that his past doesn't have any red flag warnings that may signal a character flaw that could tarnish your brand's reputation. No one has a crystal ball, and even seemingly squeaky-clean celebs—like Kobe Bryant, for example—sometimes go astray. Bryant lost many endorsements because of his indiscretion in that Colorado hotel room, and those companies, of course, had to make a quick retreat to distance themselves from him, losing millions of dollars in their future investment in him. After that incident, Bryant worked hard to reestablish his reputation; he has secured new endorsements, and seems to have regained his stature as a top NBA brand, culminating with his MVP Award for the 2007–2008 season. Some marketers even think it helped his street cred among fans.

In fact, other bad boys in the world of sports, such as Bryant's fellow NBA star Allen Iverson, seem to attract brands that are desperately looking for that type of cred. Atlanta Falcons star quarterback Michael Vick got himself into big trouble during the 2007–2008 football season, having been convicted on dogfighting charges. This proved to be *too* far beyond street cred for Nike, which immediately shelved plans for the release of a new signature shoe once Vick's antics came to light. This may be a moot point since Vick's career is most likely over because he may be too old to play when he's released from prison. And Barry Bonds, the all-time Major League Baseball home run king, has become persona non grata since allegations of his steroid use were made public. After not being re-signed by the San Francisco Giants, he is not likely to be offered a contract by any other major league team.

This type of activity is not limited to sports stars, of course. A recent report says that superstar actor Tom Cruise's couch-jumping antics may have cost *Mission Impossible 3* some of its ticket revenues.

In any case, it may be that something simply doesn't fit right between your brand and the celebrity. That's what happened to me when I tried to work with custom motorcycle builder Jesse James. Jesse was already established as a respected and influential custom designer and builder for top-end motorcycles. He was just beginning his launch of *Monster Garage*, the show that would bring his fame to the masses and launch several other custom bike and car reality shows. Jesse was interested in creating a Fender *Strat-o-cruiser* bike and he actually went as far as to meet with our Custom Shop builders (who were to create the matching guitar) over a three-day period. That was all well and good until one of our marketing guys visited his web site and saw an ad for Porn Star Clothing. I was reminded that Fender was a family-oriented company and that the backbone of our success had traditionally been the mom-and-pop stores that dotted the country. These stores—particularly those located in the Bible Belt—would certainly be offended by such an association on Fender's part, and might even stop carrying our products. I had to bring an end to the program, and we ended up going with a much less famous company for the bike, without the TV connection, of course.

Jesse's show went on to achieve cult status, and Fender eventually acquired Jackson Guitars, whose spokesperson was none other than well-known porn star, Jenna Jameson. It would have been no problem to work on a Jackson bike, and when I ran into Jesse a few years later at the SEMA Show (Specialty

Equipment Market Association) in Las Vegas,[4] he remarked how cool that Fender bike would have been. When I asked him if we could do it with the more appropriate Jackson instead, he answered, "The first one would have been no cost, but because of the show's waiting list for bikes, if you want to do it now, it would take six months and eighty thousand dollars."

End of that story.

CHAPTER 10

Promotions as an Excuse to Advertise—But We Don't Really Need an Excuse, Do We?

Factory *Authorized Sale! Back to School Sale! Super Bowl Sale! Event of a Lifetime! Sale of the Century!* Where will it end, with each ad campaign trying to top the last? We're all familiar with the tendency for anything and everything to be turned into a major blowout sales event. Case in point: over the holiday weekend leading up to Martin Luther King, Jr. Day, the *Los Angeles Times* actually ran an ad in their Sunday supplement for a chain of bed stores that announced the "I Have a Dream Sale." (I am fairly certain that sales were the furthest thing from Dr. King's mind when he made his historic speech.) But when everyone uses the same hyperbole, how do you get your brand to stand out? And is cutting prices a real sales event or even an economically wise decision, unless you are trying to clear inventory of slow-moving or discontinued products?

When I was responsible for signing new artists, the PR folks at the labels would inevitably send a release claiming that this or that new artist was the "next Dylan," the "next Beatles," or worse yet, the next "O Town," based on whoever was hot at the moment. Hardly, because the words we live by in our industry are, *itsgottabeinthegrooves.*[1] So no amount of hyping or shouting about your product is going to make your brand stand out over someone else's, particularly if you can't prove what makes yours better (that is, *different*). In fact, the old adage never rings more true, "If you want to get someone to listen to you—whisper." My take on this has always been, "And yeah, time to get creative."

When I say that a promotion is an excuse to advertise, I mean that you should create a promotional campaign that you can provide to your retailers as a reason to advertise and promote your brand over that of your competitors. If you are creative and can provide the tools like point-of-purchase displays, advertising slicks, spots, and so forth, instead of the simple worn-out discounts, you will have the upper hand. As in any industry, you will have retailers that are totally capable of creating their own effective campaigns, and who also know their individual markets, but you still need to control how your brand is presented so that the message is consistent and therefore reinforced by the retailers who are masters of the game.

I worked with such a dealer in Sacramento, California, called Skip's Music. Skip not only knew his market better than anyone, he also constantly thought up new promotions like manufacturers' expos for his customers; Weekend Warriors, where Baby Boomers could get together to meet, rehearse, and perform at his store; and Stairway to Stardom, a program for young musicians.

Skip was the first dealer I knew who created and placed his own top quality TV commercials.

I don't get too much opportunity to work with local dealers anymore in my current department because my responsibilities are primarily for the national campaigns outside our industry. But before coming to Fender, I worked for a brilliant marketing director at Washburn named Greg Bennett. He never ceased looking for new ways to promote our products in creative ways. Washburn was one of the oldest established brand names in guitars—over 130 years old already when I began there—but the brand had a really difficult time getting noticed next to the big boys like Fender and Gibson (the Coke and Pepsi of the guitar industry), as many of the electric models we were trying to promote were somewhat derivative of the big duo's most popular models. So we set out to change that by launching a series of ongoing promotions, including in-store events, personal appearances by our artists, and some unique ad campaigns.

I had just started at the company and pretty much had one artist to build promotions around: Nuno Bettencourt. He was an exceptional guitarist of Portuguese descent, whose Boston-based band, Extreme, was climbing the charts with the soft ballad "More Than Words." It was ironic because that song and their other big radio and MTV hit, "Hole Hearted," were the only really soft songs on their album "Pornograffitti."[2] The rest of the disc was made up of funky, hard-edged rock featuring Nuno's blazing guitar virtuosity. At this time, the trend was for the *guitar heroes* to be the driving force in selling your brand of guitar. Nuno's striking good looks—coupled with his stature as one of the top guitarists of the early 1990s and the hard-soft element of the band—put Washburn in a unique position. If we did an in-store meet-and-greet event with Nuno, we would bring the throngs of girls who adored him and the guys who would follow the girls but also admired him as a brilliant musician.

The band was coming through our area as the support act for Van Halen on a national tour—and I lived right down the street from the family-owned Biasco Music in the heart of the Chicago's Northwest side of Belmont and Central. Coincidentally, this happened to be roughly the same neighborhood where I grew up, and Biasco was where I took my first music lessons. Now they were one of Washburn's trusted dealers.

Unfortunately, Nuno wasn't a household name yet to many of our dealers like Biasco, so it took some prodding from me to get the Biasco brothers to finally warm up to the idea of having him appear. During the week leading up to his appearance, my young daughter Shanna, a budding Extreme fan herself, and I plastered the area with flyers announcing the event. This was my first big promo for Washburn, and the owner was worried that if no one showed up, Nuno would be embarrassed. But the Biascos came through again with several radio ads using "Get The Funk Out"—one of Extreme's heavier tracks—as the bed[3] (a prime example of the "excuse to advertise"). I met up with Nuno and the band on a boat a local soft-rock radio station had rented to take the band and lucky listeners up and down the Chicago River. I had called my friend John Starble to rent him and his stretch limo to take Nuno, myself, and Steve Hoffman from Extreme's management company across town to Biasco.

As soon as we headed out, rain began to drizzle and I thought, "Just my luck, the driest year on record in Chicago and nature picks today to rain on my parade." The rain began to let up just as we arrived at the store and I thought what I saw next was an apparition—literally *thousands* of fans lined up around four city blocks surrounding the store. Steve looked at Nuno, then at me, and in the calmest of all voices said, "I think we are going to need more security." (There wasn't a single "no neck" in sight, since we expected just a couple of dozen fans, at most). John whipped his limo around the back and we hurried Nuno inside the store. The number of fans trying push their way into that Biasco Music store was overwhelming; so much so that, fearing for Nuno's and their own lives, not to mention their precious inventory, the store managers eventually locked the doors. Now all we had to do was get Nuno safely out of the store.

Trying to accomplish this feat was the closest I have been to experiencing what the Beatles must have felt in *A Hard Day's Night*. Some of the Washburn employees who had come to help created a diversion by making it appear as Nuno was coming out the front. Like a precise military drill, we opened up the loading dock and the three of us ducked into the back seat of the waiting limousine. Suddenly someone shouted, "There he is!" which caused the herd to frantically stampede the car. We were partially blocked by the crowds at the end of the alley, which allowed the delirious, screaming fans to throw themselves on the limo. John was in the act of rolling down his driver's side window to warn the culprits not to scratch his finish when I shouted, *"You better hit it!"* and off we sped with a procession of several weaving carloads in chase. Without missing a beat, Steve calmly looked at me and said, *"I told you we needed more security."*

The next day, the press was hounding Greg Bennett to get more information on "the incident," which we now referred to as "the fiasco at Biasco." At the very least, we all made an impression in our hometown of Chicago. Not that I would recommend that type of adventure for every dealer!

We did, however, have many more successful in-stores with Nuno, and later with Dimebag Darrell Lance as well, who followed me from Dean to Washburn, and whom I regarded as the ideal artist for these types of events. He loved socializing with his fans because that's how his band Pantera had built such a huge fan base—hanging out with the loyals after the shows. Dimebag had no reservations about taking pictures with anyone who came to meet him. He would even film them as well for Pantera home videos, using his hand-held camcorder as a perpetual extension of his arm. He'd then pick up a guitar and dazzle the fans with incendiary solos during the meet-and-greets in the stores.[4]

Just like a song, my mantra is a promotion needs a hook—the one memorable thematic or musical phrase that sticks in your head. In *This is Your Brain on Music,* Daniel J. Levitin describes these as *ear worms,* taken from the German word *ohrwurm;* in other words, the method by which tunes, or hooks, get stuck in our head. Translated to a promotion, the hook would be the conceptual theme that draws the consumer's interest to the promotion. The more that advertising slogans and campaigns sound alike, just like songs, the less memorable they are.

As part of my training, Greg Bennett forced me to read many marketing classics like *Positioning*[5] and *Marketing Warfare*[6] over and over again so that we could learn how the big brands became and remained successful. *Positioning* really made an impact on both of us at the time, because even though Washburn was gaining ground in the electric guitar market, the history of the company positioned us as an acoustic brand. That's when we came up with our most dynamic and successful campaign to date.

Greg had researched cable advertising and found out how cost effective it would be to purchase national ads on MTV's newest TV series at the time, *Unplugged.* Because it was an unproven show (keep in mind that at that time MTV mainly programmed videos supplied by the record labels), national spots were dirt cheap. Local spots were even less expensive, so we could actually afford these spots for our dealers. We felt that we needed to do this to prove the campaign's worth, since so many of our dealers were still advertising like it was the 1950s. They still mainly used sales events advertised in local papers built around back-to-school discounts, since that's when bands were typically formed, having grown out of new friendships at school. We also knew our sales department at

Washburn would revert to the ancient tactics like free freight to close a sale with a dealer. We learned that to really close a sale, you had to do it from the other end—by attaining awareness and forming an emotional bond to your product so the customer would go in to a dealer's store looking specifically for your brand.

We therefore decided to create a campaign built around our equity as a renowned acoustic brand to bring both Washburn and our dealers into the modern era by advertising our guitars through national spots placed on *Unplugged*. The show's concept was to feature the major artists of the day performing their best-known songs on acoustic instruments, as opposed to recreating the original recordings on electrified instruments. Performing the songs in a stripped-down version allowed the artist to present them in a much more personal, and often sensitive, manner, which allowed the raw emotion of the song to shine through. This close emotional connection between the artist and the song could also be transferred to the guitars they used.

We started by conceptualizing and producing our own spots with the help of a local cable TV music show, *JBTV,* which had its own in-house production facility. Since we knew that major stars would be on *Unplugged* each week, we used Greg Bennett himself, a world-class acoustic picker in his own right, as our own star in the video. *JBTV* helped us re-create the quick jump edits so that our commercial would fit the MTV look and feel of the time. We ended up with top quality professional-looking ads that we began supplying to our dealers so they would be in sync with the same ads we ran nationally.

My assistant at the time was Lisa Yucht (now Lisa Bates because she married one of Washburn's endorsees, top movie soundtrack composer and producer Tyler Bates, who recently added the mega-hit movie *300* to his list of accomplishments) and she set up a program where she would personally call the local cable outlets in the dealer's market to handle details such as negotiation and placement schedule, and would add their individual store tag

lines to the local spot. Lisa also offered them a promotional rebate
when their orders hit a certain mark, at which time we would use
those funds to place additional ads for them. We even offered a
promotional checklist for dealers to follow once they got the hang
of the process. We then shipped the guitars to them, complete with
hang tags that said "As Seen on MTV's *Unplugged*"—just to make
sure the customer didn't miss the connection.

I personally flew to New York and met with the show's
producer, Alex Coletti, to get clearance to use the *Unplugged* hang
tags, and to give him Washburn acoustics for artists to use (we were
known for the acoustic bass guitar, which many artists needed for
the taping of the shows since they weren't all that common at the
time). With diverse superstars such as Bruce Springsteen, Nirvana,
Paul McCartney, Eric Clapton,[7] and yes, even KISS, it wasn't a
surprise that *Unplugged* became one of MTV's most popular shows
and spawned several hit records to the point that many all-acoustic
shows and concert segments today are still referred to as *Unplugged*.
Even if an artist didn't use a Washburn instrument on the show, it
didn't matter, because we were still able to position ourselves as the
official *Unplugged* guitar, and our sales proved it, as they nearly
doubled during the first year of the campaign. Targeting a wholly
different market, we added a second campaign with another MTV
series, *Headbanger's Ball*, featuring our artists Michelangelo and
Nuno Bettencourt. Once we showed our dealers the way, they
jumped at the opportunity to tap into our campaign. New dealers
came on in droves to be a part of it. We gave them a killer
consumer hook with *Unplugged*, and the "excuse to advertise" our
products above those of our competitors.

Although guitar heroes like John Mayer, Kenny Wayne Shepherd, and Brian Setzer are still prevalent on the scene, the trend
of store appearances is not always the best choice nowadays,

because some of these artists are too big for local in-store events. They have been replaced by national campaigns that often partner with companies outside the music industry.

I was involved with a promotion for *Standing in the Shadows of Motown*, an inspiring and award-winning documentary that launched with a full-page ad in *Rolling Stone* magazine. As part of the grand prize sweepstakes, we provided two vintage instruments that were similar to the Fender guitar and bass models regularly used by the Funk Brothers when recording all those hits for Motown. The other part of the sweepstakes was a Mitsubishi Sports model. Even with this many partners, the one consistent part of the whole contest was, once again, the promotional hook; a theme that was carried throughout.

CHAPTER 11

California Dreaming—The Essence of *The Cool Factor* in Partnership Marketing

The CEO of our company once asked me if I thought I could be as effective at what I did if I didn't live in Southern California. Without hesitation, I replied "Absolutely not!" Other cities or countries will hit on a trend from time to time, but it always seems to come back to *California Cool*. We obviously have the bulk of movies and TV productions filmed here, so our lifestyle is broadcast to the world on a daily basis. Actors and musicians from all over the world come to California to realize their dreams of stardom, and for the few who do often make California their home. New York could justifiably make an argument that they have the fashion and publishing houses, along with the movie and TV industry, Broadway shows, and major labels to promote the American lifestyle to the world. But my argument is that Southern California has all of that, in addition to year-round golden weather, which exemplifies and thus promotes the California lifestyle.

As author Timothy White writes in his engaging book, *The Nearest Faraway Place: Brian Wilson, the Beach Boys, and the Southern California Experience*,[1] "Even Paradise requires promoters, marketing salesmen, to herald not only its ethereal splendors but also its mundane perks."

California has always looked for ways to advertise its most positive attributes—the sun and the ocean, which begets, of course, surfing. From Jack London chronicling his travels—his experiences with the Hawaiian pastime of surfboarding, in particular—in the October 1907 issue of *Woman's Home Companion*, to the prime subject of White's book, the Beach Boys, California has always been a locale that has garnered considerable notice. None of this was lost on generations of Los Angeles's city fathers and public relations essayists.

The legend among the legends of surfers was Duke Kahanamoku, a Hawaiian who introduced surfing to Australia in the early 1900s just as the original California surfers spread the word along the West Coast. This trend accelerated as the automobile made it easier to travel along the beaches in search of the perfect wave. In the 1930s, Pete Peterson and Whitey Harrison[2] sneaked a trip by stowing away to Oahu and returned to California with exciting tales of the Hawaiian surf.

Advertising became the next boon to surfing when a man named Dale Velzy became a key sponsor of the sport by giving locals free boards in exchange for their endorsements. With the success of the movie *Gidget* in 1962, the rest of the nation—the young in particular—were enticed by the lure of the beach culture.

When I was growing up listening to the Beach Boys sing the merits of "California Girls," and Jan and Dean claiming that California's "Surf City" had "two girls for every boy," well, you can imagine what an impact that had on a shy, young, pubescent mind that thought that getting one girl was challenging enough. Those images were given a major boost by Walt Disney's desire to promote tourism to Disneyland by using his most popular star, not long graduated from the Mickey Mouse Club, Annette Funicello. Annette, Frankie Avalon, and the rest of the cast of blond surfer boys and beautiful bikinied babes introduced young America to the world of custom cars created by Big Daddy Roth (who was also responsible for the Rat Fink character) and the coolest surf bands of the day, like the Chantays, the Surfaris, and even the Beach Boys (they appeared as Annette's backing band in *Monkey Business*).

This trend helped Fender immensely, because these bands almost exclusively used Fender guitars. I remember my folks buying me a 1965 Fender Jaguar guitar for almost $400 because I wanted the same guitar I saw in these movies. Keep in mind that that was a small fortune back then, when you could purchase a brand-new 1964 1/2 Ford Mustang for just about $2,300.

For Fender, ad exec Bob Perine came up with a brilliant ad campaign titled "You Won't Part with Yours Either." Each ad depicted a guitarist doing exciting but nonmusical things such as getting into a jet plane, a race car, and so on, each of them with his trusty Fender guitar strapped on to his back. The most powerful images were obviously California kids (sometimes Bob used his own daughters and their friends as the models in the ads) enjoying skateboarding, motorcycle jumping, and the most recognizable of all, surfing; all had their Fender guitars with them—uniquely California imagery. Those ads still reverberate today: One of the ads even appears in the 2007 movie *Alvin and the Chipmunks* (discussed in more detail in Chapter 12). It's no secret that those images were responsible for Fender's greatest growth in that era and corporate America took note, which eventually led to CBS's purchase of the company in 1966 for $13 million.

This entire culture was constantly supported through the innovators of the day. In the late 1940s, land speed records were being broken at the Bonneville Salt Flats by young hot-rodders, including Alex Xydias, who founded the legendary SO-CAL Speed Shop in 1946 (coincidentally, the same year that a young radio shop repairman named Leo Fender from Fullerton, California, founded the musical instrument company that would bear his name). To service and publicize this new industry, *Hot Rod* magazine was launched in 1947, and its visionary editor, Wally Parks, organized street racers with the sanctioning body National Hot Rod Association (NHRA) in 1950. That same year, the first legal drag race was held at the Orange County Airport in Santa Ana, sponsored by the California Highway Patrol(!).

Filmmaker Bruce Brown's 1964 low-budget surf odyssey, *The Endless Summer*, with its simple, yet striking poster by artist John Van Hammersveld (which set the artistic tone that has been emulated by countless surf album covers and posters) actually did better than *My Fair Lady* in two weeks of test screenings in—of all places—Wichita, Kansas.

As Dick Dale, the king of surf guitar, was packing them in at the Rendezvous Ballroom in Huntington Beach, the Beach Boys were proving themselves as more than just a name by solidifying their image as the champions of surf music when they hit the national charts with "Surfin," "Surfin' Safari," "Surfin' USA," and "Little Surfer Girl." Even though great car songs like "Rocket 88" (featuring a young Ike Turner and considered by many in the industry to be the first *real* rock 'n' roll recording), "Maybelline," "Thunder Road," and "Hot Rod Lincoln" preceded the Beach

Boys, Brian Wilson and his bandmates forever linked themselves with the California culture of hot-rodding with the brilliant and exuberant recordings "409," "Fun, Fun, Fun," "Shut Down," Little Deuce Coupe," and consummating in "I Get Around," which leapfrogged the Beatles in 1964 to hit the "toppermost of the poppermost" on the Billboard national charts.

California hit the trifecta at the same time with Hollywood's discovery of "Cool California Custom Cars." We already mentioned the futuristic customs of Ed "Big Daddy" Roth, who by the early 1960s had already signed a deal with Revell to reproduce his most famous creations as model kits (on which I spent most of my hard-earned allowance). "King of the Kustoms," George Barris, relocated from Chicago in the 1940s and created his first cars for the Hollywood movie, *High School Confidential.* Following that was a long line of *Kustom* cars built for the movie and TV industry—the Beverly Hillbillies' ancient pickup, the *Munsters'* car, the Monkeemobile, the General Lee from *The Dukes of Hazzard*, the Batmobile, the Flint(stones)-mobile, the Greased Lightning from the movie *Grease*, the *Green Hornet's* car, and—not surprisingly—the Beach Boys' Little Deuce Coupe. In the 1970s, Pete Chaporous and Jim "Jake" Jacobs of Pete & Jake's Hot Rod Repair created the famous "California Kid" for the movie of the same name. In the 1980s, they designed and built rods for ZZ Top's Billy F. Gibbons, culminating in the Eliminator, as featured in the award-winning *Legs* music video. In 1997, Pete purchased the SO-CAL Speed Shop and remains close friends with original founder Alex Xydias today.

Detroit's car companies took note of the burgeoning automobile culture in California and began sprucing up their images with some of their coolest car names based on well-known West Coast locales: the Chevy Malibu and El Camino, the Pontiac Bonneville and Catalina, and the Mercury Monterey. Even the British motorcycle company Triumph struck gold when they celebrated their 1955 land speed record at the Salt Flats in Utah with the introduction in 1959 of their iconic brand, the Bonneville.

This trend wasn't limited to the automobile industry, however; the world of fashion caught on to the "California craze" as well. The young *garage* bands that rode the surf craze to the national charts were the punk bands of the 1960s. In the late 1970s, those types of garage bands evolved into the punk movement, mirroring what was happening in the United Kingdom and New York. As a reaction to the commercialization of rock music, and disco in particular, groups like Black Flag, the Dead Kennedys, the Germs, X, and Minor Threat launched a new sociopolitical and fashion movement that reverberated throughout the industry. Skateboarders—or *skaters*—and surfers embraced this music, and the small clothing and shoe companies that catered to these athletes began to gain national prominence.

Originally a surfboard label in the 1960s, Ocean Pacific's (OP) founder, Jim Jenks, extended the brand into an apparel line in 1972. Generally recognized as the first "action sports company," the company's web site also lays claim to the creation of the "Original California Lifestyle" by "uniting the entire youth culture by connecting surfing with music, skateboarding, motocross, BMX and snowboarding,"[3] intended as both functional clothing and as a fashion icon. By the mid-1970s, OP was tripling its sales each year, and was the industry leader in sales by decade's end. The 1980s brought a slip in popularity for the brand, but under the direction of CEO Dick Baker, OP reemerged in the 1990s, bringing it to prominence once again through sponsorships of athletes, musicians, and the all-important action sports competitive events.

Started as a backstreet shoe shop in 1966 owned by Paul Van Doren, the shoe company Vans has had its ups and downs (filing for bankruptcy in 1984 due in part to its reckless expansion), but has nonetheless always stressed its authentic legacy and has stayed loyal to skateboarders—and vice versa. The company purchased the Warped tour and promoted its brand by producing shows about extreme sports for NBC Sports and Fox Sports Net.[4] Corporate U.S. came knocking on the door, allowing Vans to forge sponsorship agreements with companies such as Ford and Gillette.

Another West Coaster who helped the movement along was Bob Hurley, a surfboard shaper from Costa Mesa, California, who, in the late 1970s, was working with some of the greatest surfers of the era. He was attracted to the super-long, punk rock board short styles of the hot Australian clothing company, Billabong, and established Billabong USA as a separate entity and licensee for Billabong in 1982. By the mid-1990s, Bob and his team saw a new opportunity with the modern surfer also showing love for fashion, skating, snowboarding, music, and arts. He did not renew the license with Billabong and instead launched Hurley in 1998.[5]

Keeping with the authentic surf credo of the company, an associate of mine who owned the PR company, Pacific Communications Group, that was hired to publicize the launch, told me that Bob blew off his interview with the *Wall Street Journal* because the "waves were too perfect that day" and he didn't want to miss the opportunity for some gnarly surfing. After failing for years to establish this type of credibility in the skate shoe market, Nike procured some of this authentic skater equity by purchasing Hurley in 2006 for an estimated $50 million.

Even surfwear companies founded outside of Southern California eventually established a presence on the West Coast to tap into that California cool. Quiksilver, which was founded by Australian surfers Alan Green and Jon Law, opened a small warehouse and distribution center in Newport Beach, California, under the tutelage of another top surfer, Jeff Hackman. Quiksilver remains active to this day in surfing and snowboarding by sponsoring many top events and athletes, and employing many of these top athletes in their company's ranks. In 1999, the company brought legendary skateboarder and household name Tony Hawk into the Quiksilver family when they signed him to a sponsorship agreement and purchased his company, Hawk Clothing.[6]

Volcom, another company that boasts surfer-type clothing, was created in 1991 as Stone Boardwear, Inc. by Richard "Wooly" Woolcott and Tucker "T-Dawg" Hall, in, of all places, Fargo, North Dakota. Changing its name to Volcom, Inc. in 2005, the company sponsors surfers, skateboarders, and snow-boarders, and even though it has opened stores worldwide, all of its U.S. locations are in either Hawaii or Southern California. Volcom has also, not surprisingly, launched an independent record label—Volcom Entertainment.

Another major Southern California–founded company not known for clothing nonetheless realized the importance of the West Coast style. In the 1990s, Fender's clothing line was not a major part of our sales or company initiative. Most of the items were standard fare—knit shirts and T-shirts featuring the Fender logo—pretty tame, but nonetheless typical for our industry. These styles were targeted for the dealers and our own sales reps and had little distribution outside our industry. But that all changed in 2002 when Fender signed a licensing agreement with clothing maker Defiance, whose owner, Chris Wicks, had resurrected the Da Vinci brand name. Da Vinci had been established in 1952, and was popularized by the Rat Pack. It has a timeless quality as exemplified in its catchphrase "As Cool As It Gets." Garnering wide exposure on hit TV shows like *The Sopranos* and *Two and a Half Men* (almost exclusively worn by Charlie Sheen in the first few seasons), the brand is currently more popular than ever.

Fender extended its co-licensing with Defiance to include "The Rock 'n' Roll Religion" line. Our retail store, located on fashionable Melrose Avenue in Los Angeles (which took over the Von Dutch location) was even visited by a Fender-clothing-wearing Bret Michaels on an episode of the megahit VH1 series *Rock of Love*. No longer aimed at just music industry stores, Fender-branded clothing is one of our fastest-growing divisions and is now sold in major retailers such as Macy's and Dillard's, and the international restaurant chain Hard Rock Café. Macy's is even test-marketing "Fender Boutiques" in some of their southern U.S. outlets.

Our formal affiliation with the California lifestyle began much earlier, though, than our venture into the co-branded clothing arena. Our company was introduced to events like the Warped Tour and X-Games through my assistant at the time, Alex Perez, who now heads up Fender's West Coast artist relations office since my move into entertainment marketing. Alex was a dedicated mountain biker and snowboarder himself and realized that Fender needed to explore partnerships in action sports' connection with the music industry. Thanks to the foresight of the head of the artist relations department, Bill Cummiskey, Fender was able to get in on the ground floor in sponsorship of the K2 event at Camp Woodward in 1998. K2 was a strong brand in mountain bikes, skis, and snowboards. At the Woodward event, Fender gave away guitars for the athletes who attended, and Blink 182, one of the bands Alex brought to Fender, performed.

That opened the door to our first venture into the X-Games in 2001 at First Union Center in Philadelphia, Pennsylvania. Fender provided everything from X-Games-logoed guitars as prizes for the winning athletes to the sponsorship of bands performing at the events. At that event, Alex met Bruce Crisman, who beat out many favorites to win the BMX event, and was one of the first athlete-artists with whom he built a formal relationship.

Many more of the athletes with whom Alex worked were also devoted guitar players—such as top skateboarder Ray Barbie and snowboarder Shaun White (2006 Olympic Gold medalist, as well as perennial X-Games medal winner since 2002). The combination of getting in on the ground floor in extreme sports and the one-on-one relationships built with its top athletes allowed Fender to have a premier presence at a fraction of the cost other major corporate sponsors have had to pay for similar results.

I asked Alex to put Fender's entry into extreme sports into his own words:

"I was heavily into mountain biking. Once I saw all the crazy stuff that was going on at Camp Woodward, it sparked me to get back into BMX. I'm still riding at 40. I do more mountain and road bike now, but will still go to the skate park before work to ride some BMX. I also grew up skateboarding, but not one of my better sports.

"The cool thing about the crossover was reaching people we may never reach. Most of this crowd never sets foot in a music store. We had a lot of great connections. Cool things like when a guy wins a guitar and decides he wants to learn how to play, or even better, a guy wins a guitar and he already plays; that's huge. They get good money for these contests, and also get paid very well by sponsors, but they always get stoked on winning a guitar. We've helped out skaters, bikers, surfers, skiers, snowboarders, and motocross guys. There's also been a few girls that were pro snowboarders.

"We're still involved with action sports via summer and winter X-Games. I also help out lifestyle companies like Billabong, Volcom, and Vans. They do a lot of roots-style events and some bigger TV-style events. We always help them with guitars and musical gear for onsite use or as prizes for contest winners."

Even though I was not a regular participant on Fender's behalf in the action sports events—attending only as support for Vail, Colorado's "Unvailed" competition event—nonetheless, thanks to Alex and Bill's opening the door, I saw the opportunity for another potential tie-in to the industry. I reached out to Pacific Communications Group (PCG) PR director, Jeff Green, to source out a company that would be willing to co-sponsor a music project through our on-again, off-again Fender Records. The idea was to showcase up-and-coming artists who were affiliated with, or representative of, the extreme sports world.

Fender Records had enjoyed some success as a co-branded effort with Virgin/Point Blank Records for our fiftieth anniversary CD "Guitar Legends," and Warner Brothers, with our "Choice Picks." Both collections featured major stars like Eric Clapton, Bonnie Raitt, Buddy Holly, Jeff Beck, the Beach Boys, and Sheryl Crow. The problem we experienced was that as downloads became more popular, there was less demand for these types of compilations, since fans could create their own. The only advantage would be if we could offer exciting new music or unreleased or alternate tracks (the backbone of major label re-releases) that we didn't have access to. We chose the latter, and Jeff Green came through with Ocean Pacific, who we all agreed was a perfect partner. We proceeded to cement the deal with label partner Rhino Records.

Produced by the partnership of legendary record man Spencer Proffer and guitarist Steve Plunkett (who achieved fame as guitarist for the 1980s platinum act Autograph), the first artists we approached were the athlete-musicians: world-class surfer Donavon Frankenreiter, pro skateboarder Mike V (Vallely) and his band the Rats, and pro baseball player Scott Spezio of Sandfrog, who starred in the 2002 World Series as a member of the championship winners Anaheim Angels. (World-renowned skaters Bob Burnquist and Ray Barbie were original contributors as well, but had to back out because of a conflict with one of Bob's endorsement companies regarding his potential affiliation with OP).

For the 10 days preceding Christmas 2003, with no publicity other than that on OP's and our own web site, we announced that we were looking for artists to showcase on a new Fender Records compilation. The only requirement was that these artists could not have a prior deal with any major label (the same went for the star athletes). Astonishingly, over 3,000 MP3s were submitted (our webmasters said we would have received at least 20,000 entries if we accepted CDs and tapes) on Fender. com by artists and bands from all over the world, representing a wide array of music. From those entries, the seven additional songs for this collection were chosen by an independent panel of industry experts, including Kevin Baldes of Lit and *Playboy* music editor Jason Buhrmester. Many of these experts were amazed at the level of talent we "discovered" and anticipation was running high that we had a real winner on our hands.

The following summer, "Fender Records Presents OP Emerging" was released. Even though Donavon and Reeve Oliver went on to bigger and better things by signing with major distributed labels, our experience with the CD had mixed results. Some of the artists appeared at that year's Global X-Games in Vancouver, British Columbia, and also as part of the events surrounding the Disneyland Grad Nites in Anaheim, California, but the CD unfortunately never found mass distribution as a *value added* bonus through a national clothing retailer as was originally intended.

I did have better luck on behalf of Fender with my foray into the world of custom cars and hot rods. In the late 1990s, Fender Custom Shop employee Scott Beull, whose father had been a well-known hot-rodder himself, had built a one-off custom guitar for the nearby SO-CAL Speed Shop, that featured the company's distinctive logo and red and white color scheme incorporated on its award-winning cars. I didn't know too much at that time about the history of SO-CAL, but I knew that the name was synonymous with California racing and custom cars.

Little did I know that the new owner was none other than Pete Chaporous, with whom we worked on ZZ Top's *Legs* video. When I learned that SO-CAL was founded in the same year as Fender, I felt that this was an ideal partnership to help our company reclaim its place in the history of the Southern California car culture. My boss, Ritchie Fliegler, an avid car collector and aficionado, was ecstatic about the idea, and our two companies formed a co-branded guitar program that continues today.

In 2001, our sponsor Guitar Center asked me to be on the committee for the Petersen Automotive Museum's ground-breaking exhibit, "Cars & Guitars of Rock 'n' Roll." The museum was founded and supported by Robert E. Petersen, the head of the publishing empire that promoted California car culture through publications such as *Hot Rod* magazine and *Rod & Custom*. Mr. Petersen's dream was to create an educational museum to pay tribute to the automobile.

In 1994, he opened the 300,000-square-foot automotive museum made possible by his $30 million endowment, and named in his honor. I was working up close and personally with the same famous cars I knew so well from my boyhood fascination with model car kits—designed and built by the likes of George Barris and Ed "Big Daddy" Roth. We were able to bring artist signature guitars like Eric Clapton's and Jeff Beck's to be displayed with their cars on loan to the exhibit. We also supplied several branded custom guitars such as the Ninetieth Anniversary Harley Chrome guitar; the CART guitar, hand carved by Fender artisan George Amicay and painted by famous artist Troy Lee to look like the mini-CART racer that Fender's Custom Shop created for Target's sponsorship of the 1999 inaugural race at the Chicago Speedway—and, of course, a SO-CAL-branded guitar.

Because of our involvement with SO-CAL Speed Shop, I have taken part in dozens of events surrounding California's car culture, and have worked in conjunction with other legendary builders such as Roy Brizzo ("Roy's Toys" for collectors like Jeff Beck) and the late Boyd Coddington. In 2005, I was on the team that worked on the seventy-fifth anniversary of the 1932 Roadster fund-raising event at the Petersen Museum that featured a once-in-a-lifetime pairing of guitar and (car collector) greats Jeff Beck, Jimmie Vaughan, and Billy F. Gibbons. While working on this book, I had the honor of speaking about the connection between Fender and the hot rod culture in California at the Hot Rod Restoration Show in Indianapolis, Indiana, as they honored SO-CAL founder Alex Xydias with the Petersen Lifetime Achievement award (sanctioned by Robert E. Petersen before he passed away in 2007).

Certain locales have distinct reputations and buzz words with which they are inescapably attached. Mention Colorado and you think of skiing. Chicago? The Cubs, obviously (well, that's what I think of, anyway). New York? How about big-city nightlife? Hollywood? The entertainment industry—Gotcha! California continues to be the springboard for all that is considered cool; and through movies, TV, and music, it promotes that image to the world. The traditions of the surf and hot-rod cultures reverberate through each new generation that rediscovers them and makes them their own. No matter where you are based, keeping an eye on Southern California can only help your brand take advantage of the trends that are on the horizon.

CHAPTER 12

Putting It
All Together—
Real-Time
Examples

I devote this chapter to presenting the most recent examples of partnership marketing in which I've been involved or am currently working on. The best part of the latter is that even though I am confident that these campaigns will pan out, there's just no way of knowing how everything will end. That's a little risky when you're putting it down on paper for all to see, but I'll be as just interested as you, the dear reader, to see how this all transpires.

As I stated in Chapter 5, I have had many successful promotions partnering with major labels. It seems that as of late, Universal Music Enterprises, and, in particular, their director of pop promotion, Elliot Kendall, has been aggressively searching for new ways to promote their artists. Noticing a general uptick in catalog sales of artists featured on *Rock Band* and *Guitar Hero*, Elliot approached Fender with the concept of an ad to be placed in the upcoming issue of *Rolling Stone* magazine dedicated to the "100 Greatest Guitar Songs of All Time."

Universal decided the best way to conceptualize the ad would be to link the music featured on the guitar games to the gamers themselves. They developed an ad with the catchphrase "Play the Games, Play the Music." The ad featured the distinctive Fender Stratocaster neck and headstock on the left side column, mirrored on the right side with the equally distinctive Stratocaster body design. Most readers flipping through an issue featuring great guitar songs, couldn't help but to be drawn in by the guitar imagery. Also featured in the ad were several major CDs from the guitar heroes showcased in the issue: Jimi Hendrix, the Police, U2, the Who, Nirvana, and Eric Clapton, among others. The hook for the sweepstakes was Fender's responsibility, so as with any strong campaign, I wanted to promote something that was a priority for our marketing department.

Under the direction of senior director of marketing, Richard McDonald, Fender had just launched a new initiative for guitar enthusiasts worldwide, Fender University (affectionately referred to internally as "F.U."). The program would include music workshops, hands-on educational experiences, performance opportunities, and special guest appearances. I knew from our weekly conference calls with our corporate headquarters in Scottsdale, Arizona, that this was something that needed our immediate attention because the inaugural program was just a few short months away, taking place at the Fender Center in Corona, California. The cost for enrollment was $6,500, so I thought that that would be a pretty desirable grand prize for the Universal sweepstakes in *Rolling Stone*. I was pleased when Richard approved the prize package. We were, therefore, now officially on our way.

Fortunately, I was at our headquarters attending marketing meetings, so I was able to meet one on one with Vice President of Marketing Services, Paul Jernigan. He embraced the idea as well and quickly assembled his team to work out the logistics with the label's team. Universal had just informed us that Best Buy would also be coming on board as the retail partner, so we joined forces to create a campaign that would focus on the specific goals of each partner:

- Fender would have the aforementioned Stratocaster head-stock, neck, and body prominently displayed. To Universal's credit, their art department, under the direction of Rob Jacobs, created an ad that actually appeared as if it was placed by Fender, which was pretty special for us because we had never run our own standalone ad in *Rolling Stone* (it should be noted that for the cost of that one ad, Fender could have run almost a year's worth of ads in a typical guitar magazine such as *Guitar Player*).
- Universal created a custom music player for Fender
- The sweepstakes announcement for Fender University was prominently displayed on a backstage pass icon
- On the sweepstakes page on Fender.com, visitors were encouraged to *click to purchase* CDs by the Universal artists featured in the ad
- Fender had a direct link to Best Buy for the featured artists
- *Rolling Stone* magazine sent an email blast to twenty thousand of its subscribers announcing the sweepstakes

You can tell when a campaign is hitting on all cylinders when each of the partners is genuinely enthused for the benefits they received.

Some of our partnerships require a bit more explanation than others. To clarify Fender's promotional campaign for *Alvin & the Chipmunks*, I have to give a little history. The concept of this particular film came from Twentieth Century Fox's decision that they would update the Chipmunks franchise to make them look relatable to the hip artists of today, so that new generations of children would discover them and think that, of course, the Chipmunks are cool. Therefore, instead of having front man Alvin leading a 1950s-type vocal group, these Chipmunks would be members of a rock band.

The new Chipmunk movie would require a combination of digital animation interacting with humans in a live situation. When Twentieth Century Fox contacted my department, they wanted to make sure that we could supply not only product, but also get clearances for certain Fender images that were already in the script. I knew from the start that this was a great opportunity for Fender; we would be tapping into the Chipmunks nostalgia with the generations of families that enjoyed their "Christmas Song," which was a mainstay on the radio at holiday time.

Step One required getting the right guitar for the movie. We picked a well-worn Stratocaster that had actually already had a previous life because it had been originally created for the movie *Rent*. It was perfect for this movie (Note: the guitars played by little "Alvin" in the movie obviously had to be digitized from the originals). It was also a Squier brand, an entry-level instrument, which, from a marketing point of view, was the perfect guitar for not only little Alvin, but for anyone who would be influenced enough to check out that model.

The next step was to provide the backup instruments—in particular, a keyboard that would appear in several pivotal scenes with the hero character, played by Jason Lee. For this important piece, we brought in Roland, one of our partners.

With the instruments covered for Step Two, we needed to address the clearances for certain images. Fox wanted to use the previously mentioned award-winning 1960s Fender ad campaign, "You Won't Part With Yours, Either" (see Chapter 11). It had been a fairly groundbreaking advertising campaign for a musical instrument company at the time. Everyone featured in the ad, mainly teenagers and young adults, were doing things that were very typical of young Californians at the time—and today: surfing, skateboarding, driving a convertible, and climbing into a fighter jet, all with their Fender guitars close at hand.

The famous series of ads was created by a legendary marketing director named Bob Perine. We contacted Bob's family to get clearance, because even though it was a Fender ad, the copyright belonged to the Perine estate. They gave their approval, and the ad clearly appears in scenes shot at the record label's offices.

The prop masters also wanted to create a Fender print ad for one scene. Normally, the Fender art department would have created such an ad, but in this case there wasn't enough time, so the prop masters went to our web site to capture images and logos to approximate what a Fender ad would look like on the back cover of *Rolling Stone*—and their art department nailed it.

The placements had been completed. Now fast forward to late November 2007, a month before the film's holiday release. We met with the promotional team at Fox, headed up by Jamie Hamilton, to discuss a promotional campaign. Jason Padgett, who had joined Fender earlier in the year as vice president of public relations and corporate communications and had come from a similar position at one of the top PR firms in the entertainment business, Rogers & Cowen, was with us. He was a great asset in my meetings because he really spoke the language of PR, which wasn't as much a part of my background. Jamie had the great idea to feature Alvin playing his Stratocaster in a national sweepstakes campaign for contestants to write in to pitch themselves as the "Fourth Chipmunk."

Because the movie had not yet been released when the campaign launched, we decided against using the Stratocaster guitar Alvin plays in the movie, with its distinctive "Flaming A" graphics (created digitally for the scenes). We felt it would make more sense instead to create a unique instrument that had the image of the new Alvin and the Chipmunks (recognizable from the billboards that were beginning to show up announcing the film) on the face of the guitar.

I was fortunate that my assistant, Dave Collins, had a solid background in building guitars for previous companies. In conjunction with the Jackson division at Fender, Dave worked internally with Leonardo Flores, who had a printer that could recreate the artwork for application to the instruments. Under a pressing deadline, Dave was able to make a prototype, which we showed to Jamie in her office. I guess she liked it, because the next thing we knew, we were hustled into the art department, where, within minutes, they were photographing the prototype and digitally placing it into Alvin's hands for the national ad campaign. We committed on the spot to produce 20 limited-edition reproductions of the guitar in the ad for a sweepstakes campaign that would never be duplicated for sale, making them extremely collectible. The full-page color ad ran in newspapers in 30 markets, reaching 30 million people. Everyone who worked on the campaign was cautiously optimistic that the film would do fairly well at the box office because "The Chipmunks" were a recognized franchise. There wasn't a lot of competition as far as family films went during the weekend Fox had chosen for the movie's opening. The first clue we received of impending success was the newspaper campaign that hit with some well-coordinated press junkets. The reader response for the sweepstakes was also fantastic.[1] Fender's customer services department in Scottsdale, Arizona, even called us to get a product number on the guitar because they were receiving calls from consumers who wanted to purchase the new *Alvin* signature model.

But a real home run was hit when the movie came out. It exceeded everyone's expectations by making $200 million domestically and eventually $350 million worldwide. Fender saw a major increase in sales over the previous holiday season, which, I suspect, may have had something to do with putting little Alvin and his Fender guitar in front of millions of kids and their parents, with the movie sending a very positive message about playing music. As a testament to the campaign itself, I received a call from Miramax on a movie called *Soul Man*, for which we had supplied products. When we got to the discussions regarding the promotional campaign, the marketing director pleaded, "Del, I want the Alvin and the Chipmunks promotion for my movie, too."

While I was writing this book, I had another opportunity to work with Jamie Hamilton and her staff at Fox on another promotional campaign, this time for a movie called *The Rocker*. It had originally been produced by Fox Atomic, the edgy film division of Fox, which had just been closed down, allowing big Fox to pick it up. I had a real head start on this campaign because Fox's head of placement, Kevin Arnold, had contacted me before we even began the placement process to explore what kind of promotional support we could lend to the movie's release. Kevin knew that we could do a full-line product for the two decades that the movie featured and the two different genres of bands that would be onscreen, the pop band ADD and the 1980s heavy metal hair band, Vesuvius. Both bands would feature the star of the film, comedian Rainn Wilson from *The Office*, on drums.

It didn't hurt that another one of the performers—teen sensation Teddy Geiger—was already a "Fender Guy," so that would be another opportunity to promote the soundtrack. Fender selected certain designs from our clothing and watch companies to be worn by characters in the film, a tactic that gave us exposure to styles that would then become the icons for the retail promotional campaign.

We got an even better opportunity as we got closer to the production. It turns out that in one of the film's key scenes, overprotective mom Christina Applegate tries to dissuade her angst-ridden teenage son (Geiger) from touring with the older party monster rocker "Fish," (Rainn Wilson's character). In the scene, Applegate's character reveals a little secret about her past as a fledging musician, initially by playing the game *Guitar Hero II*. The studio was having problems working out the details of the game's placement, and Gary knew that Fender's new game, *Rock Band*, would be coming out at the end of the year. He thought it would be appropriate to keep it all in the Fender family since we had committed so much product already. I was on the marketing team for the game and was aware that the team was developing just the prototype for the upcoming E3 gaming convention in Los Angeles, where *Rock Band* would debut for the hungry public. Thanks to the incredible efforts of Harmonix, the company that created the game, we were able to have the prototype flown in to Toronto for the first shoot, return to Los Angeles for the convention, and then go back to Canada to finish the shoot—whew! Before Jason Padgett and I met with Jamie, we both got to see a rough of the film, and we agreed that it looks just like a "Fender company ad"—featuring the guitar brands like Fender and Jackson, our licensed clothing on Teddy, accessories—and, of course, *Rock Band*.

What we are looking to do for *The Rocker* is to offer a download bundle to a retailer like Best Buy or Guitar Center, which would sell *Rock Band* and feature Vesuvius, the fictional heavy metal band from the movie. We would also tie in co-branded Stratocaster guitars that we have already begun producing with a flamed-out *Rocker* logo, reminiscent of the graphics one would see on 1980s guitars.

We are also looking into creating promotional items like the previously mentioned Fender-guitar-shaped shrink-wrapped T-shirts with download cards enclosed for movie music and sweepstakes prizes to be distributed through the retailer. Fox would create special promotional posters and movie trailers for participating dealers that would feature *Rock Band* and include local screenings.

This campaign wouldn't only utilize music retailers but also other retail outlets such as clothing stores that could make use of the promotional shirts and download cards. Prize packages would include a fly-and-win to the world premiere at the Rock 'n' Roll Hall of Fame, which appears in scenes from the film along with the 10-foot-high Stratocaster replicas that were painted as part of a fund-raiser we did in conjunction with the Rock Hall for the United Way. In a perfect promotional world, the premier concert would feature Rainn and Teddy recreating a performance as their characters in the film.

Fender was offered the opportunity in 2007 to participate in an event at the Sundance film festival through one of the product placement companies with which we work, Pier 3 Entertainment. Their client, Zone Perfect energy bar, was sponsoring an event titled "Where Music Meets Film," which featured both established and up-and-coming artists performing in an intimate setting at a major venue in the heart of the village called Harry-O's. Hollywood producer Kenny Griswold owns the venue and wanted to create an event where independent filmmakers get to meet these artists so they could network for future projects. I also knew that Sundance had become the premier industry showcase, so I saw a perfect opportunity for Fender to have at least some sort of presence there.

To initiate Fender's involvement in 2007, we supplied six Fender acoustic guitars engraved with the "Zone Perfect Bar" logo. These were signed by the artists and donated to raise money for music education through the Mr. Holland's Opus Fund. I sent two more for signing: one went to the Fender Center and the other to a local nonprofit in Riverside called The Unforget-tables. When I realized the level of artists who performed and autographed the instruments—Sarah McLachlan and Baby Face Edmonds, to name two—I decided to investigate how FMIC could undertake a much more active role in 2008. I began to look through my resources to find partners to both support the event and benefit from it as well.

My next step was to meet with Kenny Griswold and his partner, Dave Philips, at Kenny's historic landmark home in the hills above Hollywood. I hoped to get more information on the Zone Perfect Bar's promotions and the events they were promoting at Harry-O's. Kenny and Dave welcomed Fender's expanded involvement, which would include the Zone Perfect Bar again, and what was the Airborne Lounge, the Chef Dance, and the main concert facility, which has a capacity of 1,000.

Warner Brothers was the music sponsor for the Zone Perfect Bar event, and the Fuse TV network signed on as the media partner. Warner's offered Tyler Hilton to emcee—one of their up-and-coming artists who had also appeared on the TV series *One Tree Hill*, and who was gaining notoriety for his portrayal of Elvis Presley in *Walk the Line*. It helped that Tyler also had a new movie coming out that month, called *Charlie Bartlett*, where he plays a very uncharacteristic-for-him thug.

I recommended Tyler highly because he was one of our Gretsch artists and I had worked with him on *Walk the Line*. Furthermore, my wife had promoted Tyler on Catalina Island before he was signed to Warner's, and was actually the one who brought him to me. Tyler is an avid supporter of the Fender Center as well. That proved to be a great break for the "Where

Music Meets Film" (WMMF) event, as he was one of the best-received artists who played. He showcased his new music, and as the MC, he provided much-needed personality for the event.

Since the event would include a charitable element, I went to our CFO, Rich Kerley, to see how we could contribute. On behalf of Fender, we provided distinctive Cherry Red and Black Gretsch Electromatic guitars and added the Zone Perfect logo to the pickguards. The Gretsch guitars had a great look for the event and they tied in perfectly to Tyler Hilton, who ended up performing with and then keeping one. In fact, all of the Warner artists were very strong, including Jason Mraz, Michelle Branch, and the best-selling artist of 2007, Josh Groban.[2] Groban even chose some of the recordings from WMMF for inclusion in his new CD "Awake Live." Between the show being produced and shown on Fuse and the MySpace streaming, WMMF has accrued over 90 million views to date.

During Sundance, the main room at Harry-O's has hosted notable bands such as Metallica, and in 2008 included Maroon 5 and 50 Cent. I had been working that year with a documentary team making a film about the blues in Chicago titled *Electrified*, and the director, Phil Ranstrom, had a partnership with Les Walgreen (as in drugstore retailer Walgreen's). Les had just donated $101,000 to radio superstar Howard Stern's charity to get to appear on Stern's show to promote the film. Without a release date or distribution for his film, I told Les that the appearance would be wasted. I then informed him of our involvement in Sundance, and he seized the opportunity to jump head first into this film industry mega-event.

I promised Les and Phil that I would assist in getting an artist from our stable to appear, and immediately contacted Kenny Wayne Shepherd. Kenny occasionally tours with the legendary Howlin' Wolf guitarist Hubert Sumlin, who fit perfectly with the subject matter of the heartfelt *Electrified*, a movie based on Chicago blues on the city's famed Maxwell Street. It was appropriate that Kenny's Grammy-nominated DVD and CD soundtrack for *10 Days Out: Blues from the Backroads* documents the story of Kenny's 10 days of traveling to interview and play with the living legends of blues. The night was standing-room-only and Kenny and Hubert teamed up for a powerful perform-ance. Fender's presence was very strong, with our guitars played onstage and the giveaways of *Electrified*-logoed T-shirts (featuring the Stratocaster body design) packaged in the shape of a Strat body, and download cards inviting patrons to visit a web page for more information on the film.

Airborne paid $350,000 in 2007 for the title sponsorship naming rights for the Airborne Lounge at Harry-O's, but didn't return for 2008. We knew, based on the fee, that this was prime branding, so we determined that this would be an excellent opportunity to invite MTV Networks for *Rock Band*. The venue was perfect for MTV since it would grant the network access to artists and celebs playing the game. Dave Philips was already able to secure a co-sponsor in Ray-Ban, which would also be show-casing their new 3D-branded glasses at the Sundance premiere of *U2 3D*. Crooked X, an amazing heavy metal band made up of 13- and 14-year-olds, whom associate Spencer Proffer had brought to our attention, had a special documentary coming out on MTV, so it was determined that they would headline a show at the lounge.

Ray-Ban had the first five days to provide talent and events, leaving MTV with the remaining five. They did an excellent job filling their nights, but MTV, unfortunately, wasn't always able to have crews there to capture many of the celebrities. There were so many other events going on at Sundance at the same time, there was no way to be able to tell when a celebrity was going to play the game.

We were able to grab some photos with the cast of *American Mall* (by the producers of Disney's *High School Musical*) because we had designed a complete music store for the film in a nearby

Salt Lake City mall. The executive vice president of program enterprises for MTV Networks, Jeff Yapp, had just purchased the film for broadcast. Kenny Griswold was gracious enough to host a party during the Chef Dance (a major Sundance annual dinner event for celebrities showcasing top chefs from around the country) for Amy Redford and her father Robert and their guests after the premiere of her movie, *The Guitar*, which, of course, starred a beautiful red Fender Stratocaster guitar as the namesake of the movie's title. As a keepsake, each VIP guest received a flashing lapel pin that replicated the Fender guitar in the poster.

One more opportunity for Fender grew out of Sundance 2008. We had worked with Amnesty International through our acoustic division, under Marketing Manager Jim Bryant, to create a special acoustic guitar featuring the sixtieth anniversary logo at the first fret. These pieces had originally been fashioned for a fund-raising sales program to Amnesty members during the 2007 holiday season, but I—as well as our contact at Amnesty, Roree Krevolin—had a feeling that they were destined for bigger and better things.

We anticipated that the guitars could be offered to Fender retailers with a portion of the proceeds going to Amnesty so we could have a year-round fund-raising initiative. We also agreed that we needed a hook for this; some major artist who would be photographed with the piece, so that we could tell the story of the guitar. That moment came at Sundance when Roree brought it to Maroon 5, and the band agreed to be photographed with it and autograph it for auction. Amnesty's strength is their artist support for "Freedom of Expression," so when Roree told the story, David Bowie, Chrissie Hynde of the Pretenders, the Dixie Chicks, Dave Matthews, and Bruce Springsteen all requested in rapid succession guitars to sign. The program was then scheduled to go to Fender dealers in 2009.

The Future of Partnership Marketing—Riding the Wave of a Trend and Trying Not to Wipe Out

Primarily due to the Internet and other new developing technologies, opportunities for partnership marketing come and go in the blink of an eye. How is a company to know when to jump on, and more important, when to jump off before the financial and manpower resources invested begin to demonstrate diminishing returns? I look in this chapter at some of the opportunities on the horizon. But first . . .

In one of my favorite scenes in the Beatles' highly acclaimed first film, *A Hard Day's Night*,[1] a marketing exec mistakenly takes George Harrison for a new partner to his resident teenager, Susan, the star of his company's ad campaign. Wanting to get George's opinion on some new style shirts, the following exchange takes place:

> Marketing Exec (to his assistant): "Show him the shirts, Adrian. Now you will like these; you'll really dig them. They're *fab* and all that other pimply hyperbole."

> George: "I wouldn't be caught dead in them; they're dead *grotty*."

> Marketing exec: "Grotty?"

> George: "Yes, grotesque."

> Marketing exec (to Adrian): "Make a note of that would you, and give it to Susan. (looking at George) It's rather touching, really. Here's this kid trying to give us his utterly valueless opinion, when I know for a fact within a month, he will be suffering from a violent inferiority complex and loss of status because he isn't wearing one of these nasty things. Of course, they're grotty, you wretched nit! That's why they were designed, but that's why you'll want them."

> George: "No I won't."

> Marketing Exec: "You can be replaced, chickee baby."

> George (in a matter of fact tone): "I don't care."

The brilliance of this scene is that it played right into the collective psyche of the teenage Beatle fans who were on the inside of the joke mocking the smug, yet clueless marketing executive trying to create the next clothing trend. The whole movie took a similar *us* (the youth) versus *them* (the Establishment) perspective where our heroes, the Beatles, always won out, almost rendering the older generation irrelevant. Granted, this was 1964, in a world where the Beatles were at the forefront of a social revolution, but almost three decades later, Kurt Cobain was basically preaching the same thing to a new generation in his sarcastic tour de force "Smells Like Teen Spirit."[2]

In my opinion, we as marketers are on dangerous ground when we take for granted that we possess the power to create trends simply through marketing muscle. We can, however, utilize that muscle to anticipate a trend when it is bubbling under, and help create a greater awareness. So we are, in fact, helping to nudge the tipping point to where it will become a mainstream success, and, of course, ride the crest of that wave as it peaks.

When MTV exploded on the scene in the 1980s, it was heralded as a trendsetter. But a closer look would show that it didn't really create new trends in music like heavy metal *hair bands*, hip hop, or alternative, or new wave artists. It rather became a fresh vehicle for the labels to partner with to promote their artists that was potent enough to eventually influence radio airplay. And it just wasn't about music, as they were equally influential in fashion. But once again, they didn't create the fashion; they looked at what young people had in their closets, and gave it back to them through their network, therefore validating their trendiness. I do have to give them credit (or maybe discredit, depending upon your point of view) for being way out in front of at least one major trend—reality shows—with the launching of *The Real World*[3] way back in 1992.

TV continues to be a major force in promoting music and fashion today. The top three records of 2007 were all driven by TV exposure[4]—Josh Groban through *The Oprah Winfrey Show,* Daughtry through *American Idol*, and *High School Musical* through the Disney network. Speaking of *American Idol's* impact on sales, 2008 winner David Cook landed 11 songs on Billboard's Hot 100 singles charts immediately after his coronation. According to a recent story in the *Los Angeles Times*, that's the most from a single artist since the Beatles put up 14 in April 1964. Runner-up

David Archeletta has three songs on both the Hot 100 and digital charts.

Disney as well has become a marketing machine for their young recording artists and expect to see networks like MTV and Nickelodeon continue to follow suit with well-coordinated and network-supported campaigns. Keep in mind that Disney revived their star-making machinery back in 1989 when they brought back *The Mickey Mouse Club*, which subsequently launched the careers of future superstars Christina Aguilera, Britney Spears, and Justin Timberlake. Today, Miley Cyrus transitioned from her TV persona and alter ego Hannah Montana to become a full-fledged touring attraction expected to take in a very cool one billion dollars (yes, I said *billion*[5]) from ticket, record sales, and licensed merchandise. The Jonas Brothers are next in line but reversed the formula by being an authentic band before hooking up with the Disney machine.[6] The double-edged power of the Disney Network, coupled with Radio Disney makes for a formable promotional machine that few entertainment companies can match. Envious competitors sometimes suggest that Disney is almost a turnkey operation where almost anything they touch will turn to gold, regardless of the talent. "They own the talent; they own the distribution: they can promote all the time on television," said David Smay, co-editor of the book *Bubblegum Music Is the Naked Truth: The Dark History of Prepubescent Pop, from the Banana Splits to Britney Spears*, in a recent article in the *Los Angeles Times*. "It's almost impossible not to have a hit," remarked David.

Disney's record label, Hollywood Records, has a success rate that's unmatched in current times, but if it was that easy, every network could do it. To get more background, I contacted a longtime friend and associate at Hollywood Records, whom I have had the pleasure of working promotions with for more than 15 years, going back to when he was at A&M Records, vice president of pop promotion, Scotty Finck.

"Disney's magic is this: We utilize a principal vehicle—television, for instance—to create a familial bond between the artist and the audience. With time and repetition, the relationship deepens; it becomes visceral. The fan feels they *know* Hilary Duff, or Miley Cyrus, and that they could be family or best friends. So when the artist moves into film or music, the fan is a completely accepting and passionate supporter."

Whenever someone in marketing thinks about launching a new product or brand, the first question she may ask is, "How does my product compare to what's on the market, and more important, how does it differ?" The second part of that equation works very well with the second part of our definition of *cool* in Chapter 1: "unique when compared with the norm of the day." But that doesn't totally describe how something can retain the cool factor for decades or more. Becoming a recognized classic is one way (as opposed to an instant classic as marketers would like you believe about their product). Many times, that has to do with another marketing objective—"being acknowledged as the first, or the best" can certainly carry a product or brand a long way.

Of course, being the first and the best is the most sought-after position to be in. The Fender Telecaster guitar is recognized as the first mass-produced solid body electric guitar, and it is today still revered as one of the best. A few years later, the addition of the Stratocaster guitar was positioned as both different from, and an improvement of, the Telecaster and has pushed the brand Fender to the world's number one slot, in both recognition and sales.

Keeping with the Fender theme, *Guitar Hero* was the first musical video game with guitar controllers based on a brand name guitar, and was incredibly successful until *Rock Band* came along a few years later and offered many more features and instruments under the popular Fender brand. Even though it costs twice as much, it has closed the gap and has surpassed *Guitar Hero* in monthly sales dollars. Furthermore, consumers are using it as a primary source for downloading songs. Motley Crüe's first single from their new CD of the same name, "Saints of Los Angeles," continues to sell five downloads for every one download on iTunes. This, despite the *Rock Band* download costing twice as much!

My mom told me when I was a child, "If someone has to tell you how well off they are, they aren't." As I grew older, I realized you could substitute just about any adjective for *well off* and it would still be true—*tough, gifted, intelligent*, and so on.

Nikon just announced a new camera model called *Coolpix*. I was interested to find out more about the model because of the word *cool* in its name. Not being a professional lens man, I really couldn't tell what made this camera different or cooler from their other models, or from any other consumer camera on the market. So I did what every other person in this modern world would do, I went to their web site for more information.

Once I got there, I was bombarded with every possible "lifestyle" rotating in and out of the screen—rock climber, barrister, X-Gamer, sound designer ("Music is My Mistress"—whoa) yacht captain, nail artist (wasn't *nail technician* impressive enough?) motor bike racer, cabin attendant, anthropologist (?) and more. The first thing I thought was what precisely is a *sound designer* and a *cabin attendant?* I suspect the first is some sort of New Age name for a musician, and the latter is a maid in the Ozarks. I did notice that the attendant was actually dressed up as a stewardess, sorry, flight attendant. The point is that this group had no possible way of positioning the brand as anything cool because it was trying too hard to be everything to everyone. This is what I like to call marketing by committee, in which everyone in the room gets to throw his two cents into the pot—looks like nobody thought of coming up with a "hook" for the campaign.

Nikon is a quality company and they have tons of money to throw at this campaign to make the camera a success, but they wouldn't have to push so hard if they could just come up with a cool concept to match the name. I compared the features with other companies' similarly priced models and it was in line. It did have one feature that stood out to me called *picmotion*, which incorporates an in-camera slide show with music. Even if other cameras had that feature, here may have been the hook that Nikon could have used instead. The company's TV ads featured Ashton Kutcher interacting with adoring females, so we know what market they were targeting with the camera, which had little to do with their web site presentation. If they would have settled on a single demographic, like young women 18 to 24 years of age, and promoted the color options and focused on the music element, they would have had, in my opinion, a much stronger campaign for the launch.

It's really not fair to compare this to a revolutionary product like the iPod, but it's worth looking at that campaign just for the sake of argument. When the iPod was introduced, it was both groundbreaking and more user-friendly than anything that came before it. The ads showed a simple silhouette of a young woman against a bold contrasting background, enjoying her personal world of music through the silhouette of the iPod and its earbuds.

Simple. Effective. Incredibly successful.

I keep asking myself, "In a data-saturated world, with the average person being subjected to over 5,000 advertising messages per day,[7] in the future will brands still matter as much?" I remember there was a movement in the 1970s to provide quality products to inflation-weary consumers under the "Generic" brand, which featured a bland white label with the words "generic" and the contents. In Chicago, I used to shop at Jewel Foods, which had a dedicated generic section that had everything from tomato soup to cigarettes. At first, it was looked at as a novelty and started to catch on, but after a few years, the novelty wore off, and except for generic prescription drugs, you would be hard pressed to find these products today. What about something as generic as insurance? You would think that a consumer would purchase a policy based on features like premiums, coverage, and so forth, right? Well, if I said finish this sentence, "You're in good hands with ____," chances are you would immediately reply "Allstate."

Let's use a more current example. Aflac's name recognition increased from 12 percent to 90 percent once they started using the duck character in their national ad campaigns. Not to be outdone, GEICO added its gecko character and became the fastest-growing car insurance company in the United States, with three million new customers in 2007, nearly double their historical average.[8]

In Canadian journalist Naomi Klein's international best-seller, *No Logo: Taking Aim at the Brand Bullies*,[9] she investigates the misdeeds of the largest corporations and the various anti-globalization movements that sprang up in the 1990s, such as *Adbusters* magazine and the cultural jamming movement. An indictment of the reckless practices of international corporations such as a disregard for the environment and even their own workers in an endless pursuit of obscene profits, it's no wonder that we have seen a growing grassroots backlash against corporate greed. There is little information, however, to back up the notion that brand loyalty has been adversely affected. I think it's partly due to the feeling that there is a certain comfort level in recognized brands, and consumers find it more and more difficult to focus on new brands amid the incessant noises of advertising bombarding our senses.

When you open a can of Coca-Cola, you know exactly what it's going to taste like, plus there's a certain nostalgia associated with that first swig, which may be evocative of one's youth. The same elements work for artists. Mariah Carey's single, "Touch My Body," is her eighteenth chart-topper, which surpasses a record held by Elvis Presley for 40 years (only the Beatles have had more Number 1 hits, and they, too, are within Carey's sights). Mariah may not be the cultural icon that "The King" was, but you have to give her credit, as she has sustained her popularity for 20 years. An artist who *is* a cultural icon, Madonna, has also surpassed Presley as the artist with the most top ten singles in the modern era. Carey's fans know exactly what they will get, and Madonna's fans know that they don't always know what they will get, and so there's a certain comfort level for their respective contingents of loyal fans.

You would think that working for a company like Fender that I would have more than enough companies approaching me to partner with on co-branded promotions. It's true that we get our fair share, but I always have my antennae up looking for unique opportunities to build our brand awareness in new arenas. The following are some of the areas I see on the horizon that, in my opinion, have the greatest potential.

3-D – In 1984, John Lasseter left his animation job at Disney to join filmmaker George Lucas's special-effects computer group, which later became Pixar. The same year, Lasseter worked on his first 3-D short, *The Adventures of André and Wally B.* Through award-winning box office hits such as *Toy Story*, *The Incredibles*, and *Cars*, Pixar becomes the most successful digital animation studio. In 2008, Pixar, now a Walt Disney subsidiary, officially announced that it had committed to 3-D by releasing all of its movies in the format, beginning with *Up* in 2009.

I witnessed the latest technology when I attended the Producers' Guild screening of *U2 3D*[10] and realized that this is a whole new genre—nothing like the old-time 3-D gimmick with blue and red lenses, but a high tech delivery that will open up new doors, not just for film, but live theater events like concerts and sporting events. The producers of the U2 film think we can have this technology for our home theater systems and personal computers in the next few years, which means video games as well. Seeing how some of our guitars jumped out of the screen during the film, I can see enormous potential for product placement in this format. One drawback is that movie theater owners have been slow to convert their auditoriums to 3-D. Due to the high cost, approximately only one-third of the nation's cinemas have the capability. On a positive note, when films like *Journey to the Center of the Earth* are released in both formats, audiences choose the 3-D version by a wide margin.

Speaking at the Advance '08 advertising conference in Redmond, Washington, filmmaker James Cameron, director of the all-time box office champ *Titanic*, commented that 3-D is not just for movies, but that the real revolution will come when games and television also begin appearing in three dimensions. "Stereo production is the next big thing," Cameron said. "We are born seeing in three dimensions." He went on to add that displays for laptops, phones, and Zunes can be made stereophonic even without needing special glasses.[11] With 3-D television in the not-too-distant future, with companies ready to utilize new technology to aggressively promote their brands, the FCC is already looking into ways to inform viewers when brands are integrated into shows in exchange for money. My rule of thumb has always been the less blatant and the more organic, the better.

At the 2008 Sundance Festival, I worked with Christopher Crescitelli of Kerner Technologies, who is at the forefront of 3-D technology. I originally intended for his company to meet with MTV Networks for the possibility of transferring the *Rock Band* video game into 3-D. But through new partnerships he built at Sundance, including one with "Where Music Meets

Film" producer Dave Philips, Kerner is now being courted by some of the largest entertainment companies. The latest project in discussion is a 3-D concert film to be shot at the Smithsonian in Washington, D.C., and released through major theaters, following in the footsteps of U2. Another new technology from Kerner is FrameFree, which simply put, analyzes still images to automatically create stunning motion graphics. I was recently given a stunning demonstration by the company's CEO, Tom Randolph, and could see the incredible benefits for everything from advertising, interactive music videos, and even in creating mini-movies that can be created, then passed around and edited through the internet.

Avatars – *Virtual worlds* like Second Life are social networking sites that have immense potential for branding opportunities because of their large subscriber base. Second Life had approximately 13 million registered accounts with an average of 38,000 "residents" logged on at any particular time, interacting with one another through motional avatars. Since these residents can "own" land and other properties, they can also "purchase" brand name luxury items using real credit cards. People join these sites partly to aspire to be someone else, more successful, more popular, and so forth, so the aspirational element could be a powerful motivator for transference into the real world, not unlike brand placements in movies and TV. The true opportunity for growth will be when various social networking sites begin to link up so participants can interact in other virtual worlds.[12]

Extreme Sports – Many companies have struck gold by partnering with extreme athletes and their signature events. Extreme Sports, spearheaded by the X-Games, is the fastest-growing sport of the new century. Athletes are young, hip, anti-establishment, and have developed their own fashions, initially based on the grunge look. It is a marketer's dream, because unlike other sports heroes, fans really care about these athletes' lifestyles—not only the clothes they wear, but what music they listen to while they practice and compete.

A problem that some companies realized too late is that each year a new crop of athletes comes up. Therefore, many of their endorsements—despite costing millions in investments—may have a short lifespan of just a single year. But these athletes and their agents are smart, because as soon as a new star emerges, they negotiate a new contract with another competitor for more money. Therefore, many contracts are limited to a single year.

A second issue that companies face is that the athletes' cutting-edge image may become soiled once they become too mainstream; they essentially become victims of their own success. Just look at a company like Airwalk, which was riding high on the backs of extreme sports—and then crashed by trying to mass-market their brand everywhere and thereby lost the very consumer who made them.

Of course, there are countless brands that have achieved massive growth through partnering with extreme sports. Many athletes, like skateboarding's Tony Hawk, surfing's Kelly Slater, and motocross's Ricky Carmichael remain on top year after year. For that reason, it's best to approach the young athletes when they first begin showing promise.

This rule has always applied in the music business. This is how I approach artist relations at Fender. I seek out young artists through my contacts at labels—both independents and the majors—and check out the buzz bands as they come through town. I use my instincts to decide which artist we will support at a time when that artist needs our support the most. Whether it's a few pieces of quality gear, or simply through advertising, we begin building relationships with these artists—sometimes even before they are known to the general public. Sheryl Crow, Aly & AJ, Donovan Frankenrieter, Tyler Hilton, Jonny Lang, and

Kenny Wayne Shepherd all received their first real music company endorsements from me personally.

The Boomer Generation – Even though a large amount of advertising is aimed at a younger demographic, the Baby Boomer generation still has considerable clout, mainly because we are desperately trying to stay youthful in both appearance and how we enjoy our affluence. At a time of record high gas prices, what vehicle do you suppose the Boomers are lining up to buy? A hybrid? The 41-miles-per-gallon micro-mini Smart Car? Wrong on both accounts. How about the $40,000 2008 Dodge Challenger, a 4,140-lb., 425-hp, V-8, premium gas-guzzling Muscle Car based on the original gas hog of the 1970s? I was discussing with an associate of mine who's an exec in the music industry that the 2008 run of 6,800 cars has already been sold out and he was proud to say that he had secured number four. Chevy is following along with their re-creation of another pony car beast, the Camaro. No doubt that production run will sell out as well. But I'm one to talk. I drive a 1985 turbocharged limited run Buick Grand National, one of the fastest production cars of the era. Oh yeah, I also ride a 2002 Triumph Bonneville re-creation of the legendary 1955 motorcycle world speed record holder *Bonnie*.

When I was formulating a high end re-creation of Elvis Costello's original Fender Jazzmaster as featured on the cover of his classic debut album, "My Aim is True,"[13] his manager commented that it was a *dentist's* guitar because only white collar professionals would be able to afford it. Not that everything that Boomers desire is retro, but anything that has nostalgia for us is probably something we aspired to in our youth, but couldn't afford back then. Rhino Records has built a formidable label on the premise that archiving great classic albums and catalogs can be repackaged as boxed sets with extensive booklets that fans would be willing to pay a premium price for, even if they already have all the original music in their collections. In a May 2008 article in the *Los Angeles Times*, Geoff Boucher wrote about the partnership between the Sinatra estate and Rhino, reporting that Frank Sinatra Enterprises LLC planned to commemorate the tenth anniversary of the singer's passing and beyond with a series of entertainment initiatives.[14] Boucher writes that "what Sinatra offers to any venture is that most elusive of all auras: eternal cool." He goes on to say that, "Like Elvis Presley, James Dean or Marilyn Monroe, Sinatra's image has compass point clarity in pop culture despite the passage of time." Heading up the day-to-day operations for Sinatra Enterprises is Rhino exec Jimmie Edwards. I have had the pleasure of working with Jimmie on several projects at Rhino, so I know he knows his stuff.

If your brand has classic icons from the past, or you can tap in to the nostalgia of a retro look, you may have a product launch that goes against the modern conventional wisdom of sleeker, cheaper, and more efficient makes for success.

Charitable Causes – Just like Fender creating the Amnesty International guitar for the purpose of having a product at retail that also has a fund-raising element, I heard about a new phone that offers similar benefits. I asked Gael MacGregor, whom I interviewed for this book, to tell me about her unique phone.

> "It used to be called *Working Assets*. It's now called *Credo* and it's one percent of all the money that you pay for your phone bill goes to support progressive causes, including Amnesty International, the ACLU, [and the] World Wildlife Fund. Ben of Ben and Jerry's [ice cream] was one of the people who helped push this out to people because he said, this is the way to do it: 'Be socially responsible with the money that you spend.'

Basically, it allows you to be able to give back without having to do a whole lot of effort. At the end of the year, you have 'x' amount of money per dollars you spend on your cell phone usage year round to designate to charitable organizations. I think anything your company can do to make the world a better place, is well worth the effort. Whether it be by going green with products or manufacturing, or simply by supporting local causes, do it for the right reason and your company will be rewarded."

There are so many different programs like Credo where companies can use some of their profits to benefit charitable causes. From the grass roots artist-driven Reverb, to major global initiatives like RED, with a little research, your company should have little problem finding the right partner for your brand to support the right cause.

If I had to sum up the fundamental nature of partnership marketing, it would incorporate two key elements: "active" marketing and cross-transference between the equity of brands. Most traditional advertising is passive, meaning that it assumes that when a consumer is at the point of considering the purchase of a certain product, the advertising would present the features, price, and appeal of the advertised brand over that of a competitor's. For example, in Fender's industry, *Guitar Player* magazine is the industry bible. Our monthly ads for a certain model would present an appealing photo, but the true focus would be a presentation of the technical features such as neck width, pickup specifications, and so forth. This is product specific and works well for the small but targeted readership, who are mainly guitar players that have some grasp of why this information is important to them. Our competitors can run their version of the same ad, saying why their specs are more appealing. Also, certain players may have a preference for or loyalty to a particular brand, so a simple technical ad may have little effect on their purchasing decision.

Unfortunately, the repetition of these ads month after month has a diminishing return because they add no new information after their initial exposure to the consumer. Compare this concept to a consumer shopping for a new car who reads through *Motor Trend* magazine looking for a model that has the most desirable features within his budget. The cost per impression (advertising rate for an ad placement per reader) is much higher for this type of marketing, even though you are reaching a specific target demographic.

Active marketing takes the opposite approach by not focusing on a specific demographic or even specific features, but by reaching out to a much wider audience that includes both the targeted market and the casual consumer alike. And because you are reaching a far larger audience, it is also much more cost effective per impression. For instance, because of the national ad campaign in twenty million newspapers across the country, and the huge box office, the "Alvin" campaign described in Chapter Twelve ended up being approximately .00013 cents per impression based on the cost of the promotional instruments we supplied. Compare that to a typical ad placed in one of our industry publications which averages about three cents per impression. The casual consumer may be seduced into purchasing a product because active marketing is based on the aspirational aspect of enhancing one's life or social status by acquiring the product. In my business, this has a potential impact on a consumer who may have thought about playing guitar at one time or another, but has never been prompted enough to read a guitar magazine to research features, price, and so on. Inspiring this type of consumer to believe he can play guitar to be like the rock stars he and his friends look up to powers a brand far above the competitors.

Again, this is not product specific like passive marketing, but rather, brand specific. The logic of this is that if a consumer is influenced by the brand, he will ultimately end up buying the model he can most afford. Back to our automobile analogy: the Mustang GT garners the most publicity for Ford and is therefore one of their most aspirational models. It is no surprise that it is the hottest car featured in their company ad campaigns, but almost since its inception, the Escort was the company's best-selling car until it ceased production in 2003. It was replaced by the economy model Focus, which is now the company's best-selling car.

To illustrate the second element, the cross-transference of equity between brands, I wish to relate a recent event. A friend and associate of mine, Carson Lev, with whom I used to work when he was in licensing for the giant toy company Mattel, now works for legendary car builder Chip Foose of TV's *Overhaulin'* fame.[15] Carson brought Chip out to visit us at Fender to look at our gear to conceptualize a Cutlass Supreme for country music superstar Tim McGraw. Chip has a brilliantly creative eye and it didn't take him long to visualize the music elements from our guitars and amps that could be incorporated into Tim's custom car. We both knew this partnership could benefit both of our brands. The dedicated fans of Chip Foose and Tim McGraw would think it was so cool that a major company like Fender would be a participant in such a unique and high profile project, and the Fender devotees would be enthused that our brand would continue to associate with the best of the best in Foose and McGraw.[16]

Carson and I were talking about how lucky we were to work for such great brands, which allow us to market from the top down instead of the bottom up. When you start pushing from the bottom, you have to use all your resources to lift up a product and hope you collect enough consumers who can help you muscle it to the top. In marketing, we like to put all the various initiatives in a campaign under one convenient "umbrella." To me, that term is relatively nondescript when referring to partnership marketing. When you start at the top with a true lifestyle brand, and welcome partners that each have their own unique attributes to lend to the campaign, they become the colors of a giant rainbow that illuminates and energizes everything beneath it.

LINER NOTES

Chapter One: The Birth of the Cool—a 101 Primer

1. *The American Heritage Dictionary of the English Language,* Fourth Edition, 2000.
2. Charlie Parker, *Cool Blues*, Dial Records, 1947.
3. Miles Davis, *Birth of the Cool*, Capitol Records, 1950.
4. Michael Quinion, *World Wide Words*, worldwidewords.org/qa/qa-cool.htm, 2000.
5. Lupe Fiasco, *The Cool*, Atlantic Records, 2007.
6. Radiohead, *In Rainbows*, ATCO Records, 2008.
7. Todd Martens, "Following 'In Rainbows,'" *Los Angeles Times*, January 4, 2008.
8. *The Great Escape*, directed by John Sturges (United Artists, 1963).
9. McQueen played the character Josh Randall in 94 episodes from 1958 to 1961.
10. *Bullitt*, directed by Peter Yates (Warner Brothers/Seven Arts, 1968).
11. Issued as a tribute to McQueen wearing a similar watch in the film *Le Mans*.
12. Sheryl Crow, *Steve McQueen*, from "C'mon, C'mon," track 1, A&M Records Ume, 2002.
13. NASCAR Nextel Cup driver Dale Earnhardt, Jr. also appeared in the *Steve McQueen* video.
14. cnn.com/2004/allpolitics/10/07.
15. *The Wild One*, directed by László Benedek (Columbia Pictures, 1953). It's interesting to note that in the new Indiana Jones movie, *Indiana Jones and The Kingdom of the Crystal Skull*, Shia LeBeouf's character, Mutt Williams, is first seen onscreen in an exact replica of Brando's famous rebel garb.
16. Ever wonder where that rock band got its name?
17. *Pulp Fiction*, directed by Quentin Tarantino (Miramax, 1994).

Chapter Two: The Prime Marketing Motivators—Too Much of a Good or Bad Thing?

1. Neil Postman, *Amusing Ourselves to Death: Public Discourse in the Age of Show Business* (New York: Penguin Books, 1985).

2. Douglas Rushkoff, *Coercion: Why We Listen to What "They" Say* (New York: Riverhead Books, 1999).

3. Ylan Q. Mui, "Victoria's Revelation; Brand Is 'Too Sexy,' Chief Says" *Washington Post*, February 29, 2008.

4. iTVX staff, "Models Can't Make Hard Sell Look Attractive," itvx.net/2007/12/10/models-cant-make-hard-sell-look-attractive, (posted December 10, 2007).

5. For Heart's video for the song "In Dreams," Frank Zappa remarked that the reasons for their success was "Leave it to cleavage," no doubt inspired by the Wilson sisters' low-cut costumes.

6. Nick Roubanis, *Misirlou*, performed by Dick Dale, Deltone Records, 1962.

7. Daniel J. Levitin, *This is Your Brain on Music: The Science of a Human Obsession* (New York: Dutton, 2006).

8. Martin Howard, *We Know What You Want: How They Change Your Mind* (New York: The Disinformation Company, 2005).

9. Anne Elizabeth Moore, *Unmarketable: Brandalism, Copyfighting, Mocketing, and the Erosion of Integrity* (New York: New Press 2007).

10. Kurt Cobain, Krist Novoselic, and Dave Grohl, *Smells Like Teen Spirit*, Nirvana, from "Nevermind," track 1, Geffen Records, 1991.

11. Oliver Sacks, *Musicophilia: Tales of Music and the Brain* (New York: Alfred A. Knopf, 2007).

12. Oliver Sacks, *Awakenings* (London: Duckworth, 1973).

13. Blair Tindall, "Neurologist and author Oliver Sacks has documented extraordinary things about the brain. His new book is attuned to music's wonders." *Los Angeles Times*, December 23, 2007.

14. Janet Cromley, "Tunes as Therapy," *Los Angeles Times*, February 25, 2008.

Chapter Three: Expanding Your Brand's Identity— Partnership Marketing Outside Your Core Market

1. Author Sun Tzu, written during the sixth century B.C.E. to educate and impress the Japanese nobility.

2. Released in 1985 without the knowledge or consent of the Coca-Cola Company, *The Coca-Cola Kid* starred Eric Roberts as a marketing exec for the company, who discovers to his dismay that the brand is number one everywhere in the world except for one small town in Australia, and he is bound and determined to go there to find out why.

3. Jerry Hirsh, "Beer firms unite, seek a potent mix" the *Los Angeles Times*, October 10, 2007.

4. Brent Hunsberger, the *Oregonian* staff, powelllacrosse. com/press/96, posted March 11, 2008.

5. Randall Lane, "You Are What You Wear," *Forbes*, October 14, 1996.

6. Clayton M. Christensen, *The Innovator's Dilemma* (New York: HarperBusiness, 1997).

7. U.S. sales for video game software, hardware, and accessories were up 19 percent to $12.5 billion in 2006, according to the research firm NPD Group.

8. Roland designed and built the electronics for Fender's MIDI-capable Roland Ready Stratocaster guitar and the groundbreaking VG Strat, which won the 2007 NAMM Innovative Product of the Year award.

Chapter Four: We Will, We Will, Rock You—Marketing to the Big Beat

1. Unfortunately, record labels sometimes gave the artists cars as "gifts" in lieu of the actual royalties owed, which could have totaled many times more than the value of the car.
2. Thomas Bonsall, "Trouble in Paradise: The Story of the Cadillac Cimarron," web.archive.org/web/200012171 23800/http://www.rideanddrive.com/disasters/disasters.html.
3. John Mellencamp, Freedom Road, Universal Republic Records 2007.
4. Art worked his magic again when brought on to do the clearances for Hannah Montana's new movie. He discovered UK artist Steve Rushton, and placed three of his songs performed on camera by Steve himself in the movie. That also helped Fender place our product as Art had brought Steve to Fender prior to the movie.
5. Amy Kaufman, "No label required; Singer Ingrid Michaelson's odd rise to fame took blood, sweat and Old Navy," *Los Angeles Times*, March 8, 2008.
6. Marisa Baldi, ZYNC Music partner told me, "We loved Tim's sound from the start, but we also saw a great opportunity to stretch his potential as a songwriter by getting him inspired to write for films. Tim responded so well as he's one of those rare writers who understands the subtlety of a universal lyric that draws on emotions we all feel."

Chapter Five: The Recording Industry—An Endangered Species or Emerging Opportunity for Marketing Partnerships?

1. Brian Hiatt and Evan Serpick, "The Record Industry's Decline," *Rolling Stone* magazine, June 28, 2007.
2. Alana Semuels, "Digital music offsets drop in CD buying; Downloads rise 65% last year, down from a 150% jump in '05. The slowing growth is a worrisome sign as physical sales continue to decline." *Los Angeles Times*, January 5, 2007.
3. REO Speedwagon, *Hi Infidelity*, Epic Records, 1980.
4. The original responsibility of the A&R (Artist and Repertoire) man at labels was to sign talent and then work with songwriters and music publishers to find the perfect songs, which worked for the Sinatras of the world but had less influence later, as far as song selection went, when artists like the Beatles and Bob Dylan came along, who wrote their own songs.
5. The top-selling album of all time in the United States, as of January 2008, is the "Eagles: Their Greatest Hits 1971–1975," from Asylum Records as certified by the Recording Industry Association of America.
6. Also known as "Moondog," Freed (December 15, 1921–January 20, 1965) was known for promoting R&B music and was eventually brought down as a scapegoat in the 1950s payola scandal.
7. "Rock-Roll Fad Fades," *Idaho Evening Statesman*, December 5, 1959.

8. My brother Bruce reminded me that Ron Britain, while still on AM radio, had a show called "Subterranean Circus," which played more "underground" new music, and was a precursor to what FM would become.

9. Thankfully, Jim Ladd is still programming his own radio show under the banner of "Free Form Radio" on KLOS-FM in Los Angeles and usually leads the Arbitron ratings for his evening slot. It should be noted that Tom Petty used Jim as his inspiration for the album "The Last DJ" and its title track. Jim Ladd also hosted the final Fender Catalina Island Blues Festival in 2001.

10. "Album-Oriented Rock," en.wikipedia.org/wiki/Album-oriented_rock, posted November 2007. It should be noted that vinyl records are making a big comeback as promotional "collectable" versions of new releases. One of my favorite independent record stores, Kiss The Sky in Geneva, IL. told me that approximately 3 percent of their sales were vinyl in 2007, and in 2008, that figure increased to about 20 percent.

11. Hamer and Jackson Charvel are now part of the Fender Musical Instruments family.

12. Dannen, Fredric, Hit Men: *Power Brokers and Fast Money Inside the Music Business* (New York: Random House, 1990).

13. Matthew Hamblen, "Starbucks Serves Up Music and CD-Burning in its Café," *Computerworld*, October 14, 2004.

14. BusinessWeek Online, October 24, 2006, archived from Amoeba Press.

15. It's somewhat ironic that as New York's attorney general, Spitzer made a name for himself prosecuting the music industry for its payola practices.

16. Ken Tucker, with additional reporting by Anthony Bruno, "Nashville Boots Up," *Billboard* magazine, March 22, 2008.

17. Other tribute models from Fender's Custom Shop include Andy Summers, Jaco Pastorius, Jeff Beck, Muddy Waters, and Jimi Hendrix.

18. The Crossroads II Fender Stratocaster stand-up display won the 2008 NARM Convention's "Best POP Item" of 2007.

19. This is not just limited to artists and labels. For the Cruefest tour of 2008, MTV brought in an unrelated third party sponsor, Stride Gum, who apparently made unreasonable demands on retailer Best Buy for a huge sales commitment to promote their gum in stores. That delayed the promotional launch and eventually, the in-store consumer campaign imploded.

Chapter Six: Product Placement—The Inside Story of
Getting Your Brand into Movies and Television

1. This does not take into account barter arrangements where product is traded in-kind for placement fees.

2. This is a story that I have heard many times, but while the actual amounts may be approximate, they do fall in line with other integrations on similarly rated shows.

3. As reported on ducati.com scoopage, (c) 2008 Ducati Motor Holding S.p.A.

4. I couldn't help thinking during the first meeting with Tom Hanks that "I'm working with Forrest Gump," but he was genuinely nice to me, and patient as

well, as I learned the ropes through him and prop master Will Blount. Tom's company, Playtone, based on the fictional label in the film, we still work with, but only to the extent of engraving their logo on guitars and amps that Tom presents as gifts to his friends and associates at Christmas.

5. In a scene in *Walk The Line*, "Johnny" walks past a sleeping "Luther" and pauses to remove a lit cigarette from his lips. Tragically, that is how Luther died on August 5th, 1968, when an exhausted Perkins fell asleep at home with a lit cigarette that ignited the room. The movie has renewed interest in this true pioneer of country guitar.

6. In an early scene in the movie, "Johnny" is checking out guitars in a music store while stationed in Germany in 1953 and he seems to be fixated on a 1952 Telecaster guitar. We provided a Vintage 52 reissue for the scene; and while I was alerted by one of our employees that someone had remarked that it was impossible that a 1952 American-made Fender would be in Germany in 1953 because it would have been too rare and too expensive, keep in mind that only the body of the guitar was showing, and by the distinctive Butterscotch Blonde finish and Tele shape, this obviously dedicated Fender fan was able to correctly identify it. My reply was that the placement was taken directly from the script that had Johnny Cash's original handwritten notes on what he remembered from the store.

7. The shape of the guitar goes back several centuries when the original contours were modeled after the female form. We still refer to the parts of a guitar today as the *neck, body,* and *waist,* and some even refer to the bottom as the *butt.*

8. In the summer of 2008, Wa-Mu placed a billboard in the heart of Times Square featuring a several story high Fender Stratocaster guitar.

9. Occasionally, when I am addressing music dealer seminars for Fender, I will demonstrate the power of placements by asking what kind of car James Bond drives, and most of them reply, "BMW." I love to inform them that Ian Fleming, who created the Bond franchise, always had him in an Aston Martin, and the BMW connection was only through the car company's placement and promotional tie-ins, which cost them around $3 million.

10. *Grey's Anatomy* is a perennial top 10 primetime show, with ABC charging between $250,000 and $450,000 per 30-second advertising spot, as reported by the web site realityblurred.com.

11. Jennifer Frey, "Sort of like living inside the tube; you're watching TV and you see an actor wearing—or driving—something you'd like. The SeenOn website can make it yours." *Washington Post*, as reported in the *Los Angeles Times*, January 5, 2007.

12. itvx.net, as reported in the *Media Daily News* article by Wayne Friedman, "Product Placement: Broadcast Up, Cable Down in '07," posted December 31, 2007.

13. Place*Views, a Neilsen product placement service.

14. http://www.realityblurred.com/realitytv/archives/american_idol_Jan_14_ ad_-prices, posted February 14, 2008.

15. An average 30-second spot costs $2.7 million, as reported on money.cnn.com. publications.mediapost.com posted January 9, 2008 by Owen Mack.

16. itvx.net, Friedman, op. cit.

Chapter Seven: Event Marketing—Reaching
Your Core Demo One-on-One

1. Quoted in Martin Howard, *We Know What You Want: How They Change Your Mind* (New York: The Disinformation Company, 2005).
2. Darren Rovell, "The tangled web of sports and advertising," espn.com, May 6, 2004. Rovell also quoted Ralph Nader on the placement of the Ricoh logos on the uniform and helmet of players during the season opener between the Yankees and the Devil Rays in Tokyo, calling it "a greedy new low."
3. Information from Richard Childress, who fields cars in the NASCAR Championship Series.
4. IEG Webinar Series 2007 Sponsorship Report.
5. Cheap Trick, *At Budokan*, Epic Records, 1979.
6. The Boys and Girls Clubs of America had a major plus over other organizations because they had their own facilities that could be used for the lesson programs.
7. Sadly, Mel Taylor died not long after the NAMM event, but we continue our close relationship with the band today, which has since been inducted into the Rock 'n' Roll Hall of Fame in Cleveland, Ohio.
8. Bill Cummiskey told me that Fender has an unofficial five-year rule for sponsoring events because he feels that after that length of time we have diminishing returns because we are reaching the same audience over and over again with the same message. Fender's sponsorship of the Tempe Music Festival, Summerfest in Milwaukee, and the Catalina Blues Festival all ended after five years.
9. After the successful run of the blues festival, I asked Bettina what kind of research went into her decision to choose that genre of music before she contacted Fender, and she replied, "I like blues."

Chapter Eight: Charitable Causes—Doing Good Things
for the Right Reasons

1. Bob Geldof, *Is That It? The Autobiography* (New York: Weidenfeld & Nicolson, 1987).
2. David Crosby and David Bender, *Stand and Be Counted: Making Music, Making History: The Dramatic Story of the Artists and Causes that Changed America* (New York: HarperCollins, 2000).
3. Margot Roosevelt, "Passing along his good fortune, Chuck Feeney has donated $4 billion—very quietly—and he's nowhere near done. Just don't put his name on anything," *Los Angeles Times* March 8, 2008.
4. We did have a chance to pay Steve back for all the generosity he showed for the Fender Center. Our Senior Vice President of Operations for our U.S. manufacturing plant, Rick Anderson, was in the audience when Steve donated the guitar back, and since Steve had also spoken about honoring our troops at war, Rick decided to create a special "patriot" guitar for him, adorned with a beautifully painted waving American flag. We surprised Steve on his birthday with it, and since it was before his performance, a visibly moved Steve Miller ended up playing the guitar most of the concert that night.

*Chapter Nine: The Celebrity Quotient—How to
Wrangle It, and How to Deal With It When You Do*

1. Mercury eventually closed their offices in Chicago and Ron went on to Columbia, where he was instrumental in the careers of many other artists such as Journey.
2. foxnews.com "Report: Record Label Drops 'Idol' Runner-Up Katherine McPhee," foxnews,com/story/0,92933, 321791,00.html, January 11, 2008.
3. There's a question whether Beckham is actually bringing new fans to soccer in the United States. Many think the fans that are turning out in droves are attracted to his celebrity and may not support the team once he's gone. Another possible example of the Icarus Syndrome as discussed in Chapter Four.
4. Aftermarket vehicle accessories show.

*Chapter Ten: Promotions as an Excuse to Advertise—
But We Don't Really Need an Excuse, Do We?*

1. For you youngsters raised on digital, this was a long-time music expression used by labels to say no matter how well you promoted a record, it all came down to how good the music was. Plastic vinyl records had grooves cut in them where the phonograph needle rode, and that's how it picked up the music. So, if the record was great, it was *in the grooves*.
2. Nuno Bettencourt, *Pornograffiti*, Extreme, A&M Records, 1990.
3. Refers to the backing music under a commercial spot.
4. Dimebag was so much fun to work with, and quite the prankster. Once at dinner during a conversation, I smelled what I thought was burning cat fur. That was until I noticed that he had lit a full book of matches and set it on my pants. He captured the complete episode on his ever-present video recorder. On December 8, 2004, he was tragically shot and killed by a demented fan while onstage doing what he loved most.
5. Al Ries and Jack Trout, *Positioning* (New York: McGraw-Hill, 1981).
6. Al Ries and Jack Trout, *Marketing Warfare* (New York: McGraw-Hill, 1986).
7. Clapton's CD, "Unplugged," recorded during his appearance, sold 10 million copies.

Chapter Eleven: California Dreaming—The Essence of
The Cool Factor *in Partnership Marketing*

1. Timothy White, *The Nearest Faraway Place: Brian Wilson, the Beach Boys, and the Southern California Experience* (New York: Henry Holt, 1994).
2. *Tandem Surfing*, surfline.com/surfaz/surfaz.cfm?id=924
3. As reported on the company's web site www.op.com.
4. The *Wall Street Journal* Classroom Edition, September 2007.
5. "Hurley History," hurley.com/base/history
6. "Where They Started: The History of Quiksilver," indieclothingblog.com/2007/10/14/where-they-started-the-history-of-quiksilver/#more-162.

Chapter Twelve: Putting It All Together—Real-Time Examples

1. The campaign didn't reach just kids, because we heard some hilarious ads, including one guy who started talking on why he should be the fourth chipmunk and his voice kept speeding up until he sounded like one of the chipmunks.
2. Part of E3 was a concert with the Queens of the Stone Age at the legendary showcase club, the Troubadour, where fans could get up and play *Rock Band*, and I witnessed how it was just like watching a real concert as the audience cheered them on.
3. hollywoodreporter.com/hr/content_display/music/news/e3if6ab083ab6032af8407ed86561bd91fa?imw=Y

Chapter Thirteen: The Future of Partnership Marketing—
Riding the Wave of a Trend and Trying Not to Wipe Out

1. *A Hard Day's Night*, directed by Richard Lester (United Artists, 1964).
2. Kurt Cobain, Krist Novoselic, and Dave Grohl, *Smells Like Teen Spirit*, Nirvana, from "Nevermind," track 1, Geffen Records, 1991.
3. *The Real World* continues today, still dealing with socially relevant topics.
4. Geoff Boucher, "Finding a High Note," *Los Angeles Times*, December 21, 2007.
5. Dawn C. Chmielewski, "Disney's Latest Gig," *Los Angeles Times*, April 1, 2008.
6. *The Jonas Brothers: Living the Dream* is their reality show on Disney, and their first movie is titled *Camp Rock*, first released on the Disney Channel in June 2008.
7. Marketing Without Advertising (c) 2008 by Michael Phillips & Salli Rasberry.
8. Ted A. "bump" Davies, Jr. Paradigm Partners Webinar.
9. Naomi Klein, *No Logo: Taking Aim at the Brand Bullies* (New York: Picador, 2000).
10. *U2 3D*, directed by Catherine Owens (3ality Digital Entertainment and National Geographic World Films, 2008).
11. Ina Fried, "James Cameron: 3D heading beyond movies," news.cnet.com/beyond-binary/?keyword= 3-D, May 20, 2008.
12. I worked with Mike Nesmith on the Monkees' reunion TV special. He was the first to demonstrate the world of avatars to me, which should not have been a surprise, as his film, *Elephant Parts*, created the template for MTV . . . always ahead of the curve.
13. We ended up creating a couple of versions of his famous Jazzmaster.
14. Geoff Boucher, "Hot for the Cool," *Los Angeles Times*, May 11, 2008.
15. Chip Foose is the youngest person (age 31) ever inducted into the Hot Rod Hall of Fame (1997).
16. Fender has been an integral part of the sound of country music ever since the genre went electric in the 1950s.

INDEX